RAINFOREST COWBOYS

RAINFOREST COWBOYS

The Rise of Ranching and Cattle Culture

in Western Amazonia

JEFFREY HOELLE

UNIVERSITY OF TEXAS PRESS *Austin*

This book is a part of the Latin American and Caribbean Arts and Culture publication initiative, funded by a grant from the Andrew W. Mellon Foundation.

First edition, 2015
First paperback printing, 2015

Requests for permission to reproduce material from this work should be sent to:
Permissions
University of Texas Press
P.O. Box 7819
Austin, TX 78713-7819
http://utpress.utexas.edu/index.php/rp-form

♾ The paper used in this book meets the minimum requirements of ANSI/NISO Z39.48-1992 (R1997) (Permanence of Paper).

LIBRARY OF CONGRESS CATALOGING-IN-PUBLICATION DATA

Hoelle, Jeffrey, 1976–
Rainforest cowboys : the rise of ranching and cattle culture in western Amazonia / Jeffrey Hoelle. — First Edition.
    pages   cm
    Includes bibliographical references and index.
    ISBN 978-0-292-76134-6 (cloth : alk. paper)
    1. Beef cattle—Environmental aspects—Brazil—Acre. 2. Ranching—Environmental aspects—Brazil—Acre. 3. Deforestation—Brazil—Acre. 4. Human ecology—Brazil—Acre. I. Title.
    SF196.B6H64   2015
    636.2'13098112—dc23   2014023106

    ISBN 978-1-4773-1060-1 (pbk.)

doi:10.7560/761346

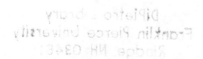

TO MY MOTHER

CONTENTS

ILLUSTRATIONS

TABLES

ACKNOWLEDGMENTS

THIS BOOK WAS CONCEIVED AND WRITTEN under the guidance of many people, and it would not have come into being without their support and perspective. Marianne Schmink, the chair of my dissertation committee, has been a source of inspiration and wisdom. In Gainesville and Acre, she served as an example of dedication in her various roles as mentor, scholar, and advocate. Brenda Chalfin provided insights from political economy and helped me navigate the Africanist literature to gain an understanding of the relationship between economy and culture from a comparative perspective. Stephen Perz, a sociologist, was central to my development of a broader perspective on Acre, giving me an opportunity to participate as a member of the field team conducting socioeconomic research during the paving of the Inter-Oceanic Highway. Michael Heckenberger served as a vital critical voice on the committee, and also provided inspiration and practical advice on research and writing.

Other members of the University of Florida Department of Anthropology were very influential in my development as a scholar. I benefited from conversations with Anthony Oliver-Smith, Clarence Gravlee, and Gerald Murray. H. Russell Bernard generously shared his broad knowledge and experience within the field of anthropology, and also provided valuable encouragement and critiques of my work. I also benefited from the perspectives of Eduardo Brondizio, Richard Pace, Jacqueline Vadjunec, William Baleé, and Ryan Adams. I appreciate the support of my colleagues at UC-Denver, Sarah Horton, Marty Otañez, Julien Riel-Salvatore, and Steve Koester, and then at UCSB, Casey Walsh, Susan Stonich, Mary Hancock, Barbara Harthorn, Stuart Tyson-Smith, and David-Lopez Carr.

My involvement with the Center for Latin American Studies and the Tropical Conservation and Development (TCD) program reaffirmed in me the belief that a multidisciplinary perspective is necessary to understand human–environment topics. Charles Wood helped me develop a solid research design that included quantitative methods and a personal interest in the rich details of Brazilian social life. It was always good to talk with Jon Dain, who encouraged my curiosity and inspired me with his energy in both Gainesville and Acre. TCD alumni Valerio Gomes, Amy Duchelle, and Rich Wallace provided friendship, support, and insights in the field. My fellow graduate students were a valuable source of inspiration, theorization, and relaxation, particularly Becky Blanchard, Ryan Peseckas, Mason Mathews, Ryan Morini, Mike Degani, Remington Flutarksi, Rafael Mendoza, and Tim Podkul. Nick Kawa has been a constant source of support. A sincere thanks as well to Jason Scott and Michael Knisley.

My research would have never materialized if not for the generous support of Acreans. Judson Valentim, the head of EMBRAPA-Acre (Brazilian Agricultural Research Corporation), provided an expert perspective on Amazonian cattle ranching, as well as institutional support and unflagging encouragement for this research. Jose Eduardo, his three sons, and Chico, all of whom are ranchers, opened up their lives to me; with their friendship I was able to overcome some of the barriers that naturally arise between Amazonian ranchers and a perceived *ecologista* from the north, and gained valuable insight into their world. Although he did not have to be, A. D. V., the president of the Acrean Federation of Agriculture, was very helpful and honest with me.

I also benefited from the help of individuals at many governmental institutions in both Rio Branco and Brasiléia, including IDAF (Institute for the Defense of Agro-Cattle Raising and the Environment), INCRA (Brazilian Institute for Colonization and Agrarian Reform), and SEAPROF (Secretariat for Agriculture and Family Production). At the Federal University of Acre, Veronica Passos and Francisco Carlos da Silveira Cavalcanti helped me navigate academic and logistical issues. Eduardo "Cazuza" Amaral Borges, of the Group for Agro-Forestry Research of Acre (PESACRE), was always open to talking with me, and helped me understand the complexity of Acre. Patricia Grijo at the Fulbright Commission of Brazil was extremely helpful, and it was as a result of her flexibility that I was able to conduct research in traditional cattle-raising centers outside of Acre. The association of the residents of the CMER (Chico Mendes Extractive Reserve) area of Brasiléia (AMOREB), along with officials at IBAMA (Institute of Biodiversity and the Environment), worked with me to gain access to rubber-tapper communities.

In the rubber-tapper community of São Cristovão, I very much appreciated the generosity and support of the following households: the Marçals; Ze Coelho Wagner and Maria das Neves; and Pedro Perto and Zefa. In the Quixadá Directed Settlement Project, Bahiana and her sons, Ney and Celio, graciously hosted me and gave me a window into their lives, as did Leopoldo, who lived on the other side of the highway. I will always remember the generous support of numerous rubber tappers and colonists whom I know only by their nicknames or first names: Tatu, João da Frontiera, Carreca, Fanhoso, Branco, Raimundo Firme, and Gilberto in Quixadá; and Carlinhos, Leni and Flavio, and Carlos in São Cristovão.

Joe, Jenny, and Annie Hoelle have patiently supported me in my journeys. In addition to giving their love and encouragement, my family provided the impetus for this research when they bought some land and a few head of cattle about ten years ago. Growing up in West Texas, and surrounded by a form of "cattle culture" that I never thought to scrutinize, I became interested in the cultures that surrounded cattle raising. My fate was sealed when I arrived at UF and began to learn more about the Amazon and the importance of cattle in debates about economic development and environmental conservation.

It was due to this connection with home, and my mom's suggestion (insistence) that I share my research, that I began to write a column entitled "Postcards from the Amazon" for my hometown newspaper. Mike Kelly and Tim Archuleta at the *San Angelo Standard-Times* helped make this happen, and guided me through the early transition to writing for the newspaper. I thank San Angeloans, and others who read my articles online, for their interest and support, for giving me the opportunity to refine my ethnographic writing skills, and for helping me to not lose sight of how to communicate with non-academics.

My wife, Shravanthi Reddy, has been a source of support and inspiration, and she has helped me become a better scholar and person. With her engineer's perspective, she always challenged me to make my work clearer and helped me to understand the logic of scientific inquiry. I also appreciate her understanding while I have been absent for months at a time, and, even when present, somewhat obsessed with cows. Thanks to baby Adhya, who, while extremely distracting, has made my life richer and taught me lessons in time management. T.R., Prasanna, and Divya Reddy provided me a hideout in their basement and so much more in the months leading up to deadlines for this book.

The American Anthropological Association granted me permission to reprint versions of two papers: "Black Hats and Smooth Hands: Social Class, Environmentalism, and Work among the Ranchers of Acre, Brazil," originally published in *Anthropology of Work Review* 33 (2) (2012), and "Convergence on Cattle: Political Ecology, Social Group Perceptions, and Socioeconomic Relationships in Acre, Brazil," *Culture, Agriculture, Food and Environment* 33 (2) (2011). I thank the editors, Michael Chibnik and Sarah Lyon at AWR and Jeanne Simonelli and Stephanie Paladino at CAFE, as well as the anonymous reviewers for their assistance in turning these dissertation chapters into journal articles.

Theresa May is a straight shooter, and I feel fortunate that I was able to work with her as editor-in-chief before she retired from UT Press. Thanks to Casey Kittrell for helping me during the home stretch.

Financial support for this research came from summer research grants from the University of Florida Working Forests in the Tropics (2007), and the Department of Anthropology Doughty Award for Applied Research (2008). Fieldwork in 2007–2009 was supported in part by participation in the NSF-HSD project "Infrastructure Change, Human Agency, and Resilience in Social-Ecological Systems" (award number: 0527511; Stephen Perz, Principal Investigator). My final season of fieldwork (2010) was funded by a fellowship from the IIE Fulbright program.

RAINFOREST COWBOYS

CHAPTER I

THE JOURNEY TO ACRE

THE SIGNS

Brazilians have colorful ways of describing the Amazonian state of Acre (fig. 1.1). Situated on the border with Peru and Bolivia in the far western corner of Brazil, Acre is so "out there" in the national imagination that it is referred to as the place "where the wind turns around" and "where Judas lost his boots." In the megacities of São Paulo and Rio, they told me, "O Acre não existe" (Acre does not exist). Acreans sometimes even mumble this to themselves, with a sigh. Those who can imagine Acre see in their minds the primordial forest and Indios, but also the settlers, loggers, miners, and ranchers of the Velho Oeste (Old West) shooting it out for resources and land. For most people, though, this remote corner of Amazonia is known for the man who put it on the map, nationally and internationally: Acre is the "Land of Chico Mendes."

When I first arrived in Rio Branco, Acre, in 2007, the billboards showing Chico Mendes were still fresh and new. I recognized the face of the rubber-tapper leader from the movies and books that told of the tappers' fight to defend their rainforest homes against invading cattle ranchers in the 1970s and 1980s. Amid international news images of trailing black smoke clouds and white cattle grazing among the charred skeletons of the forest, Mendes argued for a new alternative: people could live off the forest without destroying it.

I returned every year for the next three years, and each time I noticed that the signs were a little more faded and tattered, with older advertisements peeking through Mendes's mustachioed face and the forest behind him. By 2010, many had been painted over by ads for fashion stores, cell phone carriers, and English schools, but I could

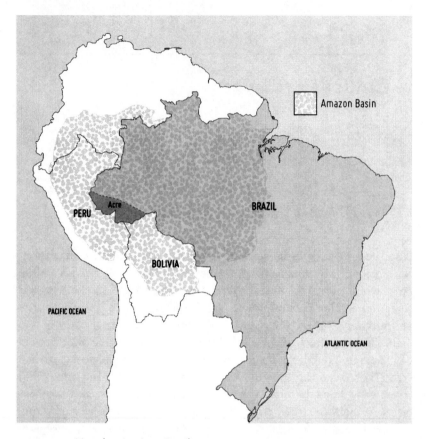

FIGURE 1.1. Map showing Acre, Brazil

still find two around town. One was alongside the Parque da Maternidade (Motherhood Park) (fig. 1.2), and the second was on a double-decker signpost by the side of the BR-364 highway in front of the Federal University of Acre: Mendes was on the upper sign, and on the lower a talking hamburger with skinny arms and legs beckoned Acreans to come to one of many *lanchonetes*, or hamburger stands, in town. When I came back to this part of the city a few weeks later to take a picture of the contrasting signs, they had both been painted over.

The signs pointed to the emerging contradictions of a political program and a global vision for sustainable development built on the legend of Chico Mendes and the rubber-tapper movement. My introduction to Acre took place during a time of social, political, and economic transition in Acre and throughout Amazonia. From 1990 to 2003, Amazonian cattle production increased at ten times the rate of the rest of the country (Arima et al. 2006), propelling Brazil to the top of the list of beef exporters in 2004. From 1998 to 2008, the count of cattle in Acre itself increased by over 400 percent, the greatest increase in all of Brazil (IBGE 2008). Much of this growth came among smallholder groups with no previous history of raising cattle, including the rubber tappers (Gomes 2009; Toni et al. 2007).

Everything that I read on the topic (e.g., Hecht 1993; Margulis 2004; Arima et al. 2006) highlighted the subsidies and incentives that made cattle more valuable than the standing forest. Little was being written about the cultural beliefs and practices that surrounded cattle raising in other parts of the world, such as the "cattle complex" (Herskovits 1926) and the "bovine idiom" (Evans-Pritchard 1944) of East African pastoralists and the "sacred cow" of India (Harris 1966). A legacy of anthropological research illustrated the deeply held beliefs, rituals, and behaviors arising from the human–cattle relationship, but in Amazonia cattle seemed to be perceived as little more than drivers of deforestation or the result of poli-

FIGURE 1.2. "Chico Mendes lives!," Rio Branco, Acre

cies and prices. To expand this view, I attempted to "look to the cow," as Evans-Pritchard had done among the Nuer, studying cattle as both economic resources and highly meaningful cultural objects.

To my surprise, I soon met self-proclaimed *caubois* (cowboys) living the *vida contri* (country life). I encountered a dedicated segment of the population, including former rubber tappers, who boasted large, shiny belt buckles, tight blue jeans, and a preference for "clean" pasture over the forest. I saw just how widespread cattle had become since the opening of the Acrean frontier to colonization and "development" some forty years ago: the ranchers' prize bulls lazed in manicured pastures, while children rode their steers to school along rubber trails deep in the forest. There was ample evidence that the growth of cattle raising had been accompanied by a "cattle culture," a cattle-centered vision of rural life that was increasingly celebrated, in both the countryside, where cow-less cowboys rode bulls in the weekend *rodeios* (rodeos), and the city, where lifetime urbanites and those displaced from the forest danced to *contri* music lamenting the idyllic rural life that lay somewhere between the city and the forest.

From the fields to the bucking bull under the *cauboi* and the leather boots on his feet to the centerpiece of the *churrasco* (barbecue), everything that I saw over the course of eighteen months of fieldwork indicated that cattle were cultural and economic objects with local and broader meanings that were both embraced and ambivalently viewed throughout Acrean society. In a setting historically, politically, and symbolically linked to the forest, it was not just the "eco-villain" ranchers, murderous *pistoleiros* (hired gunmen), or deforesters born with chainsaw in hand who were participating in this cattle culture. In fact, cattle culture was in many ways becoming inseparable from Acrean culture, revealing contradictions and fertile sites for analysis with a complex host of characters, including "carnivorous" environmentalists, small-scale cattle raisers who named and refused to eat their oxen, *caubois de vitrine* ("shop window"/urban cowboys) who owned neither cattle nor land, and members of the forest government riding their horses with forty thousand other Acreans down the Via Chico Mendes in the annual *cavalgada* (cavalcade).

To understand the appeal of cattle raising I looked to the figure of the cow in all of these situations, analyzed it from a number of angles using qualitative and quantitative methods, and then attempted to reassemble its components to enable myself to better understand the overall picture. I used a framework that emphasized the dialectical relationship between what people do and what they think, and how both are constrained by structures and reflected in material world in the form of landscapes. I thus analyzed cattle raising as an economic practice that was inseparable from "cattle culture," a suite of ideas and cultural practices that indirectly and directly valorize a cattle-centric vision of rural society.

I also followed the trails of cattle across time and scales of magnitude, from the first cattle cultures in the Iberian Peninsula to the consumption patterns and environmental concerns in the power centers of the world. I sought to capture the practices of social groups in relation to these multiscalar structures, which were political and economic, but also normative and symbolic—notions of what Amazonia *should* look like and how its residents *should* behave in relation to nature. I compared the ways that groups with unique identities and histories—from rubber tappers and urban environmentalists to cowboys and ranchers—engaged these structures from the standpoints of their own particular class, ideology, and location.

After many interviews, varied surveys, and plenty of *churrascos*, I came to perceive a mutually reinforcing system of positive signs and practices that made cattle raising socially, economically, and culturally more appealing than forest-based or agricultural livelihoods. This cattle culture is reflected in boots and belt buckles, but I also found that it is inextricable from core ideologies of nature and a complex rural sociology that can only be understood in relation to the city and the forest.

A TRIP THROUGH SOUTHWESTERN ACRE

My research began with me trying to re-envision the mighty Amazon region and Acre, Brazil, home of the forest-saving rubber tappers—not as I thought or hoped it should be, but as a place in which the cattle economy and cattle culture were increasingly apparent, but largely unacknowledged, ignored, or written off. I focused initially on what I saw: the museums, pastures, forest, *contri* bars, and slaughterhouses. I then went inside these places in search of a deeper understanding, and was gradually able to link the material world that I saw there with practices and meaning, each reflected in different ways in different people. Chico Mendes is undoubtedly the face of Acre—perhaps all of Amazonia—but here I reorient the focus to some of the other images I came across. These include a "portrait of Acre" from a conflicted past, a *pistoleiro* with a fake cowboy hat, and a photo of a *cauboi* tucked into the pages of a biology book. I begin this journey in Rio Branco, with a historical-official view, and then follow the BR-317 highway through the pastures and out to the forest. I next retrace my steps to the city, this time with a eye on cattle culture.

THE CITY OF THE FOREST

Rio Branco, the "City of the Forest," is both the capital and the largest city of the state. The work of the Governo da Floresta (Forest Government), as the state government referred to itself until 2011, was reflected in the built testaments to Acre's forest heritage and forest future, from the Arena da Floresta (Stadium of the Forest) on the Via Chico Mendes to the sleek Museu da Floresta (Museum of the Forest). These gleaming modern constructions initiated by the Forest Government rarely melded with the hodgepodge assortment of brightly painted buildings and rambling streets that surrounded them.

Amid the teeming life of everyday Rio Branco, the past was preserved in cool, quiet places around town, where you could step out of the dust and heat of the dry season. At the Museu da Borracha (Museum of Rubber) I walked through an exhibit with vivid descriptions of Acrean history, beginning with Acre's 1903 independence from Bolivia, attained with the help of the heroic rubber tappers. At the end was a life-sized display of a rubber tapper rotating a ball of rubber over a fire, working to transform the liquid latex into Amazonia's "white gold."

The first wave of rubber tappers came to Acre from drought-stricken northeastern Brazil with the onset of the "rubber boom" in the mid-1800s. From 1870 through the mid-twentieth century, Acre was one of Amazonia's most productive rubber regions (Bakx 1988). The rubber industry suffered a serious blow in the 1920s, after plantations in Southeast Asia broke the Amazonian monopoly, using seeds smuggled from the region (Dean 1987; Santos 1980). During World War II, when U.S. rubber supplies from Asia were cut off, the industry briefly rebounded, and a wave of "rubber soldiers" migrated to Amazonia from the northeast to tap rubber for the Allied war effort (Martinello 2004).

The life of the tapper was a difficult one. Locked into a system of debt-peonage, they were forced to exchange their rubber for essential goods with the *seringalista*, or rubber baron, who owned the land that they worked (Resor 1977). Following World War II, the price of

FIGURE 1.3. "A portrait of Acre," *Varadouro* magazine, December 1979 issue. Photo taken by author at the Museu da Borracha, Rio Branco, Acre.

rubber steadily declined, and the rubber barons fled the region, leaving many rubber tappers as owners of the land that they had worked (Bakx 1988:143).

In the 1970s the military government's plans to colonize the Amazon brought tumultuous changes that interrupted the rubber-tapper lifestyle depicted at the museum. The December 1979 issue of *Varadouro* magazine, which I found in the museum's archive, attests to some of the changes brought about by the arrival of migrants. In this cover illustration by Acrean artist Helio Melo, a cow has taken over the home of a rubber-tapper family, expelling them and leaving them to search for another place to live (fig. 1.3). The rubber tree (recognizable by the lines on its trunk), which sustained the rubber tapper, had been chopped down to make room for cattle pasture. This image illustrates the clash of cultures, as the forest-dwelling rubber tappers are physically and culturally displaced by foreign migrants and their cattle.

The sense of invasion was further reinforced at the Biblioteca da Floresta (Library of the Forest), a recent construction by the Governo da Floresta. In its entryway I was greeted by a dramatic wall display entitled "O Acre Como um Pasto de Boi" (Acre as a Cattle Pasture). In the first photo, a military officer aims his binoculars toward the horizon—to the Amazonian frontier, then a sparsely populated land of untapped resources and a potential security threat. Faced with unrest in the populous southern regions of Brazil, the military government opened the Amazon up to settlement by smallholders, landless populations, and urban poor (Almeida 1992; Moran 1981; Smith 1982). Entrepreneurs and ranchers from central-southern Brazil were also attracted by incentives and subsidies and worked to establish large-scale cattle ranching operations (Hecht 1993).

In the next panel of the display is a map of Brazil with red veins traversing Amazonia, to indicate the network of roads constructed to facilitate migration into isolated regions. An overburdened logging truck and a mottled Gyrolandia bull stare out from the map, symbols of the predatory extractivist business model that developed on Amazonia's "contested frontiers," where migrant groups from other Brazilian states battled for land and resources with native Amazonians (Schmink and Wood 1992). In the foreground of the map, a man with a machine gun stands behind a wooden fence denoting the entrance to a cattle ranch (fig. 1.4). The eyes of this *pistoleiro* are concealed beneath a cowboy hat, which appears to have been overlain on the original photo of the man. No doubt a creative way to conceal the *pistoleiro*'s identity, the choice of a dark cowboy hat is appropriate for the Acrean recasting of the frontier narrative, in which the forest-dwelling rubber tappers banded together to defend their forest against the villainous cattle ranchers.

Amid escalating violence in the late 1980s, the rubber tappers were able to slow down the rate of rancher deforestation and appropriation of tapper lands around the city of Xapuri, and moved toward securing rights to their land. The cause was aided by the international acclaim of Chico Mendes, who traveled abroad to speak of the rubber tappers' struggle, and drew attention to the environmental destruction taking place throughout Amazonia. Back in Acre, Mendes received death threats from ranchers angered by the rubber tappers' protests, which were preventing them from taking control of lands that they claimed.

In the aftermath of Mendes's murder, the movement attained an even broader appeal, bringing international pressure to bear on the Brazilian government (Keck 1995). The rubber-tapper movement achieved one of its primary goals with the establishment of the extractive reserve (RESEX) system. This novel land-tenure model was based on rubber-tapper patterns of resource use, in which they harvested products, such as rubber and Brazil nuts, from the standing forest. They emphasized that in these reserves people could both use the forest and contribute to its preservation (Schwartzman 1989). Following the establishment of the RESEX, similar use-based conservation units were instituted throughout Amazonia (Gomes 2009; Kainer et al. 2003). The rubber tappers became a potent symbol in an emerging global environmental movement (Tsing 2005).

All around Rio Branco and on signs along the BR-317 the same

FIGURE 1.4. Amazonian *pistoleiro* with cowboy hat. Photo taken by author of display at the Biblioteca da Floresta, Rio Branco, Acre.

symbol was painted: a tree in a box, with "Governo da Floresta" written underneath. From the Arena da Floresta to the Via Chico Mendes, with its bike lanes and potted plants, on out to the Via Verde, a highway that now encircles the city, there have been vast urban infrastructural improvements throughout Rio Branco over the past decade, and many of them have the little tree symbol stamped on them.

The "forest government" was born in 1989, when Jorge Viana assumed the governorship of Acre. Successive administrations built on the ideals of the rubber-tapper movement to promote forest-based development "to demonstrate to present and future generations that development does not depend on the destruction of the forest, but rather on its survival" (Government of Acre 1999, quoted in Kainer et al. 2003).

One of the forest government's most popular projects was the conversion of a swampy ditch running through the middle of Rio Branco into a pleasant oasis known as the Parque da Maternidade. While I was in Acre, lycra-clad women and men in sleeveless shirts walked and talked in the evenings along its extensive network of paths. Workers returned home from a day's work on their bikes, toting groceries in red and white striped plastic bags balanced in back. They passed the Museu da Floresta and the Museu dos Povos da Floresta (Museum of Forest Peoples), and O Paço restaurant, with its bow-tied waitstaff taking orders on electronic pads. Youths played soccer and volleyball on numerous sand courts between the walking paths and the canal. After an errant kick or pass, they argued about who would retrieve the ball from the ankle-high black water that bisected the park from its beginning until it crossed under the Avenida Ceará and entered the market, where sellers hawked fruits, ice cream, stacks of colorful synthetic clothing, and *pirata* cell phones.

At the far edge of the market, the black stream and the plastic bottles that floated on its surface merged with the muddy waters of the Acre River. It flowed to the Purus, Solimões, and Amazon Rivers before eventually emptying into the Atlantic Ocean some 3,000 kilometers downstream. Upriver from the park, a futuristic white pedestrian bridge carried young environmentalists from the World Wildlife Fund offices across the river to the newly renovated *mercado velho* (old market), where they often sat sipping draft beer in the fading afternoon sun.

As we follow it upstream, the Acre River meanders through the upper Acre region, through Xapuri, down to Brasiléia on the Bolivian border, and then on to Assis Brasil, before heading into Peru and its source in the Andes. The recently paved (2002) BR-317 highway roughly follows the river for some 330 kilometers through the upper Acre region (fig. 1.5). Completed under the Viana administration, the BR-317 forms part of the Inter-Oceanic Highway, which now links Brazil with the Peruvian coast. This region of upper Acre, along with lower Acre—which encircles Rio Branco and extends east to the states of Amazonas and Rondônia—is the most heavily populated and denuded part of the state.

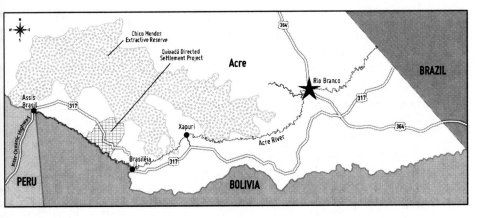

FIGURE 1.5. Map of southern Acre

This west Amazonian region is also one of the most biodiverse parts of the entire basin (Campbell and Hammond 1989; Daly and Prance 1989). Clearings have revealed geoglyphs, huge geometrically shaped earthworks that resemble streambeds from the road. These recent archeological finds are forcing us to rethink what life was like for ancient Amazonian societies (Pärssinen et al. 2009). Although it was long thought of as a virgin wilderness, contemporary researchers now highlight the role of Amerindians in shaping this ecosystem over the centuries (Balée 2006; Denevan 1992; Posey 1985) and the continued interactions between humans and ecosystem (Campbell 2007; Phillips et al. 1994).

IN THE GAPS

About 88 percent of Acre is still covered by forest, but I spent much of my time in the other 12 percent, where humped, white Brahman cattle grazed on either side of the BR-317. Elaborate gates framed the vast seas of pasture belonging to the large cattle ranches of the *fazendeiros* (ranchers). The pastures were punctuated by red-orange veins running down hills and knee-high termite mounds. The entrances to the *ramais* (unpaved side roads) were marked by the rusty soil that spilled out and eventually faded into the blacktop, chronicling the journeys of cattle trucks from colonist and rubber-tapper communities located beyond the end of the road. The *ramais* ran through the baking pastures of the colonists, many of their homesteads carpeted in stubbly grass from the front door to the farthest fence. Past the settlement project the forest thickened, the temperature dropped, and the road disintegrated into little footpaths.

Jatobá Rocha and his family lived down one of these paths. The Rochas' home sat amid fruit trees, surrounded by a two-hectare clearing planted with cassava and beans and pasture for their one bull, Tchoa. Foot trails radiated out from the homestead and through the forest, connecting the family to the rubber and Brazil nut trees upon which they and their rubber-tapper neighbors have historically depended. Jatobá was naturally hesitant to adopt cattle when I first met him in 2007, but he took the plunge and bought Tchoa a year later.

From Jatoba's house I could walk to the homes of others, and at each one heard a similar story, about how the forest did not make economic sense anymore. I saw firsthand just how useful cattle were for the isolated, poor tappers—their milk provided a constant supply of protein and they transported Brazil nuts and rubber to the side of the road for pickup. In contrast to these forest products, cattle were useful for their flexibility—they had no season and could be sold when necessary. Despite the acknowledged advantages of cattle, it was hard for the aged tappers to reconcile themselves to the growing pastures of the *seringal*.

Some days I rose before the sun came up to tap rubber with the families that I stayed with. Other days were spent fishing, hunting, working the cattle, or weeding crops. After lunch we always rested. On the long, hot afternoons of summer (dry season) we laid on the cool wooden planks of the floor or sat slumped against a wall, swatting away the ever-present *cabas* (small wasps) and asking questions about each other's lives. Airplanes often passed high above these little clearings in the forest, and my hosts inevitably spoke up or broke off our conversations to ask if I came here in one of those. They would ask what it was like, point to the sky, and wonder, "Where is that one going?" The planes were usually heading north or south, so I responded with references to places that they had heard of but never been to: the United States in the north or São Paulo, Rio de Janeiro, or Argentina in the south.

In the silences that followed, my thoughts would drift back to my flights into and around Brazil. On my first flight, from Texas to São Paulo, I passed over the Amazon at night during the dry season. It was disorienting because the light of the stars outshone the black abyss below. Glowing orange fires and nebula-like little cities occasionally broke the darkness. My mind began to fill the void with the Amazonian hyper-nature of tangled forest, watchful eyes, slithering, and buzzing. When I later headed north for Acre during the daytime, land and sky were easily distinguishable, but the ground was again monotonous, an uninterrupted mass of bumpy green carpet, with glistening rivers curling through like drunken slug trails.

It was like the flyover that often began nature programs I had seen in the United States, in which the overview sets the stage for a look beneath the green. The camera zooms in through the canopy, to a scene of exotic nature, imbued with mystery by the noises of an unseen howler monkey and a lonely woodwind. "This mysterious region is finally giving up its secrets. In the past ten years, a new species has been discovered on average every three days. But the Amazon is changing fast, threatening the animals and plants that have evolved here for millions of years." The flute whinnies and stops suddenly: "The race is on to learn more about this remarkable place before it is too late" (*Wild Amazon*, episode 1: "The Cradle of Life," National Geographic Channel).

On the plane ride to Acre that first day I found that the clearings in the forest got my attention. The pastures, roads, and cities—those spaces with which I was familiar in the "developed" world—seemed intrusive and out of place in a region that I had come to think of as the ultimate expression of the vastness of nature. These places were often the focus of Amazonian research, defined by what they are not—forest. The maps show an alarming red arc of deforestation along the southern edge of Amazonia, and gray fishbone patterns mark the settlement projects.

Once on the ground, I worked to leave that view behind me, along with the lenses of a privileged environmentalism through which a complex landscape is reduced to the green of standing forest and the red of destruction, and its inhabitants made into either eco-villains or forest guardians. The first step for me was to change the questions, and to ask why cattle made economic sense and what they meant to people, instead of asking why the area was being deforested. I learned that in the eyes of many residents of the region the forest was a vestige of a bygone time and an obstacle to development. The red-ribbon roads and geometric ranches—these represented "order and progress" carved out of a no-man's-land. I needed to view this landscape as a near reverse-negative and to see these new gaps as meaningful and important. They were created by people, individuals responding to a configuration of political and economic structures and guided by identities formed amid other ways of using the land and, sometimes, aspirations for a better life.

CATTLE CULTURE: THE *CAUBOI* IN THE BIOLOGY BOOK

Brasiléia lies some 80 kilometers away from the *seringal*, and to get there one must travel across the rubber trails, to the *ramal*, lined by smallholder colonists, and then onto the BR-317 highway, rolling alongside picturesque pastures where cowboys loll among the white herds of the ranchers.

Maria Bahiana's house was about halfway between Assis Brasil and Brasiléia. She lived in one of the settlement projects opened by the government in the 1980s. Everyone knew her and could point you down the unassuming little dirt road, lined by barbed wire and buffered by pasture, that led to her dwelling. She left her native Bahia with her husband when she was still in her teens, and made various stops along the opening frontiers. Like the other colonists in the settlement project, she came to Amazonia to get some land and make a life for herself. Shortly after arriving in Acre in 1980, her husband fell from his oxcart and was crushed under the wheels. She went it alone for almost thirty years, raising her sons and daughters and working her long fingers into a twist of knots and knuckles. In 2009, following the lead of many colonists and other rural people, Bahiana moved to the city with her sons and grandson. She kept mementos of her life tucked into the pages of an old middle school biology book. One night she pulled all the pictures out to show me, and gazed upon a black-and-white image of her deceased husband. Back when I first saw it, this photo of her eldest son, Branco, and his family struck me as an Amazonian take on American Gothic (fig. 1.6).

Here we see Branco, a *cauboi*, in his jeans, boots, and cowboy hat, and his ex-wife, with a white lamb in her arms. We sense that something else is being invoked by this photo, beyond its associations with earning a living, a driver of deforestation, or an economically rational guy responding to government incentives. As Branco stands confidently in the pasture, with cowboys and cattle in the background, the photo presents a concrete view of cattle raising, but also a man's aspirations for a way of life that is culturally meaningful.

As he stands in the pasture, amid the sunshine, in his boots—can we even say that Branco is in the Amazon? The forest is conspicuously absent from the photo; imported pasture grasses, cattle, horses, and the white lamb take center stage. His pose, his accoutrements, and his surroundings evoke a sense of control of the natural world,

FIGURE 1.6. Branco, an Amazonian *cauboi*, and family. Photo by Maria Bahiana.

of the cowboy who labors to subdue nature through the establishment and maintenance of "clean" pastures, the domestication of cattle, and the consumption of their flesh. Each of these features of the cowboy life is celebrated in Acre through cattle culture, with its *contri* songs and fashion, rodeos, and *churrascos*. Branco provides an introduction to the ways that I conceptualize both cattle raising and cattle culture—by means of an expanded focus on not only the practice and the resultant landscapes, but also the ideologies that undergird the perception of these landscapes, and the practices and groups that produce them.

The last time I saw Branco, he was competing in a *rodeio* at the Raio da Lua (Moonbeam), a few kilometers from where he had grown up with Bahiana. He was with other young *caubois*, also clad in cowboy hats, leather boots and vests, and shiny belt buckles. They were attempting to ride bucking bulls in the hopes of winning a motorcycle. After the competition, I sat with the group on a low wooden fence, and listened as they talked and compared bumps and bruises. They devoured barbecued beef and boiled manioc root from plastic plates balanced on their knees, hurriedly stuffing the last bits into their mouths as the *sertaneja* or *contri* (I use these terms interchangeably to refer to contemporary Brazilian country music) cranked up, signaling the beginning of the dance. From this little speck of light on the side of the highway, pulsating stereo speakers sent messages about an idyllic rural life floating out over the dark forest.

Rio Branco lies some 300 kilometers southeast of the Raio da Lua. Back on the BR-317 highway, we see cattle, with little white *garças* (egrets) always following close behind, moving about in the green pastures, rubbing themselves on the rough trunks of the Brazil nut trees in the morning before ambling on to the green knee-high pastures, which fade to brown in the dry summer months. These towering trees, many of them charred at the base and limbless after being burned by pasture fires, throw long, thin shadows that shrink and move from west to east as the day progresses. It is illegal to cut down these now-sterile trees, according to the "Chico Mendes Law." The landscape reflects the destructive past chronicled in *The World Is Burning* (Shoumatoff 1990) and *The Burning Season* (Revkin 1990).

Up the road in Capixaba, the highway passed the "Country Bar," with its painted sign of a woman in boots and a slim cowboy on a bucking bull. Nearing Rio Branco, we saw a new rodeo arena and dancehall called the Celeiro Beer (Beer Barn), with a wagon wheel mounted above the front door. Next to the Celeiro was a small store where I stopped once with Olessio, a ranch foreman. He needed a new belt buckle for the annual Expo-Acre celebration in Rio Branco. He chose from a selection of silver belt buckles the size of elongated saucers. They gleamed under a glass case next to smaller ones with pink accents for women, and tins of imported American smokeless tobacco.

As we approach Rio Branco, just off the Via Verde on the BR-364 (heading on to Rondonia and then to Rio de Janeiro and São Paulo), the foul smell and the black smoke announce the presence of the two new slaughterhouses. This was where Acrean cattle ended their journey from the pastures of the rubber tappers, colonists, and ranchers of southern Acre. In the pens outside of one of these slaughterhouses, I looked down on the cattle as they stood about and occasionally jostled for position, as misty water from a sprinkler cascaded over them. They slowly filtered single file into a warehouse, where they were hit over the head, strung up, split in half with a chainsaw, transformed into Acre's famed *boi verde* (green cattle), a beef marketed for its "natural" qualities. Nothing was wasted here, the manager told me, as he motioned to the rendering machine, where bones were ground and fat, sinew, and the rest were melted down and converted to ingredients for everything from toothpaste to gelatin.

On the weekend, the smell of roasting meat was heavy in the air, with *churrascos* serving as the centerpiece for social gatherings of Acreans from all social classes. A *churrasco* without beef is not acceptable to most, and, as one man told me, meatless meals "are eaten with our eyes closed." And Acreans do eat beef. Forty percent of the beef produced in Acre stays within the borders of the state, where it is consumed by Acreans, who have the highest rate of annual beef consumption in all of Brazil (Valentim 2008). It seemed that on almost every commercial block in every town there was either a butcher shop or a *churrascaria*, a self-service restaurant featuring roasted meat, as well as a pharmacy. Along with agricultural supply stores, these establishments were often decorated with scenes of majestic white bulls grazing in a verdant, mountainous countryside that called to mind a Swiss landscape. Inside a butcher shop in the humble Sobral neighborhood, a painted white bull looked out over a pasture bisected by a small stream, and down to a glass case with chunks of ruby red meat on hooks. On the wall it said, "Deus é meu pastor" ("The Lord is my shepherd").

Sobral and other neighborhoods like it are full of old rubber tappers. The city offered a better life to the ex-pioneers and the forests' huddled masses, and they built their homes on the outskirts. As Brazil emerges, those fueling urban production have access to goods beyond what they once imagined, but they also have rural roots, memories, or at least stories and songs of a purer time and place. In the first quiet slices of afternoon shade, *saudade* (longing, nostalgia) drifts over the zinc roofs of the city, skips hurriedly past the forest, and settles on a nice piece of land, maybe with a few head of cattle, in the country.

If you drove around Rio Branco you would likely hear *sertaneja* music down low in the restaurants, and louder in the *contri* bars, where local singer Bobnei belted out *sertaneja* hits, along with American country songs "Chattahoochee" and "Jambalaya." *Sertaneja* also echoed from cars parked on the sidewalk, with young men sitting in a circle and sipping *tereré* (cold *herba maté* tea), a tradition adapted from the *gaúchos* some 4,000 kilometers to the south. You could have stopped in at the recently opened "Cowboys Ranch" to buy new cowboy boots, hats, blue jeans, leather belts, or a shiny belt buckle.

At Bahamas, the most recent *contri* bar, patrons drank iced beer from little steel buckets and watched a big-screen TV playing rodeo clips and bullfighting bloopers. The volume was turned off so that they could hear a man singing *sertaneja* covers. He passed the microphone to members of the audience during the refrains of the most popular tunes. The walls of Bahamas were painted with various scenes that seemed to hearken back more to the American West than to Brazil, with cowboys roaming desert landscapes beneath fiery pink skies and tabletop mesas. The male and female bathrooms were indicated by two cowboy-hatted silhouettes leaning against a wall: one slim and muscular, the other buxom.

The Acrean landscape illustrates some of the myriad features of the growing cattle industry. The signs all point to a collection of ideas and practices that indirectly and directly valorize cattle raising. My task here is to follow the unseen threads and assemble the pieces to build toward a more complete picture of cattle raising in contemporary Amazonia.

BRIDGING THE GAPS: IDEOLOGICAL AND METHODOLOGICAL CONSIDERATIONS

In formulating a research project around this contentious topic, I endeavored to study cattle in a way that was grounded in a conceptual and methodological framework that would make my findings accessible and convincing both to scholars and to those working on issues of rural development and environmental preservation in Amazonia. I drew on perspectives from political economy and political ecology; practice theory; economic, ecological, symbolic, and cognitive anthropology; cultural geography; popular culture and literature; environmental history; and research on cattle raising in the Americas and East Africa.

As I discovered the layers, connections, and complexity involved in understanding Acrean cattle, my methods naturally evolved and expanded (see appendix B for details). I spent the first three field seasons attempting to capture the economic and cultural role of cattle in the lives of rural rubber tappers, colonists, and large-scale ranchers by conducting surveys and participant observation. I also interviewed key government officials and representatives of environmental NGOs in the city, and watched the actions of people in places where cattle were present in some form, including butcher shops, rodeos, and *churrascos*. After three trips and a year of fieldwork, I possessed comparisons of various social groups' economic practices across time, life histories, key-informant interviews, and pages of ethnographic description.

I returned home and started writing, and I found myself hanging some pretty big generalizations on anecdotes, small samples, and provocative quotes. Fortunately, I was able to acquire funding for another six months of research in Acre, and I had the time to plan out how to obtain the data needed to make the study more comprehensive. I focused on two very distinctive areas, one quantitative and the other qualitative, to help me generate the overall picture that I was aiming for.

I wanted to measure the extent to which different groups agreed with certain statements that I had heard often. For example, did cowboys and environmentalists alike associate pastures with hard work and intact forest with laziness? I thought that I understood each group and their views, but I wanted to systematically compare their responses to such questions, and to determine where the fault lines and contradictions occurred across a broad cross-section of Acrean society.

I created a survey of perceptions and activities that I thought to be indicative of cattle culture, and when I went back to Acre, I administered it to twenty members of six main social groups: rubber tappers, colonists, ranchers, cowboys, urban policy makers, and decision makers and field technicians at socioenvironmental NGOs. These data provided me with a body of empirical information within which to systematically compare social groups and gauge the extent to which cattle culture had been appropriated across a broad cross-section of Acrean society (see appendix C for questions and results).

As I prepared for my return to the field later that year, I also thought back to my initial impressions of the Amazon. I had learned so much, but I never really took the time to explain it very well to my friends and family in the United States, and I worried that in this I was in some ways contributing to the region's exoticism. We were always drawn back to the things they had seen on TV—the unbelievable *candiru* (toothpick fish), the photos of the isolated Indian tribe in Acre that swept across the Internet in 2007, and most frequently the question, "Why are they cutting down the forest?"

I could not fault anyone, because my own questions were not that different before I had the opportunity to learn more and do research in the Amazon. I wanted to find a way to share my research and show the complexity of Amazonian life, and to demonstrate how Acreans were different, but also to reveal that they were in many ways connected to and quite similar to the people of my hometown or anyone else.

I gradually learned over the course of the research that a mixed-methods approach is vital for understanding the full complexity of contemporary socio-environmental topics, in the Amazonia and elsewhere. I talked to the editors of my hometown newspaper, and we agreed that I would send biweekly "Postcards from the Amazon" from the field. In the pages that follow you will find some of these descriptive articles, quantitative data, and other observations derived from more than a year and a half of fieldwork.

CHAPTER 2

THE EXPANSION OF CATTLE RAISING IN ACRE

PRIOR TO 1975, LESS THAN 1 PERCENT of the Amazon region had been deforested (Moran 1993). This number has grown to 14.5 percent in recent years. The vast majority of the nearly seventy-five million hectares of deforested lands now serve as cattle pastures (IBGE 2008). The initial expansion of cattle into the Brazilian Amazon in the 1970s and 1980s was limited mostly to large-scale ranches in the eastern Amazon states of Pará and Mato Grosso, and was the result of land speculation and government credit and subsidies (Hecht 1993; Mahar 1989; Schmink and Wood 1992). In areas of forest extractivism, such as the state of Acre, Brazil, rubber tappers fought against the conversion of forest to cattle pasture.

Initially, raising cattle in Amazonia was profitable only because it was propped up by generous government incentives and subsidies (Hecht 1993). Although many of these subsidies and incentives have since been discontinued, new ones have emerged, and cattle raising has expanded throughout Amazonia. In 2004 Brazil emerged as the leader in global beef exports. This growth was fueled not by activities in the traditional cattle-raising areas of the country, however, but rather by Amazonian production, which increased at ten times the rate of the rest of the country during the 1990s (Arima et al. 2006). The suppression of hoof-and-mouth disease and favorable agroclimatic conditions have made the Amazon a prime haven for cattle displaced from centralized production regions where land is more expensive (Arima et al. 2006; Smeraldi and May 2008). By 2011, cattle in the Amazon accounted for 38 percent of the total national beef production.

Scholars understand the rise of Amazonian ranching to be the result of multiscalar political and economic factors that directly and indirectly contribute to the profitability of cattle raising (Arima et al. 2011; Barona et al. 2010; Margulis 2004; Moran 1993; Pacheco and Poccard-Chapuis 2012; Walker et al. 2000; Walker et al. 2009). Converting forest to pasture remains the most recognizable way of laying claim to land, gaining title to it, and increasing its value (Fearnside 2005; Hecht 1993). Regionally, expanding urban demand for beef has become a primary driver of the Amazonian cattle industry (Faminow 1998).

On the household level, cattle raising offers many advantages over other land uses, especially for poor, isolated groups. It is less risky, requires less up-front investment, and is less labor intensive than agriculture (Durning and Brough 1991). Additionally, cattle are a liquid asset that maintains value, and they are easily transported to market (Margulis 2004).

From 1998 through 2008 Acre experienced the greatest percentage increase in heads of cattle of all Brazilian states (IGBE 2010). Since 2005, improved enforcement of environmental controls has slowed Amazon deforestation (Nepstad et al. 2009), especially among large ranchers, but smallholders—including rubber tappers, who lack support for agricultural and forest extraction activities and face strict deforestation constraints—subsequently became the main drivers of cattle expansion, as cattle raising became their only economically viable livelihood (Toni et al. 2007). Governmental policy shifts have thus—inadvertently—created a generalized tendency to adopt cattle raising, even among groups previously unaccustomed to, or even opposed to, cattle (Ehringhaus 2005; Gomes 2009; Salisbury and Schmink 2007; Wallace 2004). Beneath these general trends, however, there are important differences in the ways distinct groups now understand and practice cattle raising.

This brief review illustrates the political and economic orientation of Amazonian cattle research. In this chapter I draw on this legacy to examine how the economic practices of three different rural social groups in Acre have gradually shifted to cattle raising. I analyze how groups were positioned within a political economy from 1970 to 1990, and how they have responded to structural changes in the twenty years since 1990. In addition to the critical role of political and economic factors, I emphasize the changing perceptions of cattle and intergroup relationships over the past forty years. The broader goal of this chapter is to put my research in conversation with the dominant cattle paradigm, and then to build, chapter by chapter, a better understanding of the complexity of Amazonian cattle raising.

POLITICAL ECOLOGY AND CATTLE RAISING IN ACRE

I now will draw on a comparative political ecology framework to examine the ways that political and economic factors affect different groups in unique ways across time and scale (Gezon and Paulson 2005). Political ecology builds on political economy to study the role of power relations in human–environment interactions, as well as the influence of capitalism on local systems and decisions (Biersack 1999:10).

Local economic practices are structured by political economic factors, such as governmental development policies and market fluctuations, which penetrate unequally at different levels and among groups (Blaikie and Brookfield 1987). The structural factors create the parameters, but do not determine the manner in which groups make decisions and provision for their household or the market (Chayanov 1986; Netting 1993). Perspectives from economic anthropology emphasize the importance of grounded cultural phenomena in mediating social group responses to macrostructural processes and changes (Polanyi 1958; Sahlins 1972; Wilk and Cligget 2006).

Cattle engender strong cultural beliefs in settings throughout the world (Evans-Pritchard 1940; Herskovits 1926; Harris 1966), and cattle raisers are often accorded greater prestige than those without cattle, from Africa (Schneider 1957; Spear 1993; Goldschmidt 1969) to the Americas (Bennett 1969). By focusing on cattle in more recent contexts, where broader connections are drawn out and constraints emanate from multiscalar political projects and capitalist markets, we gain a window into the ways that cattle raisers negotiate changing political economic structures and evolving meanings (Comaroff and Comaroff 1990; Ferguson 1985; Hutchinson 1996; Sheridan 2007). In summary, my framework recognizes that several factors— political and economic structures, cultural factors, including on-the-ground identities and circulating ideas of the meaning of cattle, and social relationships between groups—may affect economic practices.

ACREAN SOCIAL GROUPS AND RESEARCH AREA

Settlement projects constitute 1,955,870 hectares, or 11.9 percent of Acrean territory. Located between the CMER and the BR-317 highway is the massive Quixadá Projeto de Assentamento Dirigido (PAD), or Directed Settlement Project (DSP), where I conducted most of my research with colonists. It covers 76,741 hectares and is home to an

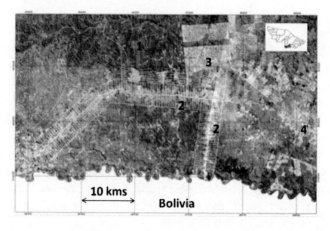

FIGURE 2.1. Satellite image of research area. Adapted from Luzar 2006 (41).

estimated 998 families (Governo do Acre 2006:116). Quixadá is criss-crossed by side roads extending up to thirty kilometers to the north of the BR-317 and to the south as far as the Acre River, which is the border with Bolivia. Households and landholdings are generally lo-cated along these side roads. Landholdings are not based on resource distribution, as was the case for the tappers, but rather were drawn by governmental officials, who settled the colonists here. The average size of colonist landholdings was around eighty hectares.

Rubber-tapper households in this sample owned about 300 hectares of land. They lived in the Chico Mendes Extractive Reserve (CMER), a sustainable-use conservation unit covering 5.66 percent of the state, with conservation units totaling 45 percent (Governo do Acre 2006: 103) (see Appendix A for more information on my research area).

None of the ranchers that I interviewed live on their ranches. They are based out of Rio Branco, and the majority of them own ranches in upper Acre, although some had ranches in the neighboring mu-nicipalities of lower Acre. A rancher, as defined in this study, owns approximately five thousand head of cattle and five thousand hect-ares of land; this total can come from one landholding or multi-ple ranches. According to figures presented by Toni and colleagues, there are eight private properties with between one and ten thousand hectares of land in the municipality of Assis Brasil, and nineteen in Brasiléia (2007:42). As previously mentioned, rancher interviews were conducted throughout the state, but these statistics, along with fig-ure 2.1, will serve to illustrate the distribution of social groups and landholdings in the primary research area.

Figure 2.1 shows the general location of the research sites and identifies the administrative units where research was conducted. The area indicated by the number 3 is a ranch that was not included in my survey. I have indicated its position here to illustrate the scale of a ranch and to show how the different land-tenure systems are situated in relation to one another. The side roads of the settlement projects and colonists' property lines are visible around the areas marked with the number 2. The RESEX (3) begins at the end of the side roads to the north. The primary line extending from right, in the city of Brasiléia (4), to left and then angling down is the BR-317 highway.

SOCIAL GROUPS, ECONOMIC PRACTICES, AND TENURE SYSTEMS BEFORE 1990

The first colonists arrived to take part in some of the nationally sponsored agricultural settlement projects implemented throughout the country in the 1970s and 1980s. They were directed by INCRA, the Brazilian Institute for Colonization and Agrarian Reform, which settled families from overcrowded and impoverished parts of the country in the sparsely populated Amazon region. These migrants were expected to convert forest to agricultural plots and grow produce for their own subsistence as well as for the market (Moran 1981; Smith 1982). Acrean colonist families reported that demonstrating "progress" through forest conversion was essential to maintaining their land in these early years.

The Brazilian government also supported the establishment of large-scale cattle ranches by offering generous fiscal incentives, attracting entrepreneurs from other parts of Brazil (Hecht 1993). The Acrean state, at that time headed by Governor Wanderley Dantas (1971–1975), courted investors from the south, and facilitated the sale of the vast rubber estates to the ranchers (Bakx 1988). Migrants, many from landowning classes in Minas Gerais and São Paulo, were drawn to the new frontier in Acre, where they could acquire cheap land and subsidies for cattle ranching.

Prior to 1990, these social groups were dedicated to distinct forms of exploiting their environment to fulfill their subsistence and economic needs: rubber tappers relied mostly on the collection of forest products (rubber and Brazil nut); colonists dedicated themselves largely to agricultural pursuits; and large-scale ranchers raised cattle.

The arrival of migrants in the form of affluent ranchers and colonists hungry for land resulted in clashes with the native rubber tappers, who were already scattered over much of southwestern Acre. Rancher legal rights, backed by the government policy of the time, were superimposed on tapper use rights. When ranchers sought to claim the land that they had purchased, and convert the forests to pastures, there was intergroup conflict (Ehringhaus 2005:5). The RESEX established in 1990 after rubber-tapper mobilization and protest served to institutionalize territorial and use rights for the rubber tappers as these related to their traditional economic practice of forest extractivism (Kainer et al. 2003; Schwartzman 1989).

From 1970 to 1990 different groups with different practices came together and came into conflict in Acre. During the process of opening the Amazon during the 1970s and 1980s, three different types of land-tenure systems were created to accommodate these distinct social groups and their specific economic practices. These systems established culturally distinct group boundaries and economic practices for rubber tappers, agricultural colonists, and large-scale ranchers, which were reinforced through governmental support for extractivism, agriculture, and cattle raising. With this focus on specific economic practices and political objectives, social groups became linked to distinct identities, practices, and spaces.

Until the 1990s cattle were essentially the domain of large-scale ranchers in Acre. Lack of technical knowledge and capital limited their adoption by smallholder colonists and rubber tappers, who also disdained cattle for their role in social conflict and environmental destruction (Bakx 1988; Toni et al. 2007). In the last twenty years, however, all groups' tenure systems have become more restrictive because of environmental laws, while their practices have continued to respond to evolving political, economic, and cultural cues. On the surface, the actions of colonists and especially of rubber tappers can be understood as diverging from their land-use practices and identities. The notion of unified group practice based on shared identity and the institutional rules of tenure systems occludes the fact that groups have always adapted to structural constraints within cultural guidelines, which are also subject to change.

The assumed unity of practice–perception–tenure also betrays the fact that the groups live side by side, interacting with and influencing one another. The essential function of cattle in the production system of each group can be distilled to the following: rubber tappers value cattle for their liquidity and view the animals as a savings account; colonists view cattle as their last option as a result of deforestation regulations that inhibit agriculture; and ranchers continue to raise cattle on a large scale for the beef market. Although groups use and think about cattle differently, their common participation in the cattle economy facilitates exchange and cooperation between them. Given these factors, I seek to answer the following questions:

(1) What political and economic factors have made cattle raising a more viable economic practice than agriculture and extractivism?
(2) How do different social groups in Acre now view cattle?
(3) Once a vehicle of conflict, how do cattle now mediate intergroup cultural and economic exchanges?

CATTLE EXPANSION IN ACRE SINCE 1990

NEOLIBERAL AND ENVIRONMENTAL POLICIES

Over the last twenty years, different social groups in Amazonia have been heavily affected by political and economic factors that are the consequences of neoliberal and environmental policies. There has been a pronounced decline in governmental support for rural family production, as evidenced by decreased support of agricultural livelihoods and the removal of subsidies for rubber (Salisbury and Schmink 2007; Toni et al. 2007). In addition to government investment in roads, these actions can be understood as part of a broader neoliberal agenda pursued by the Brazilian government (Perz et al. 2010; Perz et al. 2011). Environmental policies have also played a role in changing the practices of rural groups. Strict enforcement of deforestation and burning regulations in Acre, beginning around 2000 with Acre's "forest government," has also seriously impeded rural livelihood strategies. Each of these interventions has produced unique and unexpected effects, but collectively they have made the pre-1990 economic practices of extractivism and agriculture less competitive with cattle raising, and in some cases impossible.

Shortly after the establishment of the CMER RESEX, the government discontinued the subsidy that had propped up rubber prices for decades, undermining the viability of extractivist livelihoods. The removal of the rubber subsidy was the final straw for many extractivist families in Acre (Salisbury and Schmink 2007).

Families in São Cristovão reported that it was during the 1990s that Brazil nut became their primary source of income, replacing

FIGURE 2.2. Rubber-tapper children ride their bull home from school

rubber, and cattle began to enter the picture as a strategy for storing wealth (fig. 2.2). Cattle spread throughout the RESEX, particularly in households bordering settlement projects and ranches (Gomes 2009).

Some families in the RESEX were threatened with expulsion for exceeding deforestation limits to raise cattle. In the words of *A Tribuna* (2008), an Acrean newspaper: "The [RESEX] was born from the dreams of the rubber tappers to be protected from cattle raising. This same activity [cattle raising] has now returned to threaten them." This press account and others like it imply that raising cattle in the RESEX is a violation in and of itself; this is not the case as long as deforestation limits are observed. More than any other group, the rubber tappers feel the tensions of an evolving political economy that renders their traditional economic practices less viable than cattle raising, and they struggle to reconcile their cultural values with the material needs of their households.

There is also a disconnection between the colonists' traditional and current economic practices, but colonists, especially migrants from other regions, never had an ideological opposition to cattle. Colonists reported that up through the 1980s there was governmental support and markets for their agricultural goods, but after 1990 this was no longer the case. For most products, such as rice and corn, the

costs of getting the harvest to market outweighed potential profits. Governmental support for agriculture was not removed through
a conscious policy decision, but the colonists were essentially left
to fend for themselves after the first big push to develop the Amazon (Smith 1982). For rubber tappers settled on the smaller plots (ca.
80 hectares) of the settlement project, extractivism, which requires
more extensive landholdings (ca. 300 hectares), was never possible.

The decline in agricultural support and the impossibility of traditional extractivism on small plots of land forced many colonists to
opt for cattle raising in the 1990s. Many reported farming for their
own consumption through the 1990s, but this subsistence agriculture decreased in the early 2000s, when deforestation regulations began to be strictly enforced.

Prior to 1998, colonists and ranchers were allowed to deforest up to
50 percent of their landholdings in Amazonia, leaving the remainder
as forest reserves. In 1998, the general limit, which began to be enforced on colonists, ranchers, and other groups not residing within a
conservation unit, was lowered to 20 percent. Rubber-tapper lands re-
tain the 10 percent rule that was established with the creation of the
RESEX.

The creation of national environmental laws for the Amazon responded to growing national and international pressure, but enforcement of these laws varies from state to state. Over the past decade the
"forest government" of Acre has demonstrated the political will to
combat deforestation; it is seen by all groups as an effective enforcer
of deforestation laws. Technological advances have also contributed
to enforcement; remote sensing and the geo-referenced mapping of
properties enable governmental environmental authorities to monitor deforestation in previously inaccessible areas.

Given that policy shifts distinctly affect different social groups,
swidden agriculture is increasingly uncommon among colonists.
Most colonists have already reached or exceeded their deforestation
limits, and burning, which they consider necessary for successful agricultural production, is currently highly controlled. Tappers who
have not reached their 10 percent limit are still able to burn and plant
one hectare a year, if they obtain permission from the state environmental authority.

Those who surpass their deforestation limits are placed in "environmental debt," which restricts their access to credit and other government programs, further limiting their options, particularly those

FIGURE 2.3. Home on the range: a colonist home in the settlement project

of the colonists (fig. 2.3). Many colonists sell their land and move to the city: two of the thirteen colonist families I interviewed in 2009 sold their land later that year to a rancher, who now uses the land exclusively for grazing his cattle. Those who have stayed are struggling, and while many of them find ways to plant, either illegally or through the use of new techniques such as green manures, they invariably report being completely reliant on cattle for money to buy the staple foods that they once produced.

The concurrent application of neoliberal and environmental policies from 1990 through 2010 have thus made extractive and agricultural livelihood strategies less economically viable among rubber tappers and colonists. The regulations favor forest preservation, but have not been accompanied by the development of significant markets for forest products, or sustained governmental support for alternatives to deforestation-dependent production like swidden agriculture. In this unique configuration of factors, colonists and rubber tappers now adopt cattle or expand their herds through the conversion of former agricultural lands or clearing new forest illegally to establish pasture.

POSITIVE PERCEPTIONS OF CATTLE

Acrean smallholders are increasingly likely to view cattle in a positive light, given the material success of cattle raisers and the decline of extractivism and agriculture. In addition to the daily interactions between social groups that highlight the socioeconomic distinction of ranchers, the development of "cattle culture" in Acre reinforces positive images of a cattle-centered rural lifestyle.

Despite Acre's image as the land of the rubber tappers, and the social conflict and environmental destruction brought about by the arrival of cattle in the region, positive messages about the cattle-raising lifestyle are increasingly reinforced in popular culture. When I arrived in the region in 2007, there was one rodeo on the side of the highway in upper Acre; by 2010 there were five rodeos in the region catering largely to rural colonists and rubber tappers. In my survey of twenty members of each group, 85 percent of colonists, 65 percent of ranchers, and 50 percent of rubber tappers agreed that they enjoy attending rodeos.

The cultural constructions that surround the rodeo draw on and reinforce "cattle culture," a specific vision of the rural lifestyle in which cattle, cattle raisers, and cowboys are privileged. Positive messages about this cattle-centered lifestyle circulate and are expressed through *sertaneja* music and dress (boots, tight jeans, and plaid shirt), rodeos, and rural-themed festivals. The annual Expo-Acre fair in Rio Branco, the state's biggest festival, is largely a celebration of a cattle-based lifestyle, with hulking bulls and prize horses on display, performances by national *sertaneja* acts, and cowboys from all of Brazil competing in rodeo events. Smaller, municipal-level celebrations, also centered on a rodeo, have spread throughout upper Acre, as have stores selling *contri* clothing.

This cattle culture is present in tapper communities such as São Cristovão, where individuals have been exposed to the culture through their labor for ranchers as cowboys, the rodeo circuit, and television and radio. For example, members of each group reported that they enjoy listening to *sertaneja* music (95 percent of colonists and ranchers and 90 percent of rubber tappers). The popular cultural messages praising a cattle-based rural livelihood reach members of each group.

While the cowboy is the symbol of cattle culture, the rancher is the model of socioeconomic success in Acre. Smallholders assume

Table 2.1. Economic practices associated with selected socioeconomic terms, by social group

| | Socioeconomic Term | | | |
Social Group	"Wealth"	"Poverty"	"Progress"	"Decadence"
Rubber tappers	Cattle (85%)	Extractivism (85%)	Cattle (75%)	Extractivism (60%)
Colonists	Cattle (95%)	Extractivism (90%)	Cattle (85%)	Agriculture (55%)
Ranchers	Cattle (70%)	Extractivism (100%)	Cattle (50%)	Extractivism (85%)

that the rancher's wealth comes directly from cattle. There are also numerous examples, to the point of being scripted narratives, of upward social mobility enabled by cattle. These stories center on the poor colonist or tapper who started with one cow and is now wealthy.

Across groups, cattle raising was equated with positive descriptors, whereas extractivism and, to a lesser extent, agriculture were often viewed negatively. I asked all the respondents in each group to choose which of the three principal economic practices (extractivism, agriculture, and cattle raising) was most associated with the words "wealth," "poverty," "progress," and "decadence." The top (= sum of most chosen) responses of each group are presented in table 2.1. Positive attributes of wealth and progress are associated with cattle raising among all groups. Conversely, poverty is even more strongly associated with extractivism among all groups. Ranchers and about half of the rubber tappers believe that extractivism is associated with decadence or decline. Colonists associate their traditional economic practice, agriculture, with decline.

The perceptions of these practices extend to the members of social groups associated with them: all colonists, 90 percent of ranchers, and 85 percent of rubber tappers surveyed said that raising cattle is the practice most associated with high social status. Despite a sustained program by the Acrean government to valorize the rubber-tapper way of life and heritage, only 35 percent of rubber tappers, 15 percent of colonists, and 58 percent of ranchers felt that rubber tappers were more respected in Acrean society than ranchers. Colonists and rubber tappers are aware that their economic practices and lifestyles are not valued in popular culture or everyday perceptions to the same extent as those of cattle raisers.

The emergence of cattle raising as a viable economic practice during a time of decline in agriculture and extractivism, combined with the expansion of cattle culture, has reinforced positive perceptions of cattle raising and cattle raisers. It is not clear if perceptions paved the way for a change in practice, or if these opinions followed positive experiences raising cattle. It is apparent, however, that as the cattle economy becomes more central to Acrean social groups, cattle culture will assume a more integral role in Acrean society, combining with and overtaking other cultural traditions.

SOCIOECONOMIC RELATIONSHIPS

Twenty years ago, rubber tappers were hesitant to adopt cattle raising. It was only through time, as the memories of the conflict faded, younger generations took control of households, and political/economic factors came to overwhelmingly favor cattle raising, that they took the leap. There were also preconditions: knowledge of cattle rearing and the availability of cattle for purchase, both of which were facilitated by a social context that transitioned from one of intergroup conflict to one of interaction, cooperation, and exchange.

Interactions between groups facilitate the spread of cattle, cattle know-how, and the belief that cattle is the route to a better life in comparison to traditional agricultural or extractive livelihoods. With the help of government fiscal incentives, ranchers paved the way for the expansion of cattle by bringing cattle and a cattle industry to Acre in the 1970s and 1980s. Their success—the growth of their herds—meant that cattle were more available and affordable, and that smallholders could see cattle raising as a route to a better life. Additionally, a service industry sprouted up to support cattle raising in the small towns of upper Acre, including agricultural supply stores, slaughterhouses, butcher shops, and intermediaries to pick up and deliver cattle.

Government-supported research on improved pastures, cattle breeds, and techniques also helped, to the point that Acrean cattle raising has achieved levels of productivity unparalleled in other parts of Brazil (Valentim and Andrade 2009). Credit was available for the purchase of cattle. Some smallholders also used credit destined for agricultural pursuits to invest directly and indirectly in cattle (Toni et al. 2007). The state government went to unprecedented lengths to protect the cattle in Acre against hoof-and-mouth disease by establishing IDAF (Institute for the Defense of Agro-Cattle Raising and the Forest), part of a sustained effort by the federal government to avoid an economically catastrophic outbreak (Smeraldi and May 2008).

Essential information on basic cattle rearing, such as castration, general health, vaccination, and birthing, generally flows from migrants to native Acreans, who have less direct experience. For example, native Acrean rubber tappers in São Cristovão call on their colonist neighbors, who live along the dirt road leading to the RESEX, to help them vaccinate or castrate their cattle. Although many rubber tappers still lack knowledge of basic cattle-raising skills, some who have worked on ranches can perform these services. Many rubber tappers admitted that a lack of knowledge and environmental restrictions were the main factors that prevented them from adopting cattle.

It is common for youths in the settlement projects or rubber-tapper communities to seek work on the large ranches, where they may start as general laborers and work their way up to *peão de fazenda*, or cowboy, the most highly esteemed rural laborer. When cowboys return to their communities, they spread enthusiasm for working at the ranch, where they eat meat every day and are protected by the labor code, and for cattle, which they believe gave the rancher his wealth.

Ranchers, or their *gerentes* (ranch administrators), also enter into direct contact with smallholders, particularly colonists. These arrangements might allow calves to be fattened on rancher land or enable ranchers to rent pasturage on smallholder land to fatten their cattle. Tappers and colonists who raise cattle usually sell the calves to ranchers and intermediaries (usually members of smallholder communities) for ranchers and private entities. Selling calves, although not as economically advantageous in the long run for smallholders, makes sense because they usually have a limited amount of pasture, which is strained by raising calves to slaughter size. A calf sold at eight months for around $250 will fetch around $700 for the rancher two years later.

Such examples highlight not only the cooperative participation in the cattle industry, but also the difference in socioeconomic positions between ranchers and smallholders. Ranchers are able to make a greater profit, operating as they do at an economy of scale with direct links to the market, while smallholders are unable to engage the market on such terms. Ranchers generally have greater economic security, and so can weather ups and downs, and they usually have investments in the city as well. For smallholders, cattle are sometimes their only source of income, a savings account that must be liquidated in times of need.

Ranchers also have access to technologies and the capital to acquire them, which enables them to raise more cattle per hectare than smallholders. In the past decade, ranchers have employed herd rotation, high labor inputs, and improved grasses to increase their production. Colonists and rubber tappers do not have enough land or capital to invest in many of these improvements. The rise in cattle raising among these populations has resulted from conversion of agricultural land and/or forest to pasture.

The socioeconomic disparities between these groups remain, but have been in some cases and can be, in the minds of many, overcome through cattle. The lines that once neatly delineated social groups along the boundaries of their land-tenure systems are less discernible. The shift from intergroup relations of conflict to those of cooperation in cattle has, in addition to political, economic, and cultural changes, facilitated the spread of cattle ranching among many Acrean social groups.

CONCLUSION

The relationship between political/economic factors, cultural perceptions, and intergroup relationships, and the manner in which these collectively promoted cattle raising among different groups in Acre, underwent a number of transitions over the past forty years. The period 1970–1990 saw intergroup conflict in which separate and distinct land-tenure systems were established within a political, economic, and cultural context that encouraged group-specific economic practices. The vision of separate groups within their respective tenure systems, economic practices, and practice-based identities downplays the inherent fluidity of groups, and the complex interaction of general and group-specific cultural, political, and economic factors that have since led to a rise in cattle.

The foundation laid in the period from 1970 through 1990 paved the way, both intentionally and inadvertently, for the explosion of cattle raising after 1990. Beginning around 1990, the retraction of government policies supporting agricultural and extractivist livelihoods made cattle raising an appealing economic practice for colonists and rubber tappers. This trend was further reinforced at the end of the 1990s by the stricter enforcement of deforestation regulations, which pushed colonists in particular toward an almost singular reliance on cattle.

During this period, ranchers began amassing wealth through the growth of their herds. An industry developed to support them, and young rubber tappers and colonists sought employment on ranches. Cattle became more available, and knowledge of how to raise cattle began to circulate. The rancher also became a paradigm of success in rural Acre, while agriculture and extractivism went into decline. In the past decade, popular cultural constructions based on a cattle-centered vision of rural livelihood spread throughout Acre via music, rodeos, and dress. Cultural perceptions across groups now indicate overwhelmingly positive perceptions of cattle and cattle raisers. This confluence of cultural factors, the evolution of intergroup relations, and political/economic incentives have all contributed to a context that now favors cattle raising over other livelihood strategies.

Political, economic, and policy-oriented analyses dominate the study of cattle in the Amazon, often with a concern for slowing cattle-driven deforestation. In Acre and throughout Amazonia, cattle are simultaneously disdained for their role in social conflict and environmental destruction and desired for their singular ability to provide economic security. The positive economic features of cattle are bolstered by an idyllic cattle-centered vision of the rural lifestyle—celebrated in festivals, music, and dress—that has entered the region and is growing alongside the cattle in the fields of smallholders.

CHAPTER 3

RUMINATIONS ON CATTLE ECONOMIES
AND CATTLE CULTURES

JATOBÁ, LUANNA, AND ESPIMAR ROCHA live amid the forests of São Cristovão *seringal* in the Chico Mendes Extractive Reserve. When I met them in 2007 they had no cattle, but the next year I visited they had a white bull. Over time I witnessed the growth of their affection for this bull, named "Tchoa." The bull frequently stuck his head through the kitchen door looking for salt, which he licked out of their hands or from small heaps poured on the front step (fig. 3.1). Whenever he spotted one of them emerging from the forest, he lumbered over and stood while they rubbed his white-and-black speckled back, head, and dewlap. When Espimar knocked oranges from the trees, Tchoa stood by his side, waiting to take a piece with his raspy tongue or gobble the fruit whole.

The family cherished Tchoa, but Jatobá told me that it was the promise of his usefulness that justified their allocation of otherwise scarce resources to the beast. In 2009, they put a ring, made of old insulated wire, through Tchoa's nose, allowing them to tether and lead him. Espimar ran a rope through the ring to fashion reins, and often rode Tchoa to school. By 2010, Tchoa was pulling an oxcart with a neighboring bull, bringing rubber, Brazil nuts, and other products to the pickup point. From here the products were taken out of the forest on the side road and then onward to the paved BR-317 highway, the city of Brasiléia, and then Rio Branco.

All along the way, there are cowboys working in ranching operations. They wear leather, eat beef, and celebrate their symbolic domination of cattle in events such as rodeos. There are also people in the cities who dress like cowboys, but have no link to cattle or rural life. Sorocaba lived in Rio Branco. He was studying environmental law and had no land or cattle, yet he was "in love with the *vida contri*." In 2009 he bought himself a fine horse and debuted it at the 2010 *caval-*

FIGURE 3.1. Tchoa the bull stands at Jatobá's door

gada in Rio Branco. The *cavalgada* consists of separate groups of riders called *comitivas*—a hearkening back to the trail drives of the old
days in south-central Brazil. Sorocaba's *comitiva* was sponsored by
the Cowboys Ranch, a clothing store selling *contri* clothing, saddles,
and even Copenhagen snuff.

Each *comitiva* followed a truck pulling double trailers adorned with palm-thatch roofs and hay bales. The vehicle in front of the Cowboys Ranch group had a stage atop the trailer from which a man in a black cowboy hat and leather duster belted out Brazilian *sertaneja* and covers of American hits. Each trailer in the *cavalgada* was also laden with coolers full of iced beer, a stereo blaring *contri* music, and a *churrasqueira* (barbecue grill) crowded with sizzling beef and sausage on a stick (fig. 3.2). Riders moseyed over to the trailer in

FIGURE 3.2. The view from a trailer at the 2010 *cavalgada*

search of refreshment throughout the six-hour journey from the Acre River to the exposition grounds, their arrival signaling the opening of the Expo-Acre celebration.

While some Acreans treat their cattle as a member of the family and prohibit their slaughter, a growing number of individuals wear their skin and consume their flesh, and symbolically assert their own dominance over nature by holding onto the back of a bucking bull, connecting themselves with popular traditions practiced throughout the hemisphere.

There are thus two strains of cattle culture in Acre: one emanating from mixed subsistence uses, and the dominant *cauboi* model related to market-oriented ranching. These forms of cultural expression, which are usually reserved for the cattle complexes of East African pastoralism and American ranching, often coexist in the same Acrean household.

The objective of this chapter is to understand how distinct uses of the same resource give rise to contrasting forms of symbolic expression in Acre, and also to generate conceptual knowledge for understanding this dynamic in other settings. I compare my ethnographic data on three rural Acrean groups (rubber tappers, agricultural colonists, and large-scale ranchers) with the East African and American cattle complex literature. I show how the mode of livelihood (MoL) (ranching or pastoralism) and the mode of production (MoP) (subsistence or capitalist) structure, but do not determine, forms of symbolic expression. Features of these cattle cultures can be understood across contexts by scaling down to the level of social relations and human–animal interactions.

This local focus, however, cannot fully explain the emergence of *cauboi* cultural practices in Acre, so I examine the paths of direct and indirect diffusion that brought them to Acre. In much of the literature on frontier expansion, cattle are a key symbol of destructive development, displacement, and capitalist penetration. Yet some groups have adopted cattle raising as a source of economic security and have produced novel cultural forms, at the same time participating in a *cauboi* culture linked to capitalist exchange, production, and consumption. By examining the articulation of these two forms of cattle raising and cultural expression, I am able to situate what is occurring in Acre in relation to wider processes of capitalist production and consumption of both agricultural foodstuffs and forms of cultural expression.

CATTLE ECONOMIES AND CATTLE CULTURES

In the Americas, cattle cultures span the Canadian plains to Patagonia (Slatta 1990), but New World cattle raisers have received little anthropological attention, in comparison to Old World populations (Rivière 1972; Strickon 1965). This lacuna is particularly apparent in Amazonia, although researchers have noted the tradition and the "distinction enjoyed by the rich landowners and their gleaming white herds" (Hecht and Cockburn 1989:152; see also Hecht 2012:11; Walker et al. 2000:686–687; Smith 2002:41–74).

The strength of cultural constructions surrounding cattle stem from these animals' unique abilities to store value, adapt to novel environments, and convert inedible vegetation into human food, products, and services (Dove and Carpenter 2007; Rifkin 1993; Rimas and Frasier 2008). Although positive cultural constructions may also arise around animals with no functional or material value (in Amazonia see Descola 1994; Vivieros de Castro 1998; for overview see Mullin 1999), I focus here on materialist explanations, such as Ingold's (1980) cross-cultural examination of the herding economies of ranchers, pastoralists, and hunters. The most famous example is Harris's (1966) argument that Indians' relegation of cattle to a sacred sphere could be traced to a combination of factors, including a reliance on cattle for plowing and demographic and environmental constraints. The question is not whether the cultural constructions surrounding cattle emerge because they are "good to eat," or "good to think (with)" (Lévi-Strauss 1969:89; Harris 1985). Rather, I argue that understanding the roots of cattle cultures requires analyzing what the animals are "good for" producing—be it milk, beef, bride wealth, transportation, traction, or some combination of these.

East African pastoralism and American ranching are distinctive cattle-based modes of livelihood, each having given rise to a unique set of cultural features composing a "cattle complex" (Herskovits 1926; Strickon 1965). Herskovits's East African cattle area was defined by the presence of a complex of traits, reflected in both material culture and social and symbolic realms—including myths, rituals, behavioral mandates, and taboos (1926:241)—that was the result of a sustained reliance on a specific form of cattle raising.

Nomadic pastoralism involves herding animals over extensive areas in response to environments of marked seasonality, and daily reliance on the products of these animals, usually for subsistence ends but also for exchange in kinship-based and, increasingly, in market-based economies (Dyson-Hudson and Dyson-Hudson 1980). Within the "Euro-American Ranching Complex" (Strickon 1965), cowboys drew on common Iberian practices and technologies to work cattle, and thus structurally similar cattle cultures developed throughout the Americas (Slatta 1990). Ranching practices in Acre are similar to others across the continent, including a market orientation and the extensive use of land, usually privately owned, and hired labor (Strickon 1965).

The diversity of cattle-raising practices in Acre reflects the variety of economies encompassed by this small area. There are both large-scale ranching and a range of cattle livelihood strategies practiced by smallholders. As we have seen, many rubber tappers and colonists rely on cattle as part of a diversified livelihood strategy including forest extractivism, swidden agriculture, and wage labor. These practices change in response to opportunities and constraints, as does the extent to which production is targeted for subsistence and market exchange. In general, subsistence cattle provide smallholder households with milk and transportation of goods and people. Older cattle and calves are usually sold to intermediaries working throughout the countryside, who assemble lots of mature cattle for the slaughterhouse or sell calves to ranchers directly or indirectly (through auctions). I use "cattle raising" as an umbrella term for all of these mixed systems as well as the purer modes of livelihood—ranching and pastoralism.

In Acre we do find aspects of the cattle complexes described above in a shared setting. Further, the mixed smallholder systems found here, in which beloved cattle and nameless commodities sometimes graze side by side on the same property, do not fit neatly into either complex. It thus seems that factors beyond ranching or pastoralism give rise to certain features of the cattle complexes. Isolating and analyzing these requires decoupling the imprecise mixture of economic, ecological, and social factors composing the mode of livelihood. I look instead to the mode of production: the overarching economic system governing production, consumption, and exchange. The MoP provides a clear set of constituent social and ecological relations, from which we can scale down to the relations of production (RoP) (human/human or social relations) and the factors of production (FoP) (human/resource or ecological relations) (Marx [1867] 1977; Wolf 1982; Roseberry 1989). Such a systematic comparison makes it possible to identify the roots of different forms of symbolic expression in Acre. Given that the most comprehensive accounts of cattle cultures have come from East Africa, I use a sampling of these to understand similar relations in Acre. I limit my scope to selected foundational readings from the first half of the twentieth century ("colonial-era"), and to handful of contemporary texts dealing with economic changes and their associated cultural implications in the second half ("post-colonial"). The myriad political, institutional, and ecological variables that also play an important role in structuring cattle economies in Africa (e.g., Ensminger 1992; Galvin 2009; McCabe 2004) are, unfortunately, beyond the scope of this work.

CATTLE CULTURES IN EAST AFRICA, THE AMERICAS, AND ACRE

In colonial East Africa, pastoralism was characterized by the moving of livestock, and the family that owned and relied upon them, in accordance with seasonal variation and resource availability (Herskovits 1926). The family unit cared for cattle and consumed their products on a daily basis. As a result of this relationship of mutual dependence and cohabitation, strong emotional links developed between pastoralists and their cattle. The Nuer, for example, slept among their cattle, and in the morning washed themselves in the urine of the cow and the ash of the dung fire (Evans-Pritchard 1940). Given this intimate form of interaction between humans and cattle, pastoralists naturally demonstrated affection for their animals, created a symbolic attachment through naming, and ate them only on socially prescribed occasions (Herskovits 1926; Evans-Pritchard 1940; Schneider 1957). In contrast, in a typical Acrean ranching operation the economic value of cattle is realized through the delivery of cattle to market, where they are slaughtered for hides, tallow, beef, and other products. Owners (ranchers) command the labor of proletarian cowboys, whose aim is to secure the continued production and harvest of beef in exchange for wages. These cowboys are not invested in the cattle economically or emotionally, nor do they use them for direct sustenance or for their own eventual profit.

There is a difference, then, between cattle that are valued for what they produce and cattle that become valuable only when they are exchanged, slaughtered, and converted to products and currency. These distinctions in use value and exchange value are the defining characteristics of domestic or subsistence and capitalist modes of production (Marx [1867] 1977; Sahlins 1972). While these are useful concepts for elucidating the differences, this is not a hard and fast distinction. For example, pastoralists exchange their useful cattle in networks of mutual obligation (Deshler 1965:154), most notably as a source of bride-wealth (Colson 1955). Although Acrean smallholders usually sell their cattle, there were also occasions in which they would barbecue a calf to mobilize communal labor—essentially working their own networks of reciprocity.

In postcolonial Africa, political and economic changes resulted in an increase in capitalist forms of exchange, and these were reflected in the relationships between people and between people and cattle (Dyson-Hudson and Dyson-Hudson 1980; Moore 1993). Features associated with capitalist ranching have appeared throughout postcolonial sub-Saharan Africa (not just East Africa), including the non-ritual slaughter of cattle, the identification of cattle as commodities, and wage-laboring pastoralists becoming alienated from the means of production (Comaroff and Comaroff 1990; Ferguson 1985; Hutchinson 1996; Moritz et al. 2011). Given the deep historical and ecological roots of pastoralism, these changes have been contested and fitful. Previous cultural structures have not been completely subsumed, but the changes that have occurred show that an intensification of the capitalist MoP structures relationships between humans and cattle in such a way that specific forms of symbolic expression emerge—regardless of the context.

Among the Tshidi, the "total economy" of cattle was replaced by a cash economy. Cash was referred to as "cattle without legs," an allusion to its inability to fulfill social obligations (Comaroff and Comaroff 1990). Similarly, the famed Nuer spoke of "bloodless" money. Their loss of control over cattle was related to an overall restructuring of social and political organization and ritual practice (Hutchinson 1996). These expressions demonstrate the conflicted process of renegotiating cultural values and social relations in the transition from subsistence and socially mediated exchange to currency-based exchange, from cattle flesh and blood and connective tissue to a commodified object. These African expressions, illustrating the longevity of interaction and depth of cultural construction around cattle, indeed recall Acreans' terms for cattle: *poupança*, a savings account, and *dinheiro vivo*, live money.

In both settings we see some variation in how cattle are perceived and treated. In Africa, the MoP does not completely subsume previous forms of cultural expression, and in the Americas smallholders may name some of their cattle and sell others. While it is somewhat structured by the MoL and MoP, the defining feature of cultural expression seems to be the ways that humans interact with cattle.

Even among the Nuer, "the end of every beast [was] the pot" (Evans-Pritchard 1940:38). In this sense, it is not the ends (exchange and consumption) that matter, but the means, or the process of production—the ways that humans interact with their cattle to secure the products and services that they harvest from them. Animals that are important for their use value will require sustained training before the useful products can be harvested from them. This ecological relationship between humans and cattle, when taken within the social and economic structures that dictate the relations of production, helps to illuminate how the distinctive cattle cultures emerge, either placing value on cattle themselves or seeing them as depersonalized money on the hoof. From birth to the pot or the *churrasco*, it is the intervening form of interaction between humans and cattle that generates unique forms of symbolic expression. As further proof that it is the economic relationship, not the MoP or the MOL, we can look to the horse among proletarian cowboys in the heart of the capitalist ranching enterprise.

FACTORS OF PRODUCTION AND HORSES

In large-scale ranching systems, cowboys only separate out individual cattle that are troublesome or in need of some sort of attention. They found it perfectly natural to push around and at times abuse these nameless cattle, which in their eyes were nothing more than moving and at times obstinate commodities. On the other extreme, the cowboys usually named their horses, never ate them, and often gave them affectionate pats, hugs, and head nudges. Why?

Without a horse, it is virtually impossible for a cowboy to control cattle on the scale of or in the ways needed by a ranching operation, with its vast land and herds, limited labor, and need to move cattle from place to place. Horses serve as buffers that remove the cowboys from actual interaction with cattle, and they also transform a relatively frail but intelligent biped into a taller, stronger, and faster centaur. The horse literally puts the cowboy above the cow, elevating him symbolically above the natural world.

For the cowboy, horses are a factor of production; specifically, they are an instrument of production, an essential tool for the production of beef cattle. Similarly, pastoralists and cattle are locked in interdependency: the live cattle produce what the humans rely upon to live. As a result of this reliance, and of the hours of training and interaction required to transform a horse from wild to tame or to train cattle to pull a plow or to allow milking, bonds naturally form between humans and animals. Or, in the case of the Acrean stud bull or the *sinuelo* ("Judas cow," trained to lead the herd from place to place), there may no bond or interaction, but the services provided by these cattle contribute to overall production in ways greater than the value of their flesh.

In addition to the interconnections of economic, social, and ecological relationships, other factors, such as the availability of horses, have some role in creating unique cattle cultures. More importantly, it shows that when an animal's value as a tool or source of daily sustenance exceeds its value as a carcass, symbolic associations will form between humans and these animals, be they horses or cattle. This holds true as long as some form of sustained interaction is required in order to harvest live products or use the animals.

BAHIANA'S BARBECUE: THE ARTICULATION OF MODES OF PRODUCTION AND CATTLE CULTURES

Economic life along the Amazonian frontiers of the 1970s and 1980s followed a familiar pattern: intensification of capitalist relations of production, alienation from the means of production, and displacement of preexisting social formations (Foweraker 1981; Schmink and Wood 1992). Capitalist relations have increased in intensity across time throughout the world, but the reach of capitalism is imperfect, and thus one can find variation in local economic practices (Cleary 1993; Ferguson 2006; Wolf 1982). Different MoPs may coexist in a setting, interacting with one another in unique ways (Meillassoux 1980; Wolpe 1980). Research on the articulation of MoPs often chronicles economic and social transformations, such as the intercultural conflict resulting from such encounters (Hopkins 1978; Robben 1989). Less studied are the ways in which the forms of symbolic expression associated with distinct modes of production are negotiated by people at the sites of contact. Throughout Amazonia, groups have adopted cattle raising and adapted it to their mixed production systems (Loker

FIGURE 3.3. Bahiana, her son, and their ox

1993; Rudel et al. 2002). Here I offer an example and an examination of the ways that smallholder groups operating between the domestic and the capitalist MoPs negotiate the associated cultural features of each.

Bahiana, a colonist, lived on a side road, a few dozen kilometers up the highway from Jatobá. Her father was an agriculturalist in the arid northeast, and she grew up around cattle, before marrying and leaving home in her teens. She and her husband, who often worked as a cowboy, followed the frontier through the states of Goiás and Mato Grosso before settling near Rio Branco in the early 1980s. In 1986 she bought an 80-hectare parcel of land in the Quixadá Directed Settlement. She lived there with her sons and grandson until 2009, when she sold her land to a rancher.

Shortly after she and her husband arrived in Acre, he was thrown from his oxcart and crushed under its wheels. Despite this painful memory, Bahiana said that she had no bitterness toward her two aged bullocks, which were usually tethered to a mango tree a few feet from her front door (fig. 3.3). Her sons used the oxen to carry firewood or other cargo. In the late afternoons, after the day's work was done, Bahiana would give them a handful of salt before releasing them to join the rest of the herd, which was fenced in on the hill above her home.

Bahiana developed a strong connection with her oxen, but she did not name them, referring to them simply as *meus bois* ("my cattles"). Her sons worked the eighty head of beef cattle, distinguishing them by color and markings, sex, reproductive status, and age.

Schneider asserted that the essence of the African complex resides in a "kind of identification with cattle which leads to their association with ritual" (Schneider 1957:278). Whereas subsistence pastoralism reinforced interdependence between people, and between people and their cattle in the realm of ritual (Evans-Pritchard 1940), the capitalist relations and factors of production expressed in ranching reinforce commodified relations based on transforming labor, privately owned land, and animal flesh into currency. The conceptual distinction between humans and cattle is recreated in popular rituals, such as rodeos, in which humans symbolically assert their superiority over animals (Lawrence 1990).

An examination of a ritual that is present in both societies—the ritualized consumption of beef—illustrates how distinctive economic relationships with animals transition to the realm of ritual. In colonial-era East Africa, the slaughter of cattle was highly regulated, and restricted to ceremonial occasions, although this is changing in postcolonial times (Hutchinson 1996). In Acre, the *churrasco* is a cherished social institution centered on the ritualistic consumption of meat and commonly used to celebrate important events, such as holidays and important soccer matches. Although the ritual is present in many settings, and cattle are used therein in a variety of ways, the *churrasco* in Acre is largely made possible by commercial beef production and the consumption of a purchased commodity, and I thus classify it as a cultural expression of the capitalist ranching economy. Most beef consumers have no relationship with the animal that was raised, sold, slaughtered, subdivided, and packaged for their consumption. In rural settings, however, an entire animal may be donated or purchased for celebratory purposes, or to mobilize communal labor for large projects, such as clearing land.

Over the course of the month before she moved to the city, I was living with Bahiana and her sons, and was able to observe how she ended her relationships with her beef cattle and useful bullocks. She sold all of her beef cattle without much consideration. She could not reconcile, however, the thought of her two oxen heading to the slaughterhouse. Although she could have sold them for a handsome price, she made her son promise that he would allow the oxen to graze out the remainder of their years on his property.

Bahiana threw a farewell *churrasco* a couple of weeks before she moved. In addition to being protected by Bahiana's directive, the oxen were too big and old for the occasion, and not as appetizing as the calf she bought from one of her neighbors. Although essentially the same animals, the oxen were defined through years of use and interaction, whereas the calf was a commodity. While her oxen were unsellable, the unnamed calf was bought, slaughtered, hung from a tree, and carved up. Her sons roasted the strips of beef on a grid of barbed wire covering a pit some six feet long and four feet deep and filled with smoldering coals.

Bahiana's *churrasco* shows how forms of cattle economy and symbolic expression overlap, are reconciled, and remain distinct. Cultural constructions emanating from distinct uses of cattle coexist in the same setting, but useful cattle with which symbolic connections were formed may not transition into rituals such as the *churrasco*—an expression of the commodified exchange relationships. This example also underlines an important point: forms of symbolic expression emanating from subsistence cattle, although paralleling many features of the East African cattle complex, have not reached this level of significance in Acre. These subsistence features of cattle culture are largely subsumed by the dominant *cauboi* culture, based on ranching, which does constitute a cattle complex wherein relationships with cattle have been institutionalized in the realm of ritual.

THE DIFFUSION OF *CAUBOI* CULTURE

Bahiana's son, Tatu, was for the most part a typical colonist while on his land, where he raised beef cattle and grew crops. When Tatu headed to the city of Brasiléia, however, he transformed into a self-described *cauboi*. I can still picture him clacking down the sidewalk in his boots, black cowboy hat, blue jeans, and plaid shirt, his belt buckle glinting in the sunlight. In the city Tatu often visited his elder brother, Branco, who drove a delivery truck but "lived for" the weekends, when he rode bulls in the local rodeo circuit. The last time I saw Branco, he was competing in the rodeo described in the introduction, just a few kilometers from where he had grown up with Bahiana. There were others with few if any links to the countryside or a rural existence, such as Sorocaba, whom I describe in chapter 6.

Sorocaba, Branco, and Tatu had varying degrees of connection with the economic and ecological lifestyle of ranching represented by *cauboi* culture. They were similar in that they pursued a cattle-based lifestyle on a symbolic level through aspects of popular culture such as rodeo, *churrasco*, and clothing. In order to understand the arrival of this *cauboi* culture, dispersed across such a broad cross section of Acrean society, we must look beyond local ranching practices to multiscalar paths of direct and indirect diffusion, circulating meanings, and local factors contributing to its appropriation.

Iberian cattle arrived in the Americas in 1494, came to present-day Mexico in 1521, and spread to other parts of North and South America over the course of the next century (Bishko 1952; Dary 1981; Jordan 1993). The techniques and cultural features of cattle raising in the Americas were drawn from common Iberian roots, but became distinguishable as cattle raisers adapted to novel ecological, political, and economic contexts (Butzer 1988; Slatta 1990). These American cattle cultures share broad structural similarities arising from their common dedication to cattle ranching: an ecologic-economic pattern characterized by market-orientation, extensive scale, and the use of proletarian cowboys to work cattle (Strickon 1965).

Rich cultures developed around the practice of raising cattle, from the *huasos* and *gauchos* of the Southern cone to the *charros* and *vaqueros* of Mexico and the cowboys of North America (Slatta 1990). In Brazil, two main regional cowboy traditions emerged: the *vaqueiros* of the arid northeast, and the *gaúchos* of the southern *campanha* (pampas, or temperate grasslands). Each has unique material adaptations and worldviews, as da Cunha (1944:91–92) noted in *Os Sertões*: "The southern gaucho, upon meeting the vaqueiro . . . , would look him over commiseratingly. The northern cowboy is his very antithesis. . . . The former, denizen of the boundless plains, who spends his days galloping over the pampas, finds his environment friendly and fascinating. . . . [He] is not saddened by periodic scenes of devastation and misery. . . . The clothes that he wears are holiday garb compared to the vaqueiro's rustic garments."

Secondary Brazilian cattle cultures developed as *gaúchos* and *vaqueiros* migrated and adapted their practices to novel contexts. Migrants from the northeast brought cattle raising to the savanna region of Roraima, in northern Amazonia. In their transition from the desert to the savanna the *vaqueiros* "discarded the traditional leather clothing which, while so essential among the thorn bushes of the *caatinga*, is barely necessary on the open plains" (Rivière 1972:35).

In other cases of migration, cultural traditions were adapted to a novel ecological context. For example, cattle raising in the Brazilian *pantanal* is rooted in *gaúcho* migration and adaptation to the seasonal floodplains (Mazza et al. 1994). The *gaúcho* tradition of drinking hot *herba maté* tea (*chimarrão*) was maintained by *pantaneiros*, but they take their tea cold, as *tereré*, in response to the hot climate of the *pantanal* and influences from neighboring Paraguay. Acreans drink *maté* tea, mostly as *tereré*, but on cold mornings or during *friagens* (cold spells) many prefer *chimarrão*. I drank *tereré* and *chimarrão* in Acre and also with *pantaneiros* in the *pantanal*, and I can say that while the temperature of the drink varies, its code of etiquette and shared social function do not.

These accounts of cultural diffusion, which focus on material culture, provide a means of contextualizing the history of Brazilian cattle cultures, showing the diversity of practices that emerged in response to environmental constraints, and establishing linkages between regions, but they do not tell the whole story. Regional Brazilian traditions have exerted limited influence in Acre, and adaptation has played a limited role in the creation of *cauboi* dress. It is thus necessary to look at the specific processes of direct and indirect diffusion that brought cattle and cattle raisers to the western Amazon in the 1970s, as well as connections beyond the borders of Brazil.

Most large-scale Acrean ranchers came from the center-south region of Brazil, particularly the states of São Paulo and Minas Gerais. These *sulistas* (southerners) or *paulistas* (natives of São Paulo state), as they are referred to in Acre, established the economic and technical infrastructure necessary for the spread of the cattle industry, beginning in the 1970s. Cicero, one of Acre's largest ranchers, with more than fifty thousand head of cattle, was raised in a town in western São Paulo state that is famous for its cattle and horse-raising traditions. The King Ranch of Texas operated for many years in the area (Lea 1957), and as a young man Cicero augmented his cattle-raising knowledge by working with the Americans. His home office is adorned with numerous trophies that his sons earned in rodeo and roping competitions organized by the Americans. Cicero came to Acre with plans for a cattle ranch, as well as a love of rodeo. He passed both down to his grandchildren, who spend their evenings practicing rodeo events on the outskirts of Rio Branco. Through his training of native Acreans as cowboys to work on his ranch, he spread ranching practices, material culture, and an interest in rodeo and other cultural traditions.

Migrants brought in the infrastructure and technology necessary for the establishment of the cattle industry and planted the seeds for *cauboi* culture, but indirect paths of diffusion raised all this to another level. *Cauboi* culture was born in the town of Barretos, located in northern São Paulo state. Since the early 1900s, this was the end of the trail for *comitivas* driving livestock to market. The cowboys would then entertain themselves by competing against each other in tests of skill based on ranching practices. These informal events were institutionalized in 1955 in the Festa de Peão de Barretos (Barretos Cowboy Festival) (Dent 2009:7; Gonçalves and Iacomini 1997). North American rodeo has similar origins (Stoeltje 1989), pointing to ways that market-oriented cattle-ranching economies, building on common Iberian traditions, have given rise to similar forms of ritualized expression throughout American cattle regions (Strickon 1965). At the end of the 1980s, the growth in popularity of *sertaneja* music inspired local businessmen to transform the festival into a sort of "Texas tournament" to attract middle-class patrons who would never attend a *caipira* (hick or hillbilly) festival, but would happily come to a "country" event (Gonçalves and Iacomini 1997).

The merging of Brazilian traditions with North American country and western influences created a new image of the countryside in which consumers and country folk could celebrate rural tradition in the face of historical disdain for the backward "interior." This *vida contri/cauboi* culture has spread throughout Acre, in television, music, the rodeo circuit, and immigration. In subsequent chapters I examine the reasons for its appropriation.

CONCLUSION

I set out to describe cattle culture and to explain how it arrived in this unlikely corner of the Brazilian Amazon. "Looking to the cow" in this context, however, has required analyzing not only the distinctive productive strategies that have given rise to local forms of expression, but also the diffusion of ranching and associated popular culture and meanings, and the ways that these two economic and cultural packages overlap and interact.

By comparing foundational East African literatures with my findings from Acre, I have shown that cattle economies engender certain symbolic features across contexts. Among those raising cattle for market exchange, a feature associated with, but not exclusive to, ranching, relationships between humans and cattle tended to be impersonal. Even though Acrean subsistence uses of cattle do not share the same historical foundation and longevity as the colonial-era African cases, the intimacy of interaction and dependence produces similar results with cattle across contexts. The cases from postcolonial Africa and Acrean cowboys with their horses show that symbolic expressions may be structured but not determined by the broader economic and ecological context. In the end it comes down to an animal's designation as having use or exchange value and the constituent relationships between people and cattle required to harvest specific products.

The growth of the cattle economy and cattle culture in Acre can be interpreted in different ways. On the one hand, a rural underclass has appropriated a key symbol of capitalist intensification and used it to hold on to some forms of economic determination, despite the force of the regional, national, and global economies. The dominant *cauboi* culture, which is less about an immediate relation of production and more about a remote or partial articulation with a wider mode of production, nonetheless provides an outlet for the expression of the more intimately produced forms. Subsistence cattle production, while creating culturally autonomous forms of expression, also provides a space for these broader forms of *cauboi* culture to take root.

In closing, I want to emphasize another vital component to the understanding of the expansion of cattle raising across Acre. Cattle provide many more material benefits than other animals, and cattle raising, be its type pastoralism, ranching, or mixed subsistence, usually results in the creation of positive cultural constructions around the animals. Thus, in addition to the features that favor cattle within the current matrix of political, economic, and social factors, the near-universal economic and cultural value of cattle contributes to this appeal. Political and economic structures are key to understanding the growth of cattle raising, but culture is a critical part of the equation. Cattle raising is both economical and meaningful for Amazonians, as it is for people throughout the world.

CHAPTER 4

IDEOLOGIES OF NATURE AND HUMAN–ENVIRONMENT INTERACTIONS

IDEOLOGIES AND LANDSCAPES

TWO HOUSES

Two houses on Avenida Epaminondas in Rio Branco are separated by another. One belongs to Sorocaba, a dedicated urban *cauboi* who embodies many of the fundamental features of cattle culture. His truck can often be seen parked on the sidewalk in front of the padlocked gate set in the walls that surround his house. The interior area is similar to others in the city: it is covered in tiles from the driveway to the courtyard, around the pool, and on the little, shaded bar and grill in the back corner. There is no form of vegetation in his yard, except a few weeds between the tiles. Further down the street, at the second house, a passerby can look over the walls and see *açai* palms and ornamental plants hanging over the sidewalk. Between the walls and this house are grassy areas, a cement driveway, and concrete footpaths, which lead to a pool and *churrasqueira* (barbecue grill) in the back.

This house has long served as a meeting point for researchers and members and heads of governmental institutions. They sit around the rectangular wooden table on the shaded driveway and they talk. Many of their conversations center on coming up with new ways to provide for the economic needs of rural Acreans and, at the same time, to decrease deforestation and promote sustainable resource use.

Such discussions contributed to the policies of the Governo da Floresta with the 1988 election of Jorge Viana as governor of Acre. In 1989 his administration began to build on the ideals of the rubber-tapper movement to promote forest-based development and implemented a cultural program based on valorization of the forest and forest populations, calling it *florestania*, or forest citizenship (Schmink 2011; Schmink and Cordeiro 2008; Vadjunec, Schmink, and Gomes 2011:75).

Florestania envisions humans as coexisting with or managing the natural world with minimal impact, whereas cattle culture builds on deeply ingrained ideas of humans as separate from or clearly controlling nature. These two different houses on Epaminondas belonged to people who believed in these distinctive ideologies of nature, and I wondered to what extent the landscaping of their homes reflected these ideals. How do these urban spaces relate to the landscape of the countryside, the pastures, and the forest? In this chapter I examine ideals of appropriate human relationships with nature and the ways that these are reflected in the creation and evaluation of physical spaces in the city and the countryside.

Early Amazonian researchers explained the cultural features and social organization of Amerindian populations by focusing on the constraints of the rainforest environment (Meggars 1971; Steward 1946). Over time, scholars moved away from environmental determinism, emphasizing instead the interaction between humans and nature, and the agency of humans in constructing and managing the "natural" world (Orlove 1980; Moran 1982; Sponsel 1986; Raffles 2002). Historical ecologists, in particular, have shown that Amazonian groups had shaped what was long assumed to be pristine and primordial, further blurring the distinction between natural and cultural domains (Denevan 1992; Heckenberger et al. 2007; Posey 1985).

These perspectives highlight the dialectical relationship between humans and nature across time and the resultant landscapes, places, and spaces, which can be read as text or as a form of material culture (Balée 2006; Crumley 1994). Although much contemporary anthropological scholarship seeks to expose the fallacy of the nature–culture divide, my focus on cattle raising has convinced me that it remains central to the ways that many Acrean groups conceptualize and engage with the environment.

Cultural geographers have provided a framework for understanding the contemporary landscapes of the region, including its urban places, as expressions of historical and cultural values and political-economic structures (Cosgrove 1984; Glacken 1973; Olwig 2002; Robbins 2007; Tuan 1974). Others have focused on the manner in which non-indigenous and Neo-Amazonian groups perceive their relationships with the environment in terms of discourse, symbolism, and myth (Harris 2004; Nugent 1993; Slater 2002). I have combined features of these perspectives to analyze the landscapes and places of Acre, from the forests and pastures of the countryside to urban places that seek to symbolically recreate the rural, such as the *contri* bars. I understand the spaces that people carve around their homes to be reflections of ideologies that are physically imprinted on the material world. While the creation of such a distinctly humanized space is often oriented to functional concerns, this examination will show that maintaining a socially defined relationship with one's surroundings is also important in terms of what it says about a person. In chapter 6 I focus on the ways that urban places illustrate how people are crossing the divide and compromise in the form of *contri* places.

NATURE–CULTURE AND THE FRONTIER

The "nature–culture divide" refers to the conceptual separation between humans and the natural world in Western thought (Dove and Carpenter 2007; Little 1999). In the initial encounters between Spanish and Portuguese conquistadores, settlers, and explorers and indigenous populations in the Amazon and other parts of the Americas, Western groups envisioned themselves as agents of culture and therefore more civilized than the "primitives" and "savages" (Hecht and Cockburn 1992). External visions of Amazonia continue to be imbued with exoticism (Slater 2002; Raffles 2002) and to privilege the cultural "other" dwelling beyond the reach of civilization (Fabian 2002; Said 2003). As they have throughout colonial history, these discourses position people and nature in such a way as to justify external intervention and action, from the height of the colonial era to the present.

Throughout American history, the nature–culture divide was central to framing the Western occupation of "wilderness" and the displacement, subjugation, and conversion of the "uncivilized" (Cronon 1983; Slatta 1997; Weber and Rausch 1994; Wolf 1982). Those claiming "culture" actively created the cities and cultivated spaces where they lived, while the "savages" were thought to live in (but not actively cultivate) the wilderness, and were defined by their inability to overcome both nature and human nature.

These "savages" lived beyond the reach of civilization, and were encountered in the frontier, a zone of contact between contrasting ways of life. In the early nineteenth century, Domingo Sarmiento saw the struggle for the future of Argentina as a battle between "civilization and barbarism" taking place on the hinterland of the *pampas*, with mixed-race *gauchos* representing a form of savagery (1868). Frederick Jackson Turner saw the late nineteenth-century frontier of the United States as a site of "perennial rebirth" in which unique American identity was formed as settlers "won the wilderness," by transforming the "primitive economic and political conditions of the frontier into the complexity of city life" (Turner 1920:2).

Speaking in 1940, decades before the opening of Amazonia to colonization, Brazilian president Getulio Vargas galvanized support for the mission by using familiar dichotomous imagery: "Nothing will stop us in this movement which is, in the 20th century, the highest task of civilizing man: to conquer and dominate the valleys of the great equatorial currents, transforming their blind force and their extraordinary fertility into disciplined energy" (as quoted in Davis 1977:21). Through the guiding hand of culture, Vargas continued, the Amazonian wilderness would become, "under the impact of our will and labor[,] . . . a chapter in the history of civilization."

When the colonization of the Amazon began in full in the 1970s, the nature–culture dichotomy, now in the guise of military developmentalism, was once again central to framing the contests that took place at the frontier. Migrants, under the banner of "Order and Progress," were supported in their usurpation of the land of native groups and the transformation of the forest to pastures and fields in the name of "development" (Davis 1977; Foweraker 1981; Hecht and Cockburn 1989; Schmink and Wood 1992). The land conflicts along the frontier have diminished for the most part, but the conceptual divide between nature and culture continues to be asserted in contemporary Amazonia. Nowadays it is contested in an ideological sphere which seeks to define how people interact with the natural world.

IDEOLOGIES OF NATURE: *FLORESTANIA*, ENVIRONMENTALISM, AND CATTLE CULTURE

In their protest movement the rubber tappers argued for a new vision, in which people could live off of the forest without destroying it. With the establishment of the extractive reserve, it was and continues to be hoped that the contradictory goals of environmental conservation and economic development can be reconciled through use-based conservation initiatives (Gomes 2009; Kainer et al. 2003; Schwartzman 1989; Vadjunec, Schmink, and Gomes 2011).

Acre presents a case in which there has been a sustained attempt by the government to build on rubber-tapper practices and thereby nullify the nature–culture divide and views of the forest as an obstacle to development and those who inhabit it as culturally backward. In some ways the government's *florestania* espouses a view that is similar to non-Western perspectives in which society is less distinct or separate from nature, as indigenous groups, forests, animals collaborate in local histories and landscapes (Vivieros de Castro 1997; Descola 1994, 2013; Rival 2002). This sort of relationship with the natural world is often conflated with ideals of living in harmony with nature and the Western myth of the "ecologically noble savage" (Krech 2000; Redford 1991; see also Hames 2007).

The reconciliations proposed by the tappers appear to be yielding to traditional ideals of environmental preservation, which assert a dichotomous view of human and natural realms, with nature kept in parks and humans in cities or other clearly anthropogenic spaces (Dove and Carpenter 2007; West et al. 2006). The objective of protectionism is to maintain the natural world by preventing destructive human activities. The assumption is that humans have a propensity for destroying nature. In Amazonia, such destructive activity is often embodied by loggers, miners, and ranchers, as well as other non-indigenous and migrant groups. As this discussion will show, however, the progressive policies that were designed to focus on social equity, as well as forest preservation (Keck 1995), have been subsumed by environmental preservation's concerns (Ehringhaus 2005). The manner in which governmental authorities map and monitor the landscape to enforce deforestation regulations has in some ways reasserted the nature–culture divide through its emphasis on "forest" and "non-forest."

Much like environmental preservationism, cattle culture thrives on the assertion that humans and nature are separate. These opposed ideals each build on a nostalgic longing to be with the environment— but in a Western, anthropocentric way. While environmental preservationists are concerned with protecting the pristine landscape from the ravages of human activities, those who subscribe to cattle culture want cows and the pasture at the center of an idyllic rural life that is clearly separated from the forest, and temporally and spatially distinct from contemporary city life.

Those who raise cattle in Amazonia do not necessarily view their actions as destructive, but as part of a long tradition of engagement with the environment in which humans transform wild nature through cultivation. Some of the people that I met who defended their right to "deforest" cited biblical passages such as this one, from Genesis 1:29–30: "Then God said, 'I give you every seed-bearing plant on the face of the whole earth and every tree that has fruit with seed in it. They will be yours for food. And to all the beasts of the earth and all the birds in the sky and all the creatures that move along the ground—everything that has the breath of life in it—I give every green plant for food.' And it was so" (NIV).

For many, both secular and religious, the need to be productive is a foundational belief. Cattle culture draws on these broader beliefs of human agency in the natural world, ideals which are expressed through the conversion of "wild" nature to pastures and agricultural fields. In the region under study here, people who clearly separate themselves from undesirable forms of nature, harness the wild through cultivation, and make it "productive" are rewarded socially, and the landscapes, homesteads, and yards that they produce are judged positively.

PERCEIVING AND ENGAGING THE LANDSCAPE

PERCEPTIONS OF BEAUTY AND NATURE

When speaking about the forest, Acreans will often mention its beauty. Twenty members in each of seven different groups were asked to identify which form of landscape they found to be the most beautiful.[1] They were asked to choose one of the three most common forms of rural landscape recognized by a broad cross-section of Acrean society: forest, agricultural plot, and pasture.

As shown in figure 4.1, at least half the members of four groups found the forest to be the most beautiful form of landscape: environmental NGO workers, policy makers, urban residents of Rio Branco, and rubber tappers. Many NGO workers and policy makers value nature and the forest as a symbol of purity, and also as integral to regional and global environmental health. The eleven Rio Branco residents who chose the forest cited the importance of conserving the forest, and mentioned their perceptions that deforestation was related to climate change. To varying extents, the preference for the forest is related to environmentalist ideology and urban residence. In con-

1. Of the 140 respondents in the sample, sixteen are not included in the results here because they could not decide or chose more than one landscape.

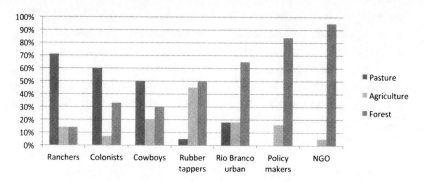

FIGURE 4.1. Survey: Which is the most beautiful landscape?

trast, the rubber tappers' preference comes from an appreciation of the forest built through sustained interaction.

The ranchers, cowboys, and colonists all found pasture—the landscape most associated with their economic practice, cattle raising—to be the most beautiful, suggesting a link between landscape, livelihood, and aesthetic appreciation (Cronon 1983; Scott 1998). Some said that a uniform pasture gave them great satisfaction because it illustrated their hard work, claiming also that it would not be appropriate to find beauty in the forest because "it is not worth anything." Members of these three groups, who did not utilize forest resources to the same extent as the rubber tappers, commonly saw the forest preserves that they were forced to maintain by the government as a "waste" of their property.

Although it is unclear why other urban residents chose one landscape over another, most Acreans were aware that "forest" is the culturally or politically correct response. Acreans often associate foreigners, especially *pesquisadores* (researchers), with efforts to "save the forest," referring to them as *ecologistas*, or environmentalists.[2] The preference for the forest may therefore have been overstated in this context. On the other hand, although most people know that choosing "pasture" would be at odds with these dominant percep-

2. Although the direct translation of "environmentalist" is *ambientalista*, this term was rarely used in Acre. Perhaps the *ecologista* label is a more accurate reflection of how many Acreans see foreign researchers, i.e., as people concerned with environmental relationships who use hard science to justify preservationism.

tions, this was still the most common response among some rural groups.

Overall, these findings show that factors such as rural versus urban residence, as well as ideological and economic considerations, play into evaluations of beauty. How do perceptions of beauty, an abstract concept, relate to the ways that groups viewed actual landscapes and the people who produced them?

CONCRETE ACTIONS: PREFERENCES FOR
THE SEPARATION OF HOME AND FOREST

Although many find the forest to be beautiful, it is also widely seen as a threat to human-modified spaces. In my survey, I asked respondents if they agreed with a statement that I often heard: "If you stop working, the forest will take over your property." There was almost 100 percent (119/120) agreement on this item. I often had to repeat the statement, which people felt to be an obvious statement of fact, not something deserving of an opinion. "Lógico!" was a common response.

Despite the fact that many urban Acreans find the forest beautiful, they do their best to keep it at a distance, even taking steps to reinforce this separation by eliminating all traces of it from their homes. In Rio Branco, most houses sit on giant concrete slabs that take up the largest portion of each lot, with the perimeter surrounded by walls. Although there were fruit trees and other ornamental plants in some homes, the homes of many urban Acreans have little if any vegetation. When I contracted dengue fever in Rio Branco, some of my friends blamed the plants surrounding the house where I was staying. Grass, fruit trees, and other individual plants are considered safe, for the most part, but excessive vegetation, especially "wild" forest species, is thought to provide a haven for mosquitoes, rats, and other disease vectors.

These functional considerations are also reflected in aesthetic preferences. Most rural homesteads are surrounded by a clearing of hard-packed dirt that is weeded and swept regularly. Some residents plant fruit trees and decorative plants, which may also have medicinal, culinary, or "magical" uses (Kawa 2012), around their homes. The insides of most of the homes I visited were largely devoid of live vegetation, but plastic plants and flowers are commonly used for decorative purposes in public and private spaces. Hotels are unique spaces, ca-

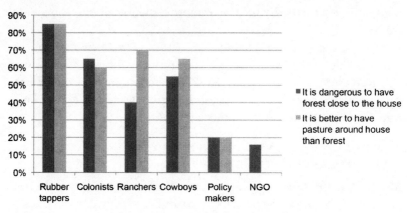

N = 20 in each group, except for NGO group, which had only 19 respondents for this question.

FIGURE 4.2. Group agreement on forest–house proximity

tering to visitors drawn to natural Amazonia while still reflecting local norms of human–nature distinction. A hotel where I often stayed in Rio Branco, for example, displays a painting that highlights a romanticized Amazonian nature, with two jaguars lazing in front of a pool of water and a waterfall. A plastic plant, sprayed and dusted on a daily basis by the maids, sits in front of the painting.

The flower shops in Rio Branco are filled with plastic flowers and roses shipped in from São Paulo. When I asked the florist why he did not sell any native flowers, he told me that no one wanted flowers from the *mato* (forest), which were not considered beautiful by most consumers. His wife, who was in the back of the store working on an arrangement, chimed in: "They are ugly. No woman wants to receive such a gift. It does not express love."

I worked from the basic premise that I'd observed in the city—the importance of separating the house from nature—and asked similar questions about residences in the forest. I asked twenty members of six groups (only 19 in the NGO group responded) if they agreed or disagreed with statements that I had heard in the countryside (fig. 4.2).

Urban policy makers and NGO workers, groups that are ideologically committed to forest preservation, downplay the importance for rural populations of maintaining a distance between house and forest. However, 85 percent of the rubber tappers and 65 percent of the colonists I interviewed—recall that these groups live in closest proximity to the forest—said that having the forest close to the home was dangerous. They cited the risk of falling trees and the increased likelihood of predators and pests entering the home.

Although I have emphasized the role of ideology and perception in landscape construction, my data show that practical matters also dictate perceptions of appropriate human interactions with nature. The contrasting perspectives of the rural and the urban groups suggest that urbanites, removed from the forest, are guided in their evaluations by ideological considerations. It is only after achieving a secure standard of living in an urban setting that an individual can contemplate the virtues, and not just the threats, of nature. This conceptual separation is reinforced in the cities by the same individuals, albeit on a less perceptible scale.

PEOPLE AND NATURE: LINKS BETWEEN LANDSCAPE AND LANDOWNER CHARACTER

For smallholders, to work the land is a basic right, one instilled in them through personal experience (Porro 2002). This perspective is also based on biblical understandings of the social function of land and its fundamental importance for producing food (Schmink and Wood 1992:181). The transformation of the land through work has also been reinforced by developmentalist policies that encourage smallholder migrants to demonstrate productivity through cultivation as a means of establishing their right to land. From this perspective, forest extractivism, based on harvesting products from the forest, is seen as an atavistic form of livelihood, better replaced by agriculture and ranching.

Despite the growth of pro-environment sentiment among much of the urban public and policy makers, rural groups are still socially and economically rewarded for their ability to transform—not to maintain—the forest. Spending time in the countryside, I heard many remarks about the character of landowners, based on quick evaluations of their landholding. This was most common among rural populations, but some NGO workers and policy makers also made similar statements when I traveled with them. They opined that a property with well-maintained, "clean" pasture demonstrates that the owner is a hard worker. Conversely, a person whose home is not clearly distinguished from the forest is described as lazy, or lacking the will to the work (falta de coragem). Figure 4.3 shows the extent to which different groups agreed with these statements (n = 20 in each group).

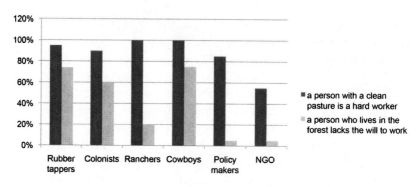

FIGURE 4.3. Group agreement on landscape–character relation

The clean pasture–hard worker association was nearly unanimous among rural groups, but somewhat lower among policy makers (85 percent) and NGO workers (55 percent). This shows that, especially among rural populations, pasture is associated with the positive value of hard work. A clean pasture is considered one of the ultimate expressions of work for two reasons: it shows the effort that transformed forest to pasture in the first place, and it indicates the continued maintenance of a cultivated space.

On the other hand, when a house is considered to be surrounded too closely by the forest, it will often be said that the proprietor lacks the will to work. Interestingly, it was the rubber tappers, the group that was often judged negatively for their forest extractivist livelihood and lifestyle, and the cowboys who agreed with this statement the most. Among the NGO and policy maker groups—urban groups who are more likely to be called "environmentalists"—there was extremely low agreement (only one out of twenty) that leaving the forest intact denotes laziness. Although the ranchers often made this sort of statement in conversation, they only agreed with it 20 percent of the time in my survey. As with many questions that were worded negatively, or could indicate a politically incorrect stance, the results do not capture the prevalence of the statement in natural speech.

PERCEPTIONS OF MEN AND WORK IN RURAL AMAZONIA

Migrants were drawn to Amazonia by marketing slogans calling it a "land without men for men without land," and men continue to be evaluated on the basis of their ability to demonstrate a strong work ethic by means of landscape transformation. Women also work, but these expressions as well as popular discourse tend to focus on men. In rural Acre, I found that a distinction is made between "men," who work, and those who fail to demonstrate their worth by transforming the natural environment. Individuals whose properties do not show a clear separation of human and natural spaces are considered to be less "manly" from the point of view of current gender roles, which assert that real men should perform physical labor.

Work and landscape transformation also served to distinguish, in the minds of some, "men" from "less evolved" people and animals. According to some ranchers, colonists, and former rubber tappers now residing in cities, the rubber tappers' "cultural underdevelopment" is the result of living in the forest, which has made them "more like the animals than men." This belief was related to a variety of local theories, from a lack of sunshine, which hindered cognitive functions, to isolation from "civilization," which limited opportunities for socialization and education. The rubber tappers often assert their own humanity in relation to a similar human–animal continuum. When describing the arrival of their ancestors in Acre, more than one rubber tapper said: "There were no people here, *só bichos e índios* [only an-

FIGURE 4.4. Cowboy in the field at sunset

imals and Indians]." It appears to be the belief of some that groups who do not transform their environment—extractivist rubber tappers and Indians—and do not labor in the *sol quente* (hot sun) lack the defining features of both "men" and humans because they have not tamed the corrupting influence of "wild" nature.

MANSCAPES

The process of work is inscribed on the body in the form of calloused hands, and on the material world through the application of culture to "wild" nature. In this way, the forest becomes a cultural landscape that is clearly recognized as bearing the mark of human intervention. The men who produce this cultivated landscape are viewed positively in Amazonia. On the other hand, the person who fails to effect this transformation and allows the wilderness to overtake culturally accepted boundaries is seen as lacking the characteristics of a good citizen. Because men usually perform this sort of work and are judged for it, I focus here on men, the way they cultivate the landscape, and the physical manifestation of this work, the "manscape."

When we imagine castaways, savages, and children raised by wolves first encountering civilization, we visualize these individuals in a bedraggled state. The first step on their road to civility is a haircut and a shave, and then a public appearance in Western—or restrictive, stuffy, high-culture—clothing. While such an individual may be the same on the inside, his symbolic transformation is illustrated by his newly "cultured" exterior in two ways: his body is now covered with clothing, and his hair is groomed.

What would you envision to be the appearance of a person with a messy yard, an overgrown pasture, or a weed-filled garden? It is likely that the neglect apparent in these human/natural spaces would be reflected in the appearance of the individual, who might perhaps wear disheveled clothing and exhibit a general lack of grooming. These unkempt landscapes, or "manscapes," are regarded as denoting internal moral failings on the part of the person responsible for managing them. Those who fail to maintain proper personal grooming are viewed as sliding away from the cultured life, and are often thought to be subversive or to embody attributes such as dishonesty, laziness, and other forms of moral corruption brought on by the inability to control that which is natural or animal-like.

In Acre, men with short, neatly cut hair are perceived as being more responsible than *cabeludos* (men with long hair) or *barbudos* (men with beards). Without exception, the many politicians, business people, and ranchers I met in Acre during my visits had short hair and were clean shaven. Those with power understood the importance of appearance, and they demanded similar standards in those tasked with serving them. So, too, did those charged with maintaining the existing social order—soldiers and policemen. Soldiers could often be seen standing at attention in front of a white wall next to the barracks in Rio Branco. (Curiously, these men wore clothing that mimicked the forest [camouflage], although it made them more conspicuous in the city.)

The ranchers I spoke with thought that long hair was part of a larger package of subversive traits associated with environmentalists and people who worked at NGOs, such as drugs, tattoos, and a fascination with indigenous culture and non-Western spirituality. Bahiana's son Ney was a different kind of *cabeludo*. He considered himself a *roquiero* (rocker); for him, long hair was an expression of a rebellious identity in the face of rural traditionalism. That said, he always wore his hair tucked in his hat when he was working in the countryside to avoid trouble (he is pictured with Bahiana in figure 3.3). *Barbudos* (men with beards) tend to be considered politically or intellectually subversive.

I cannot emphasize enough how much these traits mattered in the ways that opposed groups, such as ranchers and environmentalists, presented themselves and perceived one another. Whereas the rancher may see sloth in the bearded *cabeludo*, the *cabeludo* environmentalist, tattoo artist, and *roquiero* each felt that his self-presentation reflected a modern, cosmopolitan, or nonconformist way of life that was more enlightened. The most extreme *cabeludos* railed against the stalwarts of traditional society, and the combed hair adorning their pre-programmed heads. These individuals rejected Acrean provincialism and sought to connect themselves with large cities in the south and in the United States.

Some environmentalists in particular disagree with what they consider a pathological need to control, restrain, and dominate nature. This is interesting to consider in relation to ideas of masculinity, which require control of both the natural world and women (Ortner 1974). It is not a coincidence, then, that great pains are taken to make sure that all female body hair is managed: through the straightening of curly hair, the bleaching of arm hair, and the removal of facial hair. A procedure advertised in many salon windows as *depi-*

lação (depilation) is better known around the world as a "Brazilian wax" or simply "a Brazilian." Similar to the transformation of forest to cultivated landscape, the procedure removes all natural covering or fashions it into a geometric strip.

THE REASSERTION OF THE NATURE–CULTURE DIVIDE: ENVIRONMENTAL PRESERVATION AND THE LEGIBLE LANDSCAPE

Gaps . . . call attention to the bad transportability of demarcations of human livelihood versus nature conservation, productive farms versus forest reserves, and settled culture versus the wild.

ANNA LOWENHAUPT TSING, *FRICTION* (2005:175)

The conceptual gaps Tsing references here enabled the rubber tappers to thrive and allowed them to connect their practices with a nascent global environmental movement and challenge the long-held ideologies undergirding destructive development. Gaps, she writes, "develop in the seams of universal projects; they are found where universals have not been successful in setting the terms" (Tsing 2005:202).

Since the promise of a reconciliation, new gaps have formed. I have examined some of the actual, physical gaps in the forest of Acre, including the much-publicized clearings in the extractive reserve. There are also larger clearings—cities filled by blocks of geometric streets with rows of houses with plastic plants in their living rooms. Looking in these gaps, grouped under the rubric of "non-forest," it is increasingly clear that the ascendance of the rubber tappers to the level of international symbols of environmentalism has in some ways pushed them away from the reconciliation that they proposed with use-based conservation. These gaps reflect a reassertion of universals in the form of the nature–culture divide, capitalist expansion, destructive development, and environmental preservationism.

While the tappers fought for social justice, economic security, and environmental protection, these objectives are now largely overshadowed by environmental concerns. As Acre has come to be seen as a progressive state because of its environmental policies and its prioritization of forest preservation, it has become increasingly concerned with curbing deforestation. State governmental institutions are seen by rural groups as overwhelmingly effective enforcers of deforestation and burning laws.

Technological advances have contributed to the state's ability to enforce these laws. Remote sensing and the mapping of property lines have enabled governmental authorities to monitor deforestation in previously "invisible" or inaccessible areas (EDF n.d.). Acre was also a pioneer in zoning, completing the ZEE (Environmental and Economic Zoning) of their entire territory in 2006 (Governo do Acre 2006). This ZEE defined appropriate land uses for areas based on their topographical features, soil quality, degree of anthropogenic disturbance, and proximity and access to markets.

The ability to monitor changes throughout the state has made the government increasingly capable of influencing the practices of populations with whom its agents may never come into contact. Through mapping and surveillance, the Acrean landscape has gone from a largely inaccessible and undefined space to a landscape that is increasingly "legible" (Scott 1998) to state and national authorities. These tools give the state an unprecedented ability to enter into the lives of Amazonian groups in the name of the overarching good of environmental preservation. Amid a complex array of classifications, however, the emphasis on enforcing deforestation regulations has resulted in the mapping of the landscape simply via the dichotomous terms "forest" and "non-forest."

Members of all groups surveyed mentioned roaming satellites that could detect even the smallest new clearings, prompting the arrival of IBAMA agents to fine the offender or take him to jail. It was essential for rural producers to know how their landscape could be perceived from the sky. What size should a clearing be to avoid detection? How high or dense could *capoeira* (secondary regrowth) grow before it would be seen as forest, and thus be off-limits for use again? This awareness of an ever-present eye in the sky is generating new ways of conceptualizing the landscape. Many of the landholders I spoke with still articulated elaborate ways of classifying the composition of their land and its resources, history, development, and state of regeneration. The monitoring of the forests may not yet have an effect on the various ways that rural people categorize their land, but they are aware of the dominant classifications and adapt their practices accordingly.

CONCLUSION

The nature–culture divide continues to influence the ways that people perceive, manage, and construct the material world in the form of landscapes, dwellings, and cultural places. On an abstract level, the forest is considered beautiful by urban residents, who do not have to depend on it economically, and by rubber tappers, who have a history of interaction with the forest. Their appreciation for the forest, however, does not mean that urban or rural populations wish to live in proximity to it. Both groups take steps to separate themselves from nature, and are judged positively for demonstrating a clear distinction of human and natural realms in their landholdings, their dwellings, and even their bodies.

The prevalence of cattle culture in the material landscape, and the relative absence of any perceptible celebration of *florestania*, except in official projects, indicates that cattle culture is growing in Acre. The meanings of these landscapes and spaces reflect a desire to cross the divide that separates humans from nature, but in such a way that is highly anthropocentric. By analyzing the landscapes of Acre, from the forests and pastures of the countryside to urban places that seek to recreate the rural, we see that the nature–culture conflict of the frontier continues. The discursive battle over the future of Amazonia is based on these same tensions, and it is in these political and symbolic realms that the future landscapes of Amazonia will be determined.

This chapter has contributed to my overall objectives by elucidating how ideas guide the perception of the natural world and assign positive social value both to anthropogenic spaces and to the people who produce such locales through their practices. In addition to the political-economic structures that favor cattle raising and the economic and cultural appeal of cattle raising, discussed in previous chapters, the social perceptions associated with the nature–culture divide can be understood as further incentivizing a cattle-based lifestyle in Acre. Attempts to counter the expansion of cattle raising or to encourage use-based conservation must address each of these structures.

Members of the Acrean government recognized the importance of changing perceptions of the forest, and *florestania* was designed to do that. They acknowledged that the challenge was as much about a culture change as it was about policies promoting sustainable development. Some of their actions have actually contributed to the reimposition of the nature–culture divide on the landscape. As a result of the evaluation of use-based conservation through the lens of forest cover, a range of human-nature interactions have been reduced to "forest" and "non-forest," at least in the minds of rural people, who are altering their practices accordingly. With time and continued enforcement, it is likely that rural classifications of the landscape will also come to reflect these narrow classifications. The social and cultural objectives of the rubber-tapper vision have to some extent been subsumed by the emphasis on environmental preservation, which reasserts the distinction in a setting where there was hope for overcoming it.

CHAPTER 5

THE RANCHERS: SMOOTH HANDS, PROGRESS, AND PRODUCTION

IN THE ENTRYWAY OF the Library of the Forest in Rio Branco, there is a dramatic wall display entitled "O Acre Como um Pasto de Boi" (Acre as a cattle pasture). It chronicles social conflict and environmental destruction along the Acrean frontier in the 1970s and 1980s. In the middle of the exhibit is a near-life-size image of a *pistoleiro*, who stands in front of a ranch gate with a machine gun in his hands (discussed in the first chapter). His eyes and the top of his face are shaded by the cowboy hat on his head. The hat sits awkwardly, and its brown hue does not quite match the rest of the image. It looks as if the hat were pasted on, perhaps to protect the man's identity. Regardless of the back story, the dark cowboy hat enhances the message the photo is intended to convey. The ranchers, and their cowboys and *pistoleiros*, were the "black hats" in the revised frontier narrative, while the forest-dwelling rubber tappers were the heroes who defended their land.

Nestled in the shade of palm trees around the plaza of the Governor's Palace, there is a statue of Chico Mendes, the famed leader of the Acrean rubber-tapper movement, holding the hand of his young son. The 1988 murder of Mendes on the orders of rancher Darly Alves da Silva made international headlines. An article appearing in the *New York Times* six days after his death, under the title "Brazil Burns the Future," asserts: "Brazilian governments commonly shrug off criticism of the cowboy strand in their society. That strand is evident in the environmental holocaust sweeping the Amazon rainforest and the cold-blooded murder of a trade unionist who dared to challenge slash-and-burn land developers" (Dec. 28, 1988). In the aftermath of Mendes's murder, the ranchers' image was solidified: they are the wealthy, violent, and environmentally destructive villains of Amazonia (e.g., Revkin 1990; Shoumatoff 1990).

Not much is known about the ranchers since the time of their tu-multuous arrival in Amazonia in the 1970s and 1980s.[1] While schol-ars have made progress in demystifying the lives of ranchers in other parts of the Americas (e.g., Perramond 2010; Sayre 1999), Adams's (2010) recent work represents one of the few attempts to "study up" (Nader 1972) to this exclusive segment of Amazonian society. Not only could such information update the regional ethnographic record by incorporating the vital perspective of this powerful Amazonian group, but applied goals, such as curbing Amazonian deforestation, can be reached only with the cooperation of all groups, especially large-scale landowners (Nepstad et al. 2009).

My objective here is to increase our understanding of this enig-matic group. I analyze two interlinked features of the rancher villain label: their elite status and environmental destruction. I first exam-ine the ranchers as an elite group, as determined by their economic and political power, and then demonstrate how the ranchers conform to and challenge these classifications. I also focus on how rancher status is constructed and expressed in social situations, and com-pare subordinate rural social groups' perceptions of the ranchers. Al-though there is some idealization of ranchers as rural gentry, a survey of twenty Acrean ranchers shows that they are a diverse group com-prising both landed elites and persons of more humble origins.

Now that the land conflicts have subsided, many ranchers feel that tensions have entered the political and ideological realm as a con-test between traditional ideals associated with development, both ec-onomically and socially, and environmentalism, which they see as inhibiting economic growth, and a step backward for the country and society in general. Understanding their criticisms of environmental-ism, aside from the fact that it directly challenges the material basis of their wealth and status, requires an examination of how ranchers and other groups perceive work.

In the previous chapter I discussed landscapes and places as the products of human practices that are guided by ideologies. Here I in-vestigate the ideas of work that are central to producing landscapes and how they are linked with ideas of class. Rural Amazonian groups agree that work (trabalho) is the application of one's labor to produce food or other products. Amazonian "work" results in physical trans-formations: forests are converted to cultivated spaces in the form of

1. Rivière (1972) studied an Amazonian rancher community prior to the Ama-zonian colonization of the 1970s.

agricultural fields or pastures. But the process is also inscribed on the body, as smooth hands become calloused. Ranchers are assumed to have "smooth" hands, because they command the labor of others, a key component of elite status. Here I show how smooth hands—not marked by interaction with nature—are seen as a sign of social distinction in this context. The ranchers emphasize the social function of their production over labor and draw on developmentalist notions of landscape transformation as progress to defend their ranching livelihood and to dispute environmental ideology and policies.

THE ACREAN RANCHER AS RURAL ELITE

My sample of ranchers is confined to individuals owning large ranches—those with approximately five thousand head of cattle. Unlike rubber tappers and colonists, they do not reside in a centralized rural community, but live scattered throughout the capital of Rio Branco and go out to visit their ranches periodically.

There are challenges in gaining access to any elite group, and most of the ranchers were naturally suspicious when a foreigner and presumed *ecologista* expressed an interest in them. My first meeting with a rancher was facilitated by a government contact. I spoke briefly with the rancher in his office, and he invited me to my first cattle auction, where I was able to meet other ranchers and gradually expand my network. I made it clear that my purpose was to collect data on the cultural and economic features of the cattle industry among different rural groups, which also included, I made clear, rubber tappers and colonists. Although they were always skeptical of my real intentions, some of them gradually began to trust me to some extent. Those ranchers who chose to let me into their world embraced the fact that I was attempting to get to know them beyond the villain label, of which they are highly aware.

Out of the sample of twenty ranchers, I came to know seven of them well through participant observation, in-depth interviews, and personal interactions over the course of multiple field seasons. I visited the places of origin of two of these ranchers—in south-central Brazil—to gain an understanding of their reasons for coming to Acre in relation to their family history. I conducted ethnographic observations of some ranchers while I accompanied them on errands around town, on visits to their ranches, and during urban social events, such as auctions, barbecues, and public meetings.

Over time I began to understand the logic of their actions as it arose from their view of history, politics, and nature and in relation to their class position and associated notions of work. A description of one of the "elite" cattle auctions, where I often sat among the ranchers, provides a useful vehicle for introducing these themes and shows how the ranchers' elite status is expressed and perceived in social situations.

AN ELITE CATTLE AUCTION

On Saturdays and Sundays during the dry season months of May through August, ranchers put on *leilões de gado elite* (elite cattle auctions) to sell their purebred Nellore bulls and cows. Each auction began when the first hulking white bull burst onto the stage through a little red door. The bull's entrance was heralded by choruses from famous *sertaneja* songs and instrumental riffs from Europe's "The Final Countdown" and Van Halen's "Jump." The announcer, from his perch high above the stage and the crowd, boomed: "Reprodutor grande! Raça fina!" (Great reproducer! Fine lineage/breed!)

Once in the arena, the bulls often just stood there, huffing and staring at the sea of people in front of them. A cowboy on a skinny ledge ten feet above the stage might jab at the bull's hump, haunches, and face with a long pole, which would get the beast bucking and kicking up clouds of dust. The bulls never looked up at the cowboy but instead charged forward, and their behemoth heads and horns sometimes got stuck in the reinforced fencing. Just below the stage, dust wafted over the spectators and potential buyers, who sat around square plastic tables.

The ranchers often pushed their tables together, making one long, snaking table on the right side of the arena. These *grandes* of Acrean ranching, the *fazendeiros* (large-scale landowners), at some points paid careful attention to the bulls. Most of the time, however, they just appeared to be laughing and talking with their friends, the very picture of the *vida boa* (good life) that observers both criticize and envy. They took bites of steak and sausage with little toothpicks, dipping the morsels into piles of dry *farinha* (manioc flour). They absently held up their empty glasses, and waiters in black vests and bowties scurried to refill them with whisky, *cachaça*, beer, or soda.

When a new bull came on the stage, some ranchers might scrutinize their auction booklets to evaluate the potential quality of the bull, everything from its lineage and growth rate to its scrotum circumference, a measure of productivity. All of the auction cattle had been conceived from the frozen semen of long-deceased, legendary bulls, whose names were printed in the family trees, which went back several generations. These cattle were all certified *puro origem* (pure origin) Nellore breed, with some selling for over 14,000 *reais* (US$8,880).

There were also weekday auctions, which the ranchers only attended if they needed a *lote* (lot) of calves for quick fattening, but they often sent their *gerentes*, or foremen, to buy for them. The breeding stock at the weekday auctions was not considered "elite," but included mixed-breed cattle, gradations of the white Nellore and the Acrean *tucura*, a smaller, hardy animal with stringier meat. The *tucura* was the only kind of cattle in Acre before the arrival of the white Nellore cattle and the southern ranchers in the 1970s. The "purebred" imports have been built into the Acrean hierarchy and common perceptions as an elite stock that is more "productive" than the mixed-race Acre native.

At the long rancher table, ranchers from Minas Gerais and São Paulo, who might share kinship ties, often sat together in little clusters. The host rancher's cowboys, mostly native Acreans, and their families also attended the elite auctions, but they generally sat apart, at the smaller tables. A group of newer ranchers, both native Acreans and migrants who had been successful in business and bought ranches within the past decade, also sat around these smaller tables. There were people at the auctions who had no intention of buying cattle and owned no land. These men said that they just enjoyed seeing the beautiful animals and partaking in the free food and drink. The groups sitting at the smaller tables sometimes mixed with the traditional ranchers, but the ranchers usually came to their tables, not the other way around. When a rancher arrived, the seated individual rose quickly, and bowed slightly before extending their hands to grasp the smooth, uncalloused hand of the rancher.

CONCEPTUALIZING ELITE STATUS IN ACRE

In social settings, many ranchers exhibit cues of class distinction and a *jeito*, or way of interacting with people, that combines ease of social interaction and macho jocularity with the commanding and no-nonsense style of a person of power. As a result of their wealth and the perception that they gained or consolidated their elite status through violence against native Acreans and destruction of the forest, ranchers are both emulated and disdained in rural Acre. When other rural groups imitate ranchers, they stride purposefully with their elbows out and bark staccato orders, usually with an exaggerated *paulista* (a term applied to ranchers from outside of Acre, although it literally means "native of São Paulo state") accent.

They are an exclusive group that matches the local imaginary of an elite class, with their whiteness, southern origin, smooth hands, and expectation of deference from socioeconomically subordinate classes. It is also assumed that the ranchers possess two key attributes that denote elite status: political and economic power (Marcus 1983). Historically such elite groups were beyond the purview of anthropologists, but since Nader's (1972) call for more research, scholars have made progress in conceptualizing the upper strata of society and describing how they maintain and express power (e.g., Cohen 1981; Marcus 1983; Shore and Nugent 2002). The ranchers of Acre fit into conceptualizations of an elite class, but they also challenge them in fundamental ways.

According to a Marxian view, the ranchers evince central attributes of elite status as commodity producers who hire the labor of the proletariat and sell goods through connections with national and international capitalist classes (Cancian 1989:165). The ranchers do have greater economic power than other rural groups—cowboys, colonists, and rubber tappers—but their relationship with each group is distinct. For example, the average rancher may buy calves for fattening or rent pasturage from peasant groups who own land—the colonists and rubber tappers. These arrangements bring greater financial benefit to the rancher than the smallholders, but the relationship between the two is not coercive. Some smallholders have used rancher investments in their land to make the transition to being small-scale, independent ranchers.

Cowboys, often former colonists and rubber tappers or their sons, form another rural subordinate category: proletarians selling their labor to the ranchers. Many of these cowboys grew up in the cities, where their families may have moved as the rubber industry declined, or as a result of land conflicts with ranchers. With the transition from rubber extraction to the cattle economy in Acre, the ranchers assumed the previously dominant rural position of the *seringalista*, who controlled the labor of the rubber tappers in a debt peonage system (Bakx 1988).

All of the cowboys I interviewed felt a sense of loyalty to the ranch-

FIGURE 5.1. A rancher observes as a cowboy works cattle

ers (fig. 5.1), referring to them as *patrão* (boss), a term also used by the rubber tappers for the *seringalistas*. The cowboys, however, emphasized that they were free laborers with the ability to leave a position if they wished. In the case of the cowboys, there is a clearer relationship of domination, both historically, when they may have been forced from their lands by ranchers, and in the present, as wage laborers. The notion of economic domination is useful for conceptualizing a capitalist landowning class, but it does not capture the diversity of socioeconomic relationships between subordinate and dominant classes, or the fluidity of the smallholders here, who may move between autonomous peasant and wage-dependent proletarian categories on a seasonal basis.

The seminal writings of Pareto (1968) and Mosca (1939) emphasize the structural-political features of elite classes that allow them to maintain political power. According to Giddens, these works represent an attempt to "transmute the Marxian concept of class as founded on the relations of production, into an essentially political differentiation between 'those who rule' and those 'who are ruled'" (quoted in Marcus 1983:14). In Acre the ranchers remain economically and politically dominant in the minds of subordinate groups, but they feel that their political power has eroded with the decline of developmentalist ideology and policy.

When the ranchers arrived in Amazonia, they had a great deal of power—the ability to impose their will successfully on less powerful groups (Schmink and Wood 1992:13–14). Within the context of the frontier, Acrean ranchers could pressure state entities to act on their behalf, especially against the socioeconomically marginal rubber tappers (Bakx 1988; Keck 1995). The ranchers were also backed at that time by the developmentalist ideology and policies of colonization, which saw the ranchers' work as the vehicle for "progress" and "development" (Hecht and Cockburn 1989).

The rubber-tapper movement challenged the developmentalist discourses of "empty lands" and "technological backwardness" applied to the Acrean landscapes and people (Esteves, quoted in Kainer et al. 2003:875), stressing instead social equity, land tenure, and forest conservation as the basis for livelihoods (Allegretti 2002). Beginning in 1999, the "forest" government emphasized forest-based development and citizenship (Schmink 2011; Vadjunec, Schmink, and Greiner 2011).

The rubber tappers should have had increased political power under this administration, but many tappers feel that the images and policies of the government have not translated into political empowerment. The bottom line, many subordinate groups admit, is that money "commands" and "gets results." According to one rubber tapper: "If I go to the mayor's office to speak with her, I could wait in line all day. The rancher goes straight into her office." It is assumed that ranchers walk right through the doors that are so often closed to rural working-class groups, and that within these exclusive spaces, the ranchers are granted political favors that allow them to continue their economic and political domination.

Ranchers denied that they received preferential treatment and went out of their way to cite instances when they were specifically targeted by governmental officials for environmental and labor violations that all groups commit. Many feel that they are singled out because of the high visibility of their properties in the countryside, which denote affluence and are more easily monitored and accessed by government officials. Although smallholders think that wealth allows the ranchers to avoid sanctions through payoffs to governmental officials, the ranchers feel that they are targeted for violations by governmental officials eager to make a political statement about their solidarity with the working classes and environmentalism.

Both ranchers and subordinate groups feel that they are subjected to power structures outside of their control. Ranchers often assert that local and state government officials are puppets for an international environmental agenda, and that Amazonian forest preservation is nothing more than a pretext for developed countries to defend their economic interests by suppressing Brazilian agricultural production.

SUBORDINATE GROUP PERCEPTIONS OF THE RANCHER

While the ranchers contest these nebulous, multiscalar forces, subordinate groups' perceptions of rancher dominance are given specificity through daily interactions. On the most basic level, to be a *fazendeiro* is to own a large amount of land and accrue profits from that land through the labor of others (Wagley 1971; Harris 1956:77). As a national category, a *fazendeiro* may be the owner of a sugar plantation (Harris 1956) or a soy farm (Adams 2010), but the Acrean *fazendeiro* is exclusively a cattle rancher. Individuals owning five thousand head of cattle are considered *fazendeiros* by all groups, but the threshold for this classification varies. To be a *fazendeiro* in the eyes of all, one also must exhibit a series of characteristics that indicate economic power and a historical association with the upper strata of society.

It gradually became apparent to me that ranchers were commonly associated with a number of specific attributes. I administered a survey to measure the extent to which members of the four rural social groups associated the ranchers with the characteristics of whiteness, wealth, southern origin, land conflict, and a separation from labor. Table 5.1 shows the percentage of members in each group who agreed with the statements presented in my questionnaire.

As a result of the violent land conflicts that took place in Acre, ranchers are often associated with conflict and the displacement of native Acreans. Ninety percent of rubber tappers, the group that felt the brunt of these land contests, agreed that ranchers caused conflict. Seventy percent of colonists agreed with the conflict statement, but a little more than half of the ranchers and cowboys agreed.

When most Acreans think of a rancher, they imagine a white man. I reversed this particular statement to mitigate respondent bias, asking if ranchers were *moreno* (dark-skinned or mixed race). At least 95 percent of respondents in all groups indicated that ranchers were

Table 5.1. Agreement with statements about ranchers, by social group

	Survey Statement				
Social Group	Ranchers are moreno (mixed race).	Ranchers travel outside Acre.	Ranchers come from outside Acre.	Ranchers caused conflict in the past.	Ranchers have calloused hands.
Rubber tappers	0%	100%	100%	90%	30%
Colonists	0%	95%	90%	70%	70%
Ranchers	5%	90%	58%	53%	25%
Cowboys	5%	100%	75%	55%	10%

not *moreno*. Acreans will often use "outsider" designations to describe individuals with a light complexion: *paulista, sulista* (southerner), *gaúcho* (native of Rio Grande do Sul), *alemão* (German), and *gringo*. These descriptors highlight racial differences between foreigners and Acreans, who tend to be mixed race, as well as the assumption that white populations were born outside of the region. All rubber tappers and 90 percent of colonists agreed that ranchers came from outside of Acre, but ranchers and their cowboys (who were interviewed separately) agreed less strongly with this statement.

Acre is somewhat geographically isolated, whereas a southern origin is also associated with a connection to the economic and cultural centers of Brazil, and with modernity. Although Acreans are very proud of their state, it is generally agreed that roots in southern Brazil are socially desirable. The ability to travel outside of Acre is also an indicator of high social status, and at least 90 percent of respondents in each group agreed that ranchers can travel outside of Acre every year. Travel was often listed as an aspect of the rancher "good life," along with a new truck, a nice house in the city, a beautiful wife and/ or girlfriend, and drinking whiskey.

Elite status is thus related to a series of features that are both ascribed (race, origin) and realized through actions or behaviors (conflict, travel). With the exception of land conflict, these features are not unique to the ranchers, and describe much of the upper class in Rio Branco and across Brazil. What makes the ranchers unique is that their work is undertaken in the countryside, a setting where there are no office jobs and people must work with their hands. For many rural people, the proof of a true *fazendeiro* is written on the hands.

SMOOTH HANDS AND THE COMMAND OF LABOR

In greetings, class differences become apparent in the meeting of rough and smooth hands, which, along with other contextual evidence, such as clothing, race, and material possessions, are indicative of a life of manual labor or the power to command labor (see Schmink 1982:350). Calloused hands are seen as a physical connection to work and with the land. Maintaining "fine" hands demonstrates that one is above physical labor and makes a living by "thinking" in the city, or by commanding the labor of others in rural settings. When rural subordinate groups recounted to me their experiences in Amazonia, they often told me to look at their *mãos calejadas* (calloused hands). Their thick, deeply creased hands were often held out before they even began speaking, serving as indisputable evidence of a life of hard work.

It was often said that fine hands, those belonging to urban bureaucrats, the foreign anthropologist, and wealthy ranchers, demonstrate a disconnection from the trials of life in the countryside, and a fundamental inability to comprehend rural peoples' experience. Questions about rancher work were often met with an incredulous guffaw or statement, such as this one offered by a colonist: "Humph! The rancher has fine hands. The only thing his hands touch is the steering wheel!" Table 5.1 shows that less than a third of the rubber tappers, ranchers, and cowboys I spoke with thought that ranchers have calloused hands. Alternatively, a high percentage of colonists agree that ranchers have calloused hands. This is an indication of disagreement in conceptualizations of the rancher. While some colonists, through the acquisition of neighboring landholdings, have amassed enough land and cattle to be considered *fazendeiros*, this colonist-turned-*fazendeiro* might not be considered a true *fazendeiro* by the rubber tappers, who have a more idealized notion of them.

For many people, being a rancher means not only commanding labor and owning land and cattle in the present, but having done so as a landed elite throughout one's entire life. Self-made ranchers—those who engaged in manual labor to obtain their position, and thus have calloused hands—are not accorded the same level of prestige as the true *patrão*. In general, subordinate groups assume that ranchers come from a legacy of rural wealth and privilege. While there is some truth to this belief, I also found that there is a great deal of diversity within the rancher category.

RANCHER HISTORIES AND PERSPECTIVES

DIVERSITY OF RANCHER ORIGINS AND TRAJECTORIES

Some of the ranchers who migrated to Acre in the late 1970s and early 1980s came from traditional agricultural and ranching families, but others came with little and made their fortune in Acre. Of the twenty ranchers interviewed for this study, only four are the descendants of affluent ranching families in the center-south who came to Acre with the purpose of establishing large cattle ranches. These individuals are among the biggest ranchers in the state, with each owning more than fifty thousand head of cattle.

Zedo of São Paulo state, and cousins Ribeiro and Lui of Minas Gerais, also came from traditional landowning classes, but their families' lands had been subdivided to the point that they felt that their own prospects were limited in their homelands. Enticed by government incentives, they came to Acre—not to raise cattle, but to plant rubber trees. João, Ronaldo, Lissero, and Modesto were not affluent or members of traditional landowning families prior to their arrival in Acre. They used capital from the sale of land, or savings acquired through business ventures and professional careers, to finance their purchase of land and cattle in Acre.

Four ranchers were born in Acre, including Moroldo, who recently bought a ranch because it was a good investment, but he disliked being associated with "crude" ranchers. Almedo and Chaga owned gas stations and bought ranches with their earnings.

Some came to Acre with humble beginnings. Migdalio was born to a small farmer family in Pernambuco. He drove trucks for a living before settling in Acre. Tecides came as a cowboy and worked his way up the ranch hierarchy before acquiring his first piece of land with the help of his employer. Through profits accrued from the sale of smaller landholdings, he gradually acquired a large ranch. Three other ranchers have similar histories.

All of these ranchers now have high a socioeconomic status because they own a great deal of land and cattle, but some of them have working-class origins or acquired their initial wealth through means other than cattle. They all feel that they earned what they now have in Acre through courage and hard work. Their ideas of work were formed in relation to their family history, the developmentalist policies that encouraged their migration to Acre, broader notions of what it meant to venture to the frontier in search of opportunity, and strong beliefs about the social value of making land produce.

RIBEIRO'S STORY: HISTORY, IDEOLOGY, AND RANCHER MIGRATION TO ACRE

Ribeiro is a rancher who is widely respected by his peers, employees, and governmental officials. He was one of the few ranchers who let me accompany him in all of his daily activities and ask him difficult questions. He also allowed me to visit his hometown in the state of Minas Gerais, where I spoke with his family and other residents about his migration to Acre. Ribeiro's history illustrates some of the features that led others to become ranchers in Acre, and helps to elucidate how they understand themselves and their work in the present.

Generations of Ribeiro's family prospered in the fertile mountains of southern Minas Gerais, a land of dairy cattle and, more recently, coffee. When Ribeiro and some other now-Acrean ranchers came of age, they were members of established, economically secure, and often wealthy families. Their economic standing was derived from the land, usually cattle (mostly for milk production), agriculture, and commercial enterprises related to agricultural production.

With each generation, however, there was less available land due to a process that Ribeiro called "land reform made in the bed"—the division of parents' land between their children, eventually reducing large landholdings to small plots. After Ribeiro graduated from college with a degree in agronomy, he was eager to get to work building a future for himself, but he knew that he would have to seek his fortune somewhere else, as there was not enough land in his homeland to sustain him and the family he hoped to have in the future. Similarly, many other Acrean ranchers felt that they would be the first generation unable to achieve a standard of living equal to or better than their parents' if they stayed in south-central Brazil.

In the 1970s ranchers began arriving in Amazonia to establish cattle ranches with the aid of generous fiscal incentives offered by the Brazilian military government (Hecht 1993). The Acrean state, headed by Governor Wanderley Dantas (1971–1975), courted investors from the south and facilitated the sale of the area's vast rubber estates to the ranchers (Bakx 1988). In 1980 Ribeiro sold his *fusca* (Volkswagen Beetle) to help finance his journey, and set out for Acre with his cousin, Lui, a veterinarian. They initially planted rubber trees with the help of loans and subsidies from the government. After their rubber plants succumbed to disease, Ribeiro entered the cattle industry, which he had always intended to do at some point.

The decision by many ranchers to come to Amazonia was also related to their understanding of history. Many recalled the migration of their ancestors from Europe in search of a better life, which they achieved through hard work and, often, great suffering. Back in Ribeiro's hometown in Minas Gerais, his sister explained how their ancestors had come to Rio de Janeiro from Portugal at the end of the seventeenth century, and then struck out for what was then the wilderness of Brazil in search of gold. About 150 years ago, Ribeiro's great-grandfather decided to settle down in the town where much of the family currently resides in Minas Gerais state. Ribeiro's family thus saw his migration to Amazonia as a courageous step and an extension of their pioneer heritage.

Ranchers also tie their migration to Amazonia to a sense of patriotic duty to bring Amazonia under control and make it productive, a perspective fervently propagated during the military government's efforts to colonize Amazonia (Schmink and Wood 1992). Many ranchers see their actions in Amazonia as part of a broader historical narrative about bringing progress and development to the wilderness, a process that was romanticized in other, previous Brazilian frontier zones (Moog 1994).

Ranchers often told me that they expected to be treated more like heroes than villains. They stressed that they had not anticipated the conflicts they encountered after buying their land, nor could they have predicted the drastic shift in perceptions of the forest—from an obstacle to development to a valuable resource to be preserved. Rancher criticism of environmentalism is informed by their sense of history and commitment to traditional ideals that reinforce their class position, but many of these beliefs are shared by others (as seen through the discussion of work in chapter 4).

ENVIRONMENTAL PERCEPTIONS AND POLICY DEBATES

RANCHER PERSPECTIVES

On a tour of a slaughterhouse near the border with Rondônia, the owner pointed to an ominous-looking contraption and said: "This is where we make the *gringo moido* [ground gringo]." We laughed off his statement and I changed the subject in hurry, but the comment (and others) underscored the tensions surrounding my research, and the perceived environmentalist orientation of foreign researchers in general. From some of the more isolated places that I worked to the Federal University of Acre, some Acreans voiced their concern that my research was part of an international plan to preserve Amazonian resources until they were needed by the "First World."

It was supposedly a map from an American geography textbook that detailed imperialist plans to occupy Amazonia. Some had seen the map through chain emails, while more had heard about it secondhand. According to this apocryphal text, which I found on the Internet, the "FINRAF" ("Former International Reserve of the Amazon Forest"), comprising the majority of the Amazonian basin, was formed when the United States and United Nations assumed (uncorrected from the original text) "possession of these valuable lands to such primitive countries and people who should condemn the lungs of the world to disappearance and destroying in few years" (see Mitchell 2010).

For many Acreans, not just the ranchers, the emphasis on forest preservation is puzzling and extremely frustrating. Agriculturally oriented smallholders were especially angry about this sudden and drastic shift in policy. They blamed environmentalists in the United States and Europe, as well as Brazilian governmental officials on the national, state, and municipal levels, for the constraints that have forced them to change the ways that they use and perceive their land. For ranchers, as well as members of other groups, all the trouble started with Chico Mendes. Their criticisms once again return to the theme of work.

ENVIRONMENTALISM AND THE LEGACY OF CHICO MENDES

On December 22, 1988, Chico Mendes was murdered in his home by the son of rancher Darly Alves da Silva. In an interview on the national television program *O Fantástico* twenty years after Mendes's assassination, Darly explained his actions to the host, saying: "Ninguém matou Chico Mendes. Quem se matou foi ele mesmo" (No one killed Chico Mendes. He got himself killed).[2]

I will examine the ranchers' interpretation of this statement, but

2. *Fantástico*, Dec. 14, 2008.

first a few notes are required on how they feel about Darly Alves da Silva, based on the conversations I had with a handful of ranchers with whom I established sufficient rapport to broach this heated topic. They made a point to say that Alves da Silva was a criminal before he arrived in Acre, a bad apple that has given the whole group a "dirty name." They also emphasized that the land conflicts that did occur were the result of the inherent confusion of the situation, in which a rancher bought a property and then had to find a way to come to terms with the rubber tappers, who also had legal use rights to the land. All of the ranchers that I interviewed stressed to me that they worked with the rubber tappers to find a peaceful solution to these issues.

No rancher defended the actions of Alves da Silva, but some offered an explanation of his enigmatic words about the murder of Chico Mendes. They said that in the rural context it is generally agreed that interfering in the affairs of others is not well regarded by most landowners, and that inhibiting the work of others is seen as a form of aggression and an insult. One rancher said about Chico Mendes: "It is all a myth. He was a bum [*vagabundo*]. Anyone can start a problem, but it is hard to solve one. Interfering—keeping a man from working—is bad, real bad." Presented in this way, in a conscious invocation of a working-class discourse, the conclusion is meant to be that Mendes did not work and, through his insistence on saving the forest, he inhibited the ability of others to work.

Many ranchers feel that rubber-tapper history has been turned into a fairy tale that is used by "them" to justify the shackling of the Acrean economy for "their own personal benefit." When pressed to explain how conservation benefits "them" and who they are, ranchers mentioned: the current state and national government of the Worker's Party, academics and environmentalists, the Catholic Church in the 1970s–1980s, international conservation entities and their Brazilian puppet NGOs, North American and European business interests, and the liberal media based out of Rio de Janeiro.

They contrast their frustrated ambitions in Amazonia with American westward expansion, in which there were few limitations, and the nation and people subsequently prospered. While some ranchers admire the pioneer spirit of North Americans, they also resent the contemporary *gringos*, whose actions toward Amazonia are not motivated by an authentic concern with the environment, but rather are indicative of international powers that "have theirs and don't want

us to have ours." They focus their ire on local and national governmental officials, who are thought to be in the pockets of these international entities. Amazonia's inability to "progress," they say, is the
result of politicians who, by promoting international conservation interests, stifle the ranchers' ability to produce affordable food, which
they claim they can do more efficiently than smallholders.

Smallholders may defend themselves against environmental violations in the name of providing food for their family, and thus be
viewed somewhat sympathetically, but wealthy ranchers have no
such moral high ground on which to stand. Although they are not
"workers," ranchers frame their opposition to environmentalism
through a discourse of work. One rancher has a bumper sticker on
his truck that says: "Já comeu hoje? Agradeça a um fazendeiro"
(Did you eat today? Thank a rancher). Migdalio, the trucker-turned-
rancher, asked me: "What do people eat that doesn't come from the
earth? Where does Marina's food come from?"[3] In their use of work
discourse, they deemphasize physical labor, focusing on how their actions and initiative produce vital food for society.

Many ranchers are active in the ongoing debates surrounding
the Brazilian forest code, which currently requires that Amazonian
ranchers and colonists maintain 80 percent of their land as forest reserve. Lissero is the head of an organization that has been fighting
for revisions to the code. When I first met him in 2007, he was de-
fiant about any form of environmental regulation. In 2010, the last
time we talked, he had softened his stance, saying: "Deforestation is
too politically incorrect these days. You can't argue against the forest
anymore. Now we are focused on trying to get the forest code revised
so that it is more reasonable."

Ribeiro likewise expressed a position that demonstrates that the
ranchers are searching for a balance between economic and environmental concerns, and attempting to link their ideals of work and production to social concerns in order to engage with political debates
about environmentalism: "There are one billion people in the world
now living in hunger and the world's population continues to grow.
They call the Amazon the 'lungs of the world' because of the forest,
but maybe we need to also think about the 'stomach of the world'—

3. He is referring to Acre native Marina Silva, a former rubber-tapper leader
and Brazil's minister of the environment from 2003 through 2008.

all those hungry people. Here we can produce the food that the world needs."

By tapping into the discourse of work, which is centered on production, and aligning themselves with a nationalistic stance in which they are to be seen as doing what is best for all sectors of Brazilian society, the ranchers seek to eliminate their class distinctions and remove the villain label, and give themselves a moral and ideological foundation from which to confront environmental legislation.

CONCLUSION

The ranchers at the apex of the rural social hierarchy in Acre are believed by subordinate groups to have both wealth and political power; these perceptions are reinforced in social situations, in which ranchers exhibit elite cultural symbols, behaviors, and characteristics historically associated with the landowning classes. At one time the ranchers did exercise economic and political power, with the backing of ideology and policy. They no longer enjoy these benefits, but they have remained economically dominant, despite the ascendance of subordinate groups. The ranchers nowadays contest perceptions that they have political influence, pointing both to their disfavor in the halls of state power and to international economic and environmental interests that seek to constrain them.

Although all ranchers are considered to have high social status and to be "above" physical labor, this is a diverse group of both landed elites and persons of more humble origins. In general, rancher and subordinate group perspectives are similar in that they view work, as informed by biblical and developmentalist ideas of land and production, as an essential activity. The ranchers' class position, however, is determined in large part by their separation from physical labor, which puts them in opposition to the working-class rural groups. Ranchers seek to demonstrate that they do in fact work, pointing not to labor but to production. Ranchers use the concept of work as production to oppose environmental legislation by claiming for beef production a positive social function; they insist that by producing a large amount of food more effectively than smallholders, they increase access to affordable foods among the lower classes, and also benefit the national economy by increasing food security.

Amazonian deforestation has been framed as an issue that threatens the future of humankind. It is only natural that in such a contest the good and the bad have been clearly defined. Traditional anthropological realms of inquiry and ideological commitments, however, need not eschew thoughtful analysis of a society's more powerful groups. Issues of access will remain with elite groups, but if preserving the Amazon forest is of such pressing global importance, it will be essential to have a clear understanding of the perspectives of all of those involved, especially those with the greatest on-the-ground political and economic power in the region.

CHAPTER 6

THE CITY AND THE *CONTRI*

BRAZILIANS LONG FOR THE COUNTRYSIDE

On most Sundays, and other days and times that follow no discernible pattern, my neighbor cranks up his *sertaneja* music.[1]

One minute, stadium-filling *sertaneja* duos strum their guitars and harmonize about falling in love, looking for love, losing love, and bull riding. The next minute, romantic ballads once heard by a generation through the radio waft over the walls of our street.

He sprinkles in some music from the old days, folk songs about the simple joys of rural life coupled with sharp criticisms about the changing times.

He even has a CD composed entirely of a cowboy blowing on a *berrante*, or bull's horn, like they used to do on cattle drives. He played that one for the entire neighborhood to hear last weekend.

I always know when he is coming down the street, because the country crooning grows like an approaching train, reaches a peak, and then dies as he squeals to a stop in front of his house. His truck straddles the curb and is covered with stickers that say things like "Yes Cowboys," the name of a Brazilian Western wear store.

With his music, his truck, and his stickers, my neighbor seemed like he could help me understand the country—or, as they say here, *contri, cauboi,* or *sertaneja*—lifestyle.

Although I have written about all sorts of topics lately, the purpose of my research here is to understand the culture surrounding cattle in the Amazon. So I had to meet this neighbor.

I clapped my hands out in the street to get his attention, as is the custom here.

1. From the series "Postcards from the Amazon"; published in the *San Angelo Standard-Times* on July 1, 2010. The original content of the article has been maintained, with minor editorial changes.

The sound barely reached above the music he was listening to that day, but his dad heard me, let me in, and pointed me to the back of the house.

There sat my mysterious neighbor, the embodiment of cattle culture in Acre.

He was sitting at a little white plastic table, where he was watching old videos of team penning competitions and thumbing through his music collection.

"I am Leonardo," he said with meaty hand, a sweaty brow, and a huge smile, "but you can call me Sorocaba."

Behind him, in his brick *churrasqueira*, some *picanha* [top sirloin], the most beloved cut of meat in Brazil, roasted and dripped grease onto the coals.

As we nibbled on the *picanha* and sipped *cachaça*, I began to learn more about this "*vida contri*" that Sorocaba so loves.

"I am from the city, but I have always liked this country stuff. I think it all started for me and other people my age when the soap opera *Pantanal* was on TV. I was only 5 when I saw that show, but it made a mark on me and an entire generation. It awoke in us an interest in the countryside."

Before that, soap operas were always set in the city, and the tradition and purity of the country life appealed to Sorocaba and others of his generation.

From an early age, he began to follow the rodeo, wear boots and jeans, and ride horses.

The rodeo in Barretos now draws around 2 million people every year, including Sorocaba and his friends. Two of his buddies, Humberto and Gladson, were talking one day while on a fishing trip and decided to open up a store in Acre where people could get the kind of things they saw in Barretos.

Last month they opened up "Cowboys Ranch," a store that specializes in all things *contri*, with saddles, lassos, and fancy cowboy boots.

There is a constant stream of customers at Cowboys Ranch, and there are regulars, like Sorocaba, who come every afternoon to "meet up, hang out, and tell stories."

They practice lassoing chihuahua-sized metal bulls in the middle of the floor, one nabbing the head, the other the hind legs.

There is a circle of heavy wooden chairs near the front window (fig. 6.1). In the middle is a leather-encased cooler filled with iced water and lemon wedges. A cup made from a bull horn is filled with dried *herba maté* leaves. Sorocaba and his friends sit around in the afternoons refilling the communal horn with cold water, drinking the refreshing *tereré*. In the temperate south, they drink *maté* with hot water. When it made its way north into the tropics with the spread of cattle and cowboys, people started to drink it cold.

Sorocaba and all his friends are excited about Expo-Acre, the annual agricultural fair and the state's biggest party. They are planning to ride their horses from the center of town to the fairgrounds for the opening ceremonies. Over the next week, Acreans will come to see some of Brazil's biggest country music acts, cowboys competing in the rodeo, and the state's prize bulls and cows on display.

Everyone gets dressed up for Expo-Acre, but they aren't dressed in the garb

FIGURE 6.1. Sorocaba at the Cowboys Ranch

of the *gaúchos* of southern Brazil or the leather-clad *vaqueiros* of the spiny, dry northeast. They are dressed "Texano" style, with cowboy boots, blue jeans, plaid shirts, tooled leather belts, felt hats, and big belt buckles.

Those who look really sharp, Sorocaba says, are described as "*bem* Texano" (really Texan), and those who have good cowboy skills might be complimented by being called a "*cauboi* Texano," a true Texas cowboy.

They can get all their country gear, even some Copenhagen snuff, for 25 *reais* (US$14) at Cowboys Ranch.

Sorocaba will be all decked out for Expo-Acre, and if I had seen him before, I would never have imagined that his first taste of the country came from a soap opera, that he doesn't own land or cattle, and that he is studying environmental law.

Sorocaba can't see it happening any other way: "I can only say that I could never live another life. Just like we don't ask to be born white or black, tall or short, I can't change that I was born *sertaneja*. I think in Acre, where cattle raising is so strong, and in Brazil in general, we are all linked to the countryside, whether we like it or not."

He has witnessed the growth of *sertaneja* and *contri* in Brazil at a paradoxical time when both cattle raising and agricultural production, on the one hand, and migration from the country to the city, on the other, have skyrocketed.

There is nostalgia for life in the country, a longing for the tradition and simplicity of a bygone era that can be, to some extent, both nurtured and soothed by listening to country music, wearing boots, and watching soap operas and rodeos. All this comes together in the Rio Branco evenings. In the bar, Bobney's band sings a sped-up version of "Jambalaya." People sip cold *tereré* in the shade of trees as the tropical sun goes down. Sorocaba ropes a tiny little metal bull at the Cowboys Ranch.

All these little scenes combine to make up Sorocaba's beloved *vida contri* in the middle of the Amazon.

Thus far I have been working toward an understanding of why cattle culture has taken root in a place with such a short and contested history with cattle, one so strongly linked to rubber-tapper history and progressive environmental policies. How can we understand its growth among those at the *cavalgada*, such as Sorocaba, who lived in the city?

CONTRI PLACES IN CITY SPACES

Sorocaba owned no land and rarely left the city, but he connected with the *contri* life on a symbolic level through activities such as horse riding, drinking *tereré*, and wearing boots. Even though Sorocaba was studying environmental law, and would one day, it is assumed, work in some way to defend the "environment," he would never engage with the forest as an acceptable social space. Like many Acreans dissatisfied with life in the city, and longing for something more "authentic," Sorocaba found a reconciliation of the urban and rural in urban *contri* places that approximate what can be understood as a culturally appropriate vision of rural life. These *contri* spaces reflect a vision of human-centered existence in a cultivated countryside, and are usually, but not always, linked with cattle culture.

Rural landscapes are constrained by political and economic structures and practical concerns, as well as cultural preferences and ideals. Landscapes can be mapped and measured, but what about cultural places in the city? Do *contri* bars in Rio Branco or the rodeo arenas scattered across upper Acre tell us something? Although many urbanites did not view the forest and its wild plants and animals in a positive light, and sought to distance their homes from it, they did not seek to escape nature in all its forms. In fact, many searched for an escape from the confines of modern urban life and longed to connect with an idealized form of human–nature interaction. The ways that many do this suggest a compromise of sorts, but one tilted heavily in favor of clearly anthropogenic spaces.

Here I describe *contri* places and *cauboi* culture as emerging forms of compromise between persistent spatial and ideological dualisms associated with the forest and the city. I focus on places of compromise that people carve out of city venues, such as Sorocaba's little slice of the countryside in his backyard, the Cowboys Ranch, and even temporary events such as the *cavalgada*. I also measure the extent to which people who subscribe to this particular vision of rural life demonstrate it through the boots, belt buckles, and cowboy hats that they wear.

ON THE EDGE: *CHACARÁS* AND *RANCHOS*

The outskirts of Rio Branco are lined with *chacarás*, where people with means seek respite from the "stress, crime, and noise" of the city in a semirural milieu that is not without urban conveniences. *Chacarás* are usually small pieces of land with a house sitting among fruit trees, manicured lawns, gardens, and artificial ponds stocked with fish. Although not explicitly related to cattle culture, the *chacarás* are a form of compromise between rural and urban, and going to them evokes a sense of escaping the modern strictures of the city and relaxing in the simple countryside.

Ranchos are small landholdings similar to *chacarás*, but with land for cattle and/or facilities for rodeo competitions. At the Rancho Sinuelo, on the periphery of Rio Branco, young urban professionals meet up after work to practice roping and other rodeo-related activities. They sit along the fence, passing the bull's horn filled with *tereré* and sliced lemons. This relaxed scene in the setting afternoon sun is punctuated by the explosive release of calves from the chute, followed closely by a man on horseback. His aim is to rope the calf before it gets to the end of the run. Their conversations meander from evaluations of each performance to annoying friends and love interests. Some of the men dip smokeless tobacco.

The Rancho Tijolo has the only covered rodeo arena in all of Acre. The Tijolo hosts country music concerts and roping competitions, and people come to practice rodeo events in the evening. The owner came from the state of Goiás, and had the distinction of opening up Acre's first *motel*, a walled-in meeting point for paramours, with rooms paid for by the hour. With earnings from his *motel*, he was able to buy a ranch and create the Tijolo. He explains this as a business venture, but also as a way of connecting with the rural life and bringing some of his traditions to Acre.

The *ranchos* provide a valuable rural space for these exclusively urban men, which allows them to participate in activities in which they can connect with the perceived traditions and tranquility of rural life. They can escape the annoyances of modern life in the city, but they do not have to give up its conveniences or deal with the difficulties of a rural life on the land. In these "rural" spaces on the edge of the city, these men have constructed a socially appropriate way of engaging the countryside and selectively appropriating some features of the cattle-based lifestyle.

CAUBOIS DE VITRINE AND CONTRI BARS

Such "rural" places need not be in the outskirts of the city or provide fenceposts to lean on, but can be created wherever a group of friends sit down and symbolically participate in cattle culture. In the evenings, groups of people congregate on the edge of the Parque da Maternidade or on the sidewalk in front of their houses, drinking *tereré* and, usually, listening to *sertaneja* music. It was rare to see people drinking *tereré* on the street when I first arrived in 2007, but it became more conspicuous with every year. In 2013 a store opened that was dedicated solely to *tereré* and associated paraphernalia.

Sorocaba and his friends all meet up at the Cowboys Ranch to drink cold *tereré* in the evenings. They pass the cup around as they sit in the wooden chairs in front of the glass window, which provide a good view of the street. There is some irony in the fact that these urban *caubois*, who tend to be "all hat and no cattle," are referred to as *caubois de vitrine* (shopwindow cowboys, recalling the U.S. "rhinestone cowboy").

Contri- or *sertaneja*-themed bars, which draw heavily on Barretos's rodeo and American "Western" themes, increased in number over the course of my fieldwork. At the most recently opened *contri* bar, Bahamas, patrons drink icy beer from little steel buckets and watch a big-screen TV showing rodeo clips and bullfighting bloopers, while a man sings covers of *sertaneja* hits. Visiting Bahamas is not like going to the countryside and encountering the fearsome inhabitants city residents sometimes associate with the "interior": back-

Table 6.1. Agreement with statements about social aspirations, by social group

	Survey Statement		
Social Group	It is not a dream of most Acreans to own land.	It is the dream of most Acreans to own cattle.	It is the dream of most Acreans to be a rubber tapper.
Rubber tappers	5%	95%	25%
Colonists	5%	84%	5%
Ranchers	0%	95%	0%
Cowboys	5%	100%	5%
Policy makers	10%	85%	10%
NGOs	5%	85%	0%

ward forest dwellers, machete-toting colonists, violent ranchers, jaguars, and disease-carrying insects. At Bahamas, people sing about the beauty and simplicity of country life and the perennial search for love. They dress like cowboys, those masters of their domain who roam the frontier—as painted on the walls—and ride ferocious bulls—as shown on television.

A PIECE OF LAND

Most Acreans interviewed would one day like to actually own property in the country. My findings suggest that urban dreams of a "piece of land" are firmly centered on cattle (table 6.1). The figures indicate that the current culturally acceptable way of engaging the land is through a reliance on cattle, not as a rubber tapper practicing forest extractivism. It is worth noting that rural and urban residents alike, including the policy maker and NGO groups, agree that it is the dream of many Acreans to own land and cattle, but that aspirations for a rubber-tapper way of life were relatively uncommon, despite the fact that NGO and policy maker groups found virtue in many features of rubber-tapper existence. This points again to the challenges facing any attempt to implement an alternative cultural program, such as *florestiana*. A forest-based rural life is neither economically viable nor culturally appreciated.

CONTRI DRESS: FUNCTION, MEANING, AND CHOICE

Urban "rural" places are not strict reflections of economic activities in the way that a pasture represents cattle raising—they are symbolic re-creations of a way of life, and they rely to a greater extent on perceptions of appropriate or desirable human–environment interactions. The people who choose to frequent them believe that such contexts embody something that is culturally appealing. Note, for example, that my Acrean environmentalist colleagues told me that they would not be caught dead at Bahamas. I never saw them wearing the clothing associated with cattle culture.

To what extent then do different groups actually participate in this form of rural expression? I made a list of activities, behaviors, and practices that I believed to be associated with cattle culture, and then confirmed with key informants that it was accurate. Here I focus on one of five themes: wearing *contri-*, cattle-, or rodeo-themed clothing.[2] The aim here is to learn to what extent people participate in cattle culture, and also to determine the rationale for that participation or nonparticipation.

Wearing *contri*-style clothing—an ensemble including big belt buckle, cowboy hat, boots, tight jeans, and plaid shirt—is highly associated with cattle culture in the minds of many Acreans. Choosing this form of dress amid the many fashion alternatives represents an individual's conscious decision to link her- or himself with cattle culture, although there are some exceptions. For example, boots are the article of clothing perhaps most associated with cattle culture, but they are also the most common footwear worn by people who work in the countryside, especially during the dry season. Boots have some symbolic meaning, but they are also functional and often the only form of dry-weather footwear available in rural supply stores in the small towns of upper Acre. There are thus at least three factors to consider: meaning, function, and choice.

At least 70 percent of members of all the rural groups I surveyed report wearing boots (table 6.2). This practice is less common among

2. My list of cattle-culture activities comprised twenty-one items grouped according to five themes: (1) consuming beef; (2) wearing *contri-*, cattle-, or rodeo-themed clothing; (3) participating in a cattle-based lifestyle; (4) watching/listening to cattle culture–themed programming or music on TV/radio; and (5) participating in popular cultural events. I discuss these themes in chapter 9.

Table 6.2. Reported use of *contri* clothing, by social group

	Social Group					
Item Worn	Rubber Tappers	Colonists	Ranchers	Cowboys	Policy Makers	NGOs
Boots	70%	90%	80%	100%	30%	20%
Contri-style clothing	0%	15%	20%	100%	10%	0%
Belt buckle	10%	10%	15%	95%	0%	0%
Cowboy hat	5%	20%	30%	80%	5%	5%

urban populations, such as the policy makers and NGO workers, who may nonetheless wear them when visiting rural areas.

A large, shiny belt buckle, on the other hand, is not a functional necessity. Its use implies a conscious symbolic connection with cattle culture, with which it is unequivocally associated. Ninety-five percent of cowboys report that they wear a belt buckle—sometimes when working (usually an old one), but mostly when they go the city or attend cultural events such as dances and rodeos. The three ranchers who reported wearing a belt buckle did so only for cultural events, but most ranchers rejected all forms of *contri* clothing because of its link with the working class and their desire to keep a low profile. Environmentally oriented policy maker and NGO groups clearly reject the belt buckle. Only 10 percent of colonists and rubber tappers reported wearing such a belt buckle, although a larger percentage of them wear boots and cowboy hats, items which again might be the only forms of such functional clothing available in their local markets, but which are nonetheless linked with cattle culture.

Members of the NGO group and policy maker group are very aware that their use of such accoutrements could be viewed as a form of approval for a way of life that many of them in fact do not wish to endorse. The rubber tappers in my group, on the other hand, often wore baseball caps and T-shirts emblazoned with rodeo themes. When I asked them if this reflected a preference or an endorsement for the cultural meanings behind the image, they often said no. Some had inherited a hat or bought a shirt because they thought it was *bonito* (beautiful) or liked its design or color. When rubber tappers went to the small towns, the same limited selection of hats and shoes was for sale in every store. Their options were further limited by what they could afford. These considerations applied less to NGO employees in Rio Branco, whose purchases were influenced less by buying power and availability and more by the message conveyed by their clothing.

DEVELOPMENT AND DISPLACEMENT

The growth of cattle culture in the urban landscape and in popular culture shows that people do seek to cross the divide between urban and rural, but the spaces that they increasingly choose privilege a human-centered view of nature. In urban "rural" places, a compromise of sorts has been reached, in which a socially appropriate rural way of life is reflected in the cultural landscape. These spaces seek to connect with a mythologized rural past and disassociate Acreans from rural life as it actually exists in Acre, especially forest life. Yet if the city is so difficult or unpleasant, why have so many rural people moved there in recent years, in Acre and throughout Brazil? A visit with Maria Bahiana reveals the complexity and interconnections of rural and urban lives.

COUNTRY RESIDENTS MOVE TO THE CITY

If you wandered around Acre near the Bolivian border, you would probably come to know Maria Bahiana (Maria from Bahia).[3] You could just say "Bahiana," and everyone for miles around would know that you were talking about the tough, talkative lady who lived down a dirt road at the bottom of a hill with her sons and grandson.

Bahiana grew up in the arid northeast state of Bahia. Along with her husband, she followed the frontier through the Amazon before settling in Acre in 1982.

Life wasn't easy for Bahiana, especially after her husband died in an oxcart accident twenty-five years ago.

"There was no man here to help me. Ask anyone. I provided for these kids on my own. I raised them alone.

"Look at my hands—they are calloused from working the land, from sweating in the *roça* [farm] to provide the kids with food."

Her hands show the struggles of a woman who has lived for over sixty years

3. From the series "Postcards from the Amazon"; published in the *San Angelo Standard-Times* on May 15, 2010.

in the country. They are large and rough and seem out of place compared to her slight frame and her black hair, which is always pulled back tight in a bun.

A year ago, I arrived at Bahiana's house to learn about the life of the colonists, families who settled in the Amazon over the past thirty years on plots of land of about one hundred acres.

I stayed a month in her house with her two youngest sons and her grandson. Some things stick out in my mind from that time.

Two enormous white bulls with rings in their noses stood outside her door and always came when she called them. She washed clothes in the little creek behind the house, the slapping of clothes on a plank echoing for miles around. Everyone stopped at her house to hear the latest, tell of their troubles, or get some free advice, even if they didn't want it. She would tell you all about it in her distinctive way of talking, with singsong phrases that go up and down in pitch, often followed by long sighs.

But, there was more going on than I realized. On that first day that I arrived, a man was sitting with her at the kitchen table. I later learned that they were negotiating the sale of her land. My month with them would be their last month in the countryside. It wouldn't be a typical month for a colonist family, but I would learn that there really isn't anything typical about a colonist's life, and things change every day.

Throughout Acre, many people who live in rural areas are moving to the cities. They do this for a number of reasons, most often citing the availability of health care, education, and job opportunities that are limited or nonexistent in the many rural communities of the Amazon.

In Bahiana's case, she had painful kidney stones and needed surgery. She was nervous about being so far way and not being able to get to the hospital in time.

She also didn't want to deal with the fights surrounding her inheritance. She wanted to sell the land now and divide the money while she was still around and see her children enjoy it.

In general, she was tired of life in the country.

"This is no place for an old person. It is tiring to fight with the mud and rain, and to always have to take care of the animals."

At this point in her life, the benefits of the city outweigh the tranquility of life in the country.

A week before she moved to town, her family had a big barbecue. We dug a big rectangular hole in the ground six feet long and four feet deep.

One of her sons offered a calf for the event. We strung it up on a tree branch and dressed it with a machete. The meat was rubbed with salt and laid across a grid of barbed wire that covered the hole, and was then left to roast. When it was ready, we ate the salty hunks of meat and squeezed lemon juice on top.

Relatives and friends from the city came with immaculately white shoes. They had taken their shoes off when they left the highway and carried them down the dirt road until they got near the house, where they washed their muddy feet. They arrived at the house looking good, their clothes and shoes spotless.

Most of them had only been living in the city for a little while, and they longed to get back, away from the "noise, dust, and crime of the city."

The truth is, once most people move to the city, they don't come back to the country. They all want a place in the country—a place to relax on holidays and weekends, but not to work and live.

Bahiana has been in the city for almost a year now and the house where she raised the boys is now boarded shut. The man who bought her land is not interested in the house. He bought it only for the pasture where his cows now graze.

Bahiana's surgery went well, and she is in good health again. Next time I will tell you about her life in the city.

MOVING ON IS PART OF THE CITY LIFE

A year ago, Bahiana, who had lived in the country all her life, packed up and moved to the city.[4]

The images we have of the Amazon region undoubtedly are associated with the forest, but the majority of people who live here are in cities, which are swelling with migrants from the countryside.

Most of them despise the idea of leaving a life on the land, but the city offers people things that they cannot get in their isolated rural properties, such as education, health care, and wage labor.

Bahiana's new house in the city is painted light green and orange. It sits on a dirt road a few blocks off the main highway.

The first time I arrived here, I was saddened to see the way that her life in the country, which I found to be difficult but noble, had translated over to the city.

The dogs that once had run free in the forest were chained and moved only to follow the little slivers of shade that tracked across the hard-packed yard. Instead of bathing in the clear little stream behind the house, the family now clean up in a dark bathroom, with only a little window covered in screen chiseled into the concrete wall.

My tour of her house on this first day was accompanied by the Backstreet Boys, whose greatest hits blasted from the house behind her. They played the CD straight through seven times. Life in the city didn't seem so great to me.

4. From the series "Postcards from the Amazon"; published in the *San Angelo Standard-Times* on June 5, 2010.

FIGURE 6.2. The view from Bahiana's front porch in the city

I have gotten used to it here, but it isn't really fair to say that her life was better in the country. If I have a hard time understanding her decision to come to the city, they think I am completely crazy for choosing to leave the comfortable American life they see every day on TV to come here.

My preference for a tranquil, "pure" life in the forest is based on daydreams made possible by good health, education, and financial security. It is a romanticism disconnected from the everyday trials of living in the Amazon, or anywhere in the countryside, for that matter.

Initially, at least, Bahiana hated life in the city. "I cried every day for the first few months," she said.

Gradually, as she healed from her surgery, she began to like it.

"I rested my body and my mind. I didn't even know my head was tired, but now I do. It was stressful out there for me. I always worried about taking care of the animals and when the boys were not around, I worried about criminals."

Although she doesn't miss the life in the *colonia* anymore, her sons do. One has found a job in the city. He works ten hours a day, six days a week delivering drinking water on a motorcycle. He makes about $250 a month. He would prefer to go back to the *colonia*, where he could make that much selling one calf a month with a lot less work. On his day off, he heads straight for his relatives' house in the country.

FIGURE 6.3. Bahiana looks out the front window

It was kind of lonely for Bahiana in the country. She loves to talk to people and she gets to do that more now in the city.

Last week, a tiny woman whom Bahiana knew from the *colonia* came to the city to process some documents. She ate lunch with us, gripping her spoon with her whole hand. I don't think she ever talked, but she laughed her head off at Bahiana's claims that I was her long-lost white son from southern Brazil.

Bahiana doesn't always need to have a person to talk to. I could hear her in one of her son's bedrooms last week. She was folding a pile of clothes that he had left on the floor.

"I don't know when these boys are going to learn. I am not always going to be around to fold their clothes and clean up after them. Oh, but don't worry about it, really. I will take care of it. Lazy bums (*sigh*)."

She gets all the work done early so that she can watch the *novelas* (soap operas) around lunchtime and then again in the evening. These are wildly popular in Brazil and the streets are mostly empty when they begin, around 7 p.m. I have arrived at people's houses during *novela* time, sometimes the first American they have met, and they are very interested to know me, but only during commercial breaks.

Not surprisingly, then, Bahiana also talks to the *novelas*. She judges the morality of people's actions, evaluates their looks, and laughs when a wrongdoer gets what he deserves. She interprets the not-so-subtle cues that someone is falling in love or is being deceived, telling them the secrets that they should know: "She doesn't love you—she just wants your money!"

On a Sunday (the only day without *novelas*), I sat with Bahiana, her sons, and her grandson watching bloopers and practical jokes. We howled together at the men getting racked by errant swings at the piñata and misfired soccer balls, and a levitating corpse prank.

Later, when the TV was finally turned off, I saw Bahiana running her finger over a photo of her late husband.

"If he was still around we'd be two happy old-timers, I tell you."

Bahiana admits that it hasn't been easy for her, but she is proud that she took what was dealt and made it work.

Moving has made her life better in a number of practical ways, but it is not always about where you are as much as who is with you, or in Bahiana's case, who has already moved on.

Through her words, and her laughter and tears, Bahiana has shown me that people are not so different from place to place, even in the Amazon. She also illustrated to me that people generally will choose to better their life if they can. For Bahiana, and many others in this region, this means moving to the city.

SAUDADE IN THE CITY

To understand the growth of cattle culture in Acre, you have to understand that the cities are made up of a range of people, from Sorocaba to Bahiana. They have different experiences, to say the least, but they are united by their urban residence at this particular time in this particular place. As the cities of Amazonia grow, no one wants a true life in the forest nor are they completely satisfied in the city. They are searching for a compromise. The same processes that brought cattle and migrants to Amazonia in the 1970s have created the demographic, economic, social, and political preconditions for the once-rejected messages that resonate in the present.

Many Acreans say that modernity and progress arrived with the state highway in the 1970s, when it was linked to the rest of Brazil by the construction of the BR-364. From this point, Acre started to "develop"—muddy paths became paved roads, water and electricity became more consistently available, and scarce goods became more prevalent. The arrival of migrants also spurred land conflict and the displacement of the native rubber tappers, many of whom fled to the city (Bakx 1988). The cities of Acre are filled with people who left behind their rural homes in the search for a better life in the city (Schmink and Cordeiro 2008), paralleling general trends in Amazonia and Brazil in the late twentieth century (Browder and Godfrey 1997). The development processes that began with the opening of the Amazon to colonization created the roads and electric lines that would bring new ways of using the land and associated cultural messages of rural life from the center to the periphery.

Bahiana, who made several stops along the frontier in search of land, was eventually drawn to the city by the availability of health care, education, and security. She and others who have moved to the city often romanticize what they left behind, recalling feelings of autonomy and tranquility. Lifetime urbanites, such as Sorocaba, also experience a longing for the countryside, and their unfamiliarity with the hardships of rural life makes it an even more appealing escape—imagined scenes of purity and tradition contrast with the "crime, noise, and hustle" of the city. Some city dwellers in traditional population centers in southern and south-central Brazil criticize the processes of modernization that left them separated from the land and searching for an idealized rural past (Dent 2009; Oliven 2000).

Most Acreans explain their feelings with the word *saudade*, which connotes a mixture of longing, missing, and nostalgia—in this case for the countryside and rural life. For many, this *saudade* has found an outlet for expression in *cauboi* culture, which offers a way of symbolically reconnecting or connecting with an idealized rural past or less complicated present—a mythical "golden age" of sorts that in fact never existed (Williams 1975).

Given the historically urban and international (European) preferences in Brazilian forms of popular culture, a bias apparent in the immensely popular evening *novelas* (Kottak 1990; Pace 2009; Pace and Hinote 2013), the international connections of *cauboi* culture bolster the appeal and legitimacy of this form of rural expression throughout Brazil, especially in Acre. This national and international sense of connection is important, given Acre's marginal status in relation to the rest of Brazil. Although Acreans are fiercely proud of their state, many agree that it is "o fim do mundo" (the end of the world).

Although it never corresponds exactly with experience, *cauboi* culture is the only form of rural identity that is positively valued and thoroughly institutionalized throughout Brazil. It links people with an assertive rural folk celebrated from Acre to São Paulo, and beyond the borders of Brazil. Few if any Brazilians want to be associated with the *caipira* represented in the Festas Juninas (June Festivals), with their missing teeth, freckles, and patched clothes. Fewer still would seek to play up their connections with groups perceived as the rural Amazonian extreme backwoods cousin of the quaint *caipira—caboclos* (backwoodsmen), *ribeirinhos* (riverine peoples), rubber tappers, and indigenous groups.

It is important to stress that the city and the forest are extremes that represent not only different spaces but also different evolutionary and temporal stages in the minds of many. Forest dwellers are considered to be corrupted by their contact with nature and thereby become less human, while urbanites become soft and depraved due to their estrangement from honest work. The country, however, is a place of hard work, self-sufficiency, fresh air, cool evenings, and foods like grandmother used to make. Although it never existed in Acre, it is somehow just a generation ago.

Many who remain in the countryside find that it bears little resemblance to the descriptions in *sertaneja* songs. Nonetheless, *cauboi* culture gives voice to a specific form of ecology in which humans demonstrate their control over nature through the creation of anthropogenic landscapes. These messages resonate with the developmentalist ideology and policies that encourage Amazonian settlers to convert the forest to productive spaces. Acre, with its current emphasis on forest preservation and environmentally friendly livelihoods, frustrates the drive to "develop" and "progress," and many rural Acreans report that they feel unjustly constrained by environmental laws limiting burning and deforestation. *Cauboi* culture provides an oppositional voice to environmental preservation, regarding such conservation efforts as an affront to the self-reliance that is central to the identity of many rural producers, especially the migrants who came to Amazon to build their future.

While many have moved to the city, Brazilian agriculture has expanded, putting the nation on the top of lists of global production and export in many agricultural commodities, including beef. The national-level growth of *cauboi* culture can be seen as part and parcel of the economic and demographic ripples of capitalist processes of rationalized, industrialized, mechanized, and commodified production and the growth of the emerging middle class with its rural roots. While it is increasing in popularity, it would be an overstatement to say that this lifestyle is accepted uncritically, as people lament the loss of both economic and cultural production. Agricultural commodities are largely produced in a way that is not reflective of the family-centered productive practices that once characterized rural cultural subjects (McCann forthcoming).

In my own brief time in Acre, I have seen people move from marveling at all of the products in the supermarket to complaining about the lack of taste of storebought chicken and corn. For many, the very medium that is supposed to valorize this bygone rural life seems even more plastic and formulaic than the food. The slick new singers of *sertaneja* are not like the previous generation's old storytellers, who, despite untrained voices, had "heart" and rural sensibilities. In these expressions it is possible to see just how interconnected the mass production of both economy and culture are, as they are both, in the minds of many Acreans, moving away from the idyllic rural life that they pretend to represent and toward a commodified, mass-produced package, be this tasteless corn or contrived music.

THE BEND IN THE BRIGHT RIVER

Brazilians have seen the *bangue bangue* movies, and these certainly influence the shape of cowboys' dreams, but there is also something timeless about the cowboy. Although working-class rural or independent laborers are not accorded the same level of mystique and prestige in Brazil as they are in the United States, they are more respected or captivating than the farmer tied to the soil. In contrast to the *caipira* is the cowboy, figure of agency, physical power, and masculinity. In the words of the Brazilian classic *Os Sertões* (*Rebellion in the Backlands*): "The awkward rustic unexpectedly assumes the dominating aspect of a powerful, copper-hued Titan, an amazingly different being, capable of extraordinary feats of strength and agility" (da Cunha 90).

The popularity of the American cowboy/country culture and the

Argentine appreciation of the *gaúcho* only really emerged after the actual way of life was eclipsed by the constraints of modernity and the logic of capitalist production (Slatta 1990). It is with increasing urbanization that the cowboy becomes something more: a mythical and idealized masculine image, an individual who is in control and free from the constraints of the modern world (Hobsbawm 2013). A masterful passage by Joan Didion from *Slouching towards Bethlehem* captures this transcendent essence:

> When John Wayne rode through my childhood, and perhaps through yours, he determined forever the shape of certain of our dreams. . . . And in a world we understood early to be characterized by venality and doubt and paralyzing ambiguities, he suggested another world, one which may or may not have existed ever but in any case existed no more: a place where a man could move free, could make his own code and live by it; a world in which, if a man did what he had to do, he could one day take the girl and go riding through the draw and find himself home free, not in a hospital with something wrong inside, not in a high bed with the flowers and drugs and the forced smiles, but there at the bend in the bright river, the cottonwoods shimmering in the early morning sun. (Quoted in Rimas and Fraser 2008:156–157)

Cauboi culture is perhaps most perceptively understood as the best rural alternative. In and of itself, it does not represent anyone, but some parts of it resonate with and provide the much-needed form of expression that urban and rural Acreans have been looking for. Its direct connection with the cattle-ranching economy certainly provides an opening for it to grow, but in the end its emergence and urban appropriation were related to broader economic transformations that engender displacement and *saudade* for a rural life that is somehow more authentic than the present but more modern than the forest.

CONCLUSION

Displaced or drawn to the city, those who now live there express *saudade* for life in the countryside. *Cauboi* culture represents the countryside as an anthropogenic space that is located somewhere between the atavistic forest and the modern city. It is inextricable from the economic processes occurring throughout Brazil, and the commodified, mass-marketed production of both food and culture. Acreans are not oblivious, of course, to these processes, and just as they criticize the tasteless foods of the supermarket, many deride the formulaic music of current *sertaneja* stars. Although this manufactured *cauboi* culture does not correspond exactly with their memories of their rural past or their present station in life, it nonetheless provides a means of reconnecting symbolically with the rural life.

CHAPTER 7

HERE'S THE BEEF: SYMBOL, SUSTENANCE, AND HAMBURGER CONNECTIONS

BEEF A SPECIAL TREAT IN THE FOREST

It was midmorning on a Saturday in June in western Amazonia, and the mist had long since burned off the forest, the chickens had become sluggish, and the million little sounds of the rainforest morning had died down.[1] Jatobá, Luanna, their son, Espimar, and I closed up the house and headed out for the *churrasco*, or barbecue.

We left the clearing that surrounded Jatobá and Luanna's house on a little path into the forest. It felt like it was suddenly evening, as the heat and light of the blazing sun were muted by the canopy overhead. Fifteen-foot-wide trees went straight up for a hundred feet without a single limb before extending their branches into the canopy. We passed vines a foot thick that climbed all the way to the top and meandered from tree to tree.

We followed the rubber trails, little paths that connect around fifty to one hundred rubber trees, or about as much as a tapper can tap and later harvest in one day. We crossed creeks and muddy rivers that will rage when the rains come, balancing on felled trees that served as bridges.

As we walked, we came into clearings in the forest where other families lived, and they would offer us sweet coffee from a thermos. Some joined our caravan to the *churrasco*. After a three-hour walk, we arrived at the house of one of Jatobá's "closest" neighbors, Carlos, who was hosting the barbecue.

Carlos slaughtered one of his cows for the party. It was to be a celebration and a chance to see friends, but Carlos also needed help. The promise of beef lured friends from miles around to help him clear some land for planting. The guys were happy to work all morning, knowing they would feast in the afternoon.

For the rubber tappers, who live deep in the forest, eating beef is a rare treat.

1. From the series "Postcards from the Amazon"; published in the *San Angelo Standard-Times* on Aug. 14, 2010.

FIGURE 7.1. Pedro Perto (standing) and his daughters enjoy some grilled meat at the *churrasco*. Mauro (seated) cuts the beef off a skewer. Carlos's house is visible in the background.

When they eat meat, it is usually hunted. The local favorite is a small deer, which weighs around forty pounds.

They also eat armadillo. Every time I mention that people eat armadillo in Acre, [Americans] worry about leprosy, but I haven't ever heard of that being a problem in Acre. When I asked if eating armadillo causes any health problems, Leni, who had just fried some up for dinner, told me drily: "Eating *tatu* [armadillo] can cause backache."

I added this one to my list of folk beliefs and food taboos, along with others that I had learned, such as that peanuts and celery are sexual stimulants, but passion fruit somehow makes you sleepy. Later, when I was in the city, I told a friend about my anthropological discoveries and found out that Leni was pulling my leg. He explained the old joke to me: "Eating armadillo makes your back hurt because it is so little that you have to bend over to catch it."

In addition to armadillos, they eat turtles, wild pigs, *pacas*, and a lot of animals and birds that we don't have [in the United States].

Although many of them now raise cattle, their cows are too valuable to eat. They use them to carry goods, such as rubber, and the milk provides a steady source of protein. Some kids even ride their steers to school. When they do sell their cattle, it is usually in times of emergency, when they need immediate cash. Eating beef, then, is a luxury for most rubber tappers.

By the time we got to Carlos's house, the women were in the kitchen and scattered throughout the house, talking, cutting the meat into smaller pieces, and peeling manioc root. The men had finished clearing the field and were relaxing in the shade of a tree, trying to be patient with the first pieces of meat on the grill. They were crouching near the barbecue pit, which was literally a pit—a hole five feet deep and big enough for a coffin. Coals smoldered on the bottom, grilling the thin cutlets of meat laid across a barbed-wire grill at foot level (fig. 7.1).

As night settled in, Carlos's tiny house on stilts provided the only light except for the stars above, thousands of little pinpricks in the black sheet that covered us all. In the corner of the house, next to a kerosene lamp, a battery-powered radio played an old *forró* (traditional accordion-driven music from northeastern Brazil) cassette. The glowing house swayed and seized with the rhythm of their dance steps—a slide and step that sounded like a huge broom sweeping and then a collective stomp as they planted their feet again.

Old Pedro Perto, who limped the entire hike over, was floating around light as air with his wife, Zefa. Teenagers danced awkwardly with the few potential girlfriends and boyfriends who lived within a day's walk, their happiness over-coming any initial hint of embarrassment. When we left just before dawn, the stars were slowly beginning to disappear, but the house was still swaying and there was meat on the grill.

BEEF: GOOD TO EAT AND GOOD TO THINK

From the cow grazing on the pastures in the countryside to the hole-in-the-ground *churrascos* in the *seringal*, the poolside gatherings of the rancher and the hamburger stands in the city, beef is at the center of Acrean social life. As a commodity that circulates, is widely consumed, and is associated with many and varied meanings (and double meanings), beef provides a means of connecting people, places, ideas, and actions.

Claude Lévi-Strauss famously asked if the cultural constructions surrounding animals emerge because of their material value ("good to eat") or from cognitive and cultural affinities with certain animals, which may be "good to think (with)" (Harris 1985; Lévi-Strauss 1969:89; see Mullin 1999). The relationship between the material and the symbolic, as well as the ways that group practices are enacted through structure and agency, has been a guiding theme thus far, as we put together the pieces of cattle culture. Beef is uniquely positioned in this matrix: with its connotations of strength and status, it provides the nutritional and symbolic fuel for development in the city and the country. The way that cattle and beef metaphors are used shows that cattle are "good to think" with in terms of providing a conceptual means to express features of Acrean society and to re-assert structural relationships between the sexes, status within male groups, and social class. Unfortunately, such expressions usually produce negative outcomes: sexual domination, gender inequality, and infidelity.

Overall, the social practices and perceptions surrounding beef provide an explanation as to why Acreans increasingly choose beef over other foods. An examination of these sociocultural features can thus reveal the demand that fuels deforestation. As I will show, however, beef has many roles in this dynamic, and is in many ways the impetus for development and the center of cattle culture.

THE HAMBURGER CONNECTION: FROM MCDONALDS TO MCNALDÃO

The expression "hamburger connection" was coined by Norman Myers in 1981 to draw attention to the importation to the United States of cheap beef from deforested lands in Central America (Myers 1981). Other scholars have subsequently highlighted the complicity of American fast-food chains in Latin American forest destruction in provocatively titled studies, such as "The Cattle Are Eating the Forest" (DeWalt 1983), *Hoofprints on the Forest* (Shane 1986), "Rain-forests and the Hamburger Society" (Nations and Komer 1983).

During the 1970s and 1980s, demand for beef in Latin American countries was less of a concern, as middle-class buying power was limited by economic crisis (Jarvis, quoted in Hecht 1993:688). While the role of international markets was important in understanding this growth, it may have been overstated, as Latin American beef exports accounted for less than 5 percent of U.S. beef imports in that period (687). Following Myers's original postulation, subsequent studies have shown that production and consumption dynamics vary across time and are affected by international as well as national and regional drivers (Edelman 1995).

Up until the 1990s, most of the beef produced in the Amazon was consumed within the region, which imported beef until 1991 (Kai-mowitz et al. 2004). Much of the growth in the Amazonian cattle industry in the 1990s was attributable to the growing demand for beef in Amazonian cities, which quadrupled from 1972 to 1997 (Faminow 1998:115), although government subsidies and incentives had some impact as well.

In the early 2000s, Brazil emerged as the world's leading exporter of beef (Smeraldi and May 2008). The majority of the growth in the country's cattle industry occurred in the legal Amazon, which accounts for 41 percent of the Brazilian national herd (Smeraldi and May 2008). From 1998 to 2008, the amount of cattle in the state of Acre increased by over 400 percent, the greatest percentage increase in all of Brazil (IBGE 2008). The upper Acre region, where data for this analysis were collected, is now classified as a "deforestation hotspot" because of cattle-related activities (FAO 2006). Prior to 2009, there was no way of ensuring that Amazonian beef came from illegally deforested land, but Brazilian authorities have implemented a certification program to identify beef sources (Brazilian Federal Public Ministry 2012).

Greenpeace Brazil's (2009) *O farra do boi na Amazonia* (English title: "Slaughtering the Amazon") recently drew attention to the link between cattle and deforestation, slave labor on ranches, and illegal slaughterhouses.[2] This report and others by international environmentalist NGOs and the popular press call attention to cattle-driven deforestation by focusing on the complex commodity chains that implicate remote consumption patterns of soy and beef in ongoing Amazonian deforestation. While these analyses provide useful information, the powerful images that circulate via news stories and the Internet are perhaps more effective in conveying a sense of urgency, and drawing attention to the role of first-world consumption patterns in rainforest destruction.

THE LINKS IN THE INTERNATIONAL "hamburger connection" chain have been well documented by researchers, environmentalists, and the popular press. Here I focus on local consumption patterns in Acre. After all, almost 40 percent of the beef raised in Acre does not leave the state. Acreans are the highest per capita consumers of beef in Brazil, eating on average 45 kilograms (99 pounds) of beef per year, which is much higher than the national average (37 kilograms) (Valentim 2008).

What are the factors that explain the Acrean love of beef? To answer this, it is helpful to look at the beef consumption patterns of different Acrean groups (table 7.1). On average, beef was eaten less than one day a week by rubber tappers, but nearly every day by the cow-

2. The literal translation of "O farra do boi na Amazonia" is "The festival of the oxen in Amazonia."

Table 7.1. Frequency of beef consumption, by social group

	Rubber Tappers	NGOs	Policy Makers	Colonists	Ranchers	Cowboys
Beef consumption (days/week)	<1.0	3.8	3.9	5.6	5.9	6.6

$p < .05$

boys. All groups buy their meat—with the exception of the cowboys, who slaughter a cow every week to provide food for the ranch, and can eat beef every day free of charge. The rubber tappers' low consumption is the result of a lack of access but also reflects their cultural preference for game meat. It is noteworthy that the members of the environmentalist NGO group eat beef almost four days a week. This is considerably less than cowboys, ranchers, and colonists, but the number is nevertheless surprising, given that many in this group are keenly aware of the fact that their own consumption of beef directly supports the cattle industry that many of them oppose on ideological and political grounds.

YOU ARE WHAT YOU EAT I: BEEF CONSUMPTION, CLASS, AND STATUS

When my interviews were canceled or I was waiting for permission to go to the field, I often went to the Boi Gordo butcher shop in Rio Branco. I liked talking with the butchers and learning about how they classified the cuts of beef and determined quality. Watching the customers was one of the things that convinced me that beef was in many ways the key factor to understanding the cattle culture and the cattle industry. I will always remember the unmatched enthusiasm of people coming in to buy beef, especially on Fridays and before anticipated soccer matches. On those weekends, the smell of *churrasco* was heavy in the air.

Over the course of my fieldwork, I went to *churrascos* hosted by rubber tappers, colonists, ranchers, UFAC professors, journalists, workers at environmentalist NGOs, and government officials. It was in these settings that I learned of certain similarities that seemed to be a part of the ritualized consumption of beef that is the *churrasco*, including a gendered division of labor, beef-related double entendres, and suspicion directed toward those who refused to eat beef. A *churrasco* was a social event and a statement of social status. Groups offered different cuts of beef at their *churrascos*, and this said something about their social standing or their aspirations. When a whole cow was killed, for instance, the guests with some prestige were given cuts better than the children received.

I worked with key informants and butchers to rank the cuts of beef from most (most delicious or choicest) to least preferable or tasty. I then classified beef cuts into four categories of quality, on a scale from one, "high quality" (e.g., *picanha*), to four, "low quality" (the least desirable cuts, including organs, bones, and hooves). In general, the best cuts are the most expensive, usually because they are relatively limited in relation to the overall amount of meat on the carcass, but this does not always hold true. The lowly hooves, for example, were at the bottom of the preference rankings, despite being relatively limited in comparison to the leg to which they were attached. I asked respondents in six groups: "Which cut of beef do you prefer?" The results, in table 7.2, summarize the average quality value of beef preferred by the twenty members of each of the six social groups. As seen in the table, higher-class groups (ranchers, policy makers, and NGO workers) who live in the city and cowboys prefer cuts of beef in the top

Table 7.2. Quality of beef consumed, by social group

Social Group	Average Quality of Beef Consumed
Rubber tappers	2.5
Colonists	2.35
Cowboys	1.70
NGOs	1.45
Ranchers	1.25
Policy makers	1.25

$p < .05$

Note: Figures for beef quality are based on the assignment of numerical values to four groups, with high quality = 1, medium-high quality = 2, medium-low quality = 3, and low quality = 4.

two categories. Rubber tappers and colonists are out of the highest-quality meat range, with an average preference in the medium range.

My question about preference was to some extent hypothetical, but it is true that preference also implies some basis in lived experience. I assumed that people would name the cuts of beef they had come to prefer over time and that most would choose *picanha*, which is widely considered the best cut, if they were able to. I thus considered beef preferences to be a proxy for class positions—a person's ability to buy a certain cut of beef depends on socioeconomic position, and through repetitive consumption that person forms a basis for preference.

The figures I obtained also reflect participants' degree of access to beef. The cowboys have exaggerated access to beef because of their employment on ranches. The rural groups had lower scores compared to urban groups. It is more difficult for rural groups to buy, transport, and store meat. Even if they slaughtered a cow, rubber tappers do not have the means to store such a large quantity of meat. Colonists reported that they ate more beef after an electrification project gave them the ability to store it in their refrigerators.

Many cultural celebrations are premised not on the quality of the meat, but on the connection with regional tradition. I went to a *festa de gaúcho* (gaucho festival) in the town of Nova California, where there was a large population of southerners (*gaúchos*). We ate racks of beef ribs that had been roasted on iron poles stuck in the ground above a line of coals, in the tradition of the *gaúchos*. A huge slab of ribs was laid on our table and we shared a knife, cutting off pieces of the crisped, fatty meat. Beef ribs are not considered to be a high-quality cut of meat; the appeal stems from a connection with tradition and culture. Similarly, many urban and rural Acreans will prepare *mocotó* (hoof) or tail stew for annual holidays and celebrations.

I was staying at a ranch in upper Acre on the day that a calf was slaughtered for the employees (the foreman, cowboys, fence builders, and their families). This weekly event provided the employees with food to eat over the following week. A small crisis erupted when the rancher was confronted by one of the cowboys, who complained that the *capitaz* (foreman, the highest rank in the ranch hierarchy after the rancher) was taking more than his share of *picanha* each week. The cowboy threatened to quit unless the rancher ensured that the meat was distributed equally—not only in terms of its weight, but in terms of its quality.

The situation caused quite a rift on the ranch because the *capitaz* felt that his access to the highest-quality cuts of beef was a natural expression of his high rank and status as the longest-tenured cowboy on the ranch. Beef provides sustenance, but the significance and distribution of the various cuts is important in terms of delineating status.

YOU ARE WHAT YOU EAT II: BEEF PERCEPTIONS

STRENGTH AND DEVELOPMENT:
FROM THE EGG TO THE *BIFE*

I never went to a celebration centered on the consumption of chicken or rice and beans. Although these foods might be served as complements to the main dish at a *churrasco*, they were not accorded the same level of stand-alone importance. Different foods are associated with positive social values, which are in turn connected to perceptions of taste and the amount of energy or strength that they give a person, particularly for individuals who make a living through physical labor.

In this ordering of foods, beef is at the top, followed by the "weaker" pork, chicken, and fish. Game meat is considered a delicacy by some and a health risk by others. A simple meal of rice, beans, and *farinha* (manioc flour), commonly eaten by the rubber tappers, is considered to be fundamentally lacking by most. Chicken is more expensive than many cuts of beef, but this does not add to its allure in the minds of most. The perceived nutritional value of different foods is also reflective of class position, and eating beef is considered to be an indication of socioeconomic advancement by lower- and working-class groups.

The sense of an individual "developing," or advancing, socioeconomically is also related to an overall process of societal development. The now-widespread availability of beef is considered by many to be an indicator of their improved standard of living. Many Acreans described what for them was a significant cultural memory: waiting in line to buy beef in the time before the influx of cattle. They would get in line before daybreak, and were unable to choose specific cuts. Acreans can now be picky and selective about the cuts of meat they purchase, which is for many a sign of the development of the state.

Eating beef instead of other foods shows that an individual is also "developing." The administration of Brazil's president "Lula" (Luiz Inácio da Silva, 2003–2011) oversaw a period of socioeconomic advancement for many in Brazil. One man described it as a time of transition from the *ovo* to *bife* (from egg to beef cutlet) in the *marmita* (lunch pail) of Brazilian workers. The egg in the *marmita* was also known as the *bife de olhão* (big-eye)—evoking the envious or jealous (big-eyed) person looking on as another enjoys beef.

In group settings, it is important to have a piece of meat, preferably beef, on one's plate, as this signifies social status and a shared understanding of the symbolic and material benefits of beef. During lunchtime, urban workers and cowboys sometimes make fun of those who do not have meat to eat, by mocking their inability to buy it or questioning their ability to work throughout the afternoon. Among members of lower social classes, both urban and rural, eating beef is considered a marker of social status and a provider of the strength and sustenance required for working.

MCNALDÃO'S HAMBURGERS, "MEGA POWER," AND A BULLDOZER

Many Acreans agreed that some form of protein, be it the lowly egg or any cut of beef, in the diet is essential, to provide one with the strength to work in the afternoons and also for overall health. A steady diet of beef, they say, makes a person, particularly a man, *forte*, meaning both "strong" and "stout," or *gordo* (fat), which is not necessarily an insult but an indicator of status and health.

If I had to name a symbol that captured local notions of strength, as well as the celebrated and highly critiqued ideals of Amazonian "development" associated with beef and cattle raising, I am not sure if I could do better than the bulldozer that adorns this sign on McNaldão's hamburger stand in Rio Branco (fig. 7.2), located in a park a few blocks away from the central market. The curved yellow "M" points to the universally recognized first letter in the name of the American fast-food giant that is so often targeted in deforestation propaganda. At the right, the all-caps words "mega power" are stamped above a bulldozer chugging through what appears to be a forested landscape.

In their most basic form, Acrean hamburgers consist of a bun, a skinny beef patty, a thin slice of *presunto* (ham) or *apresuntado* (ham-like product), and sometimes lettuce and canned corn. The biggest burger on the menu at McNaldão's is the "Super McNaldão Mega Power," 500 grams of beef and eleven other ingredients, including sausage, a hot dog, bacon, a fried egg, and a chicken cutlet. Little

FIGURE 7.2. McNaldão's hamburger stand in Rio Branco

packets of mustard and ketchup sit on the table, and people squeeze them onto their hamburgers, bite by bite. The hamburgers get pretty big and unwieldy when other ingredients are added. A little stack of napkins usually stands next to the condiments. These napkins have the curious quality of being almost completely nonabsorbent, and are really useful only for scraping sauces off the side of your mouth or corralling a spill by crumpling a bunch around it.

There are cheeseburgers as well, usually denoted on the menu with the word "xis" or the letter "X," which sounds like the English word "cheese" in Brazilian Portuguese. Thus, a *xis-tudo* (cheese-everything) contains the core ingredients and everything else—a fried egg, bacon, corn, one or two hotdogs split down the middle, a thin cut of *bife*, and sometimes even beets and peas. Such a meal is bound to be fortifying, but the effect can be increased by drinking the juices that are usually available at the hamburger stands. Native Amazonian foods, such as açai juice and the guaraná powder with which it is sometimes coupled, are also thought to increase strength.

COMPARISONS OF BEEF PERCEPTIONS

To what extent are the perceptions of strength, sustenance, and other positive attributes accorded to beef shared by different Acrean social groups? Table 7.3 gives an answer. One hundred percent of the cowboy

Table 7.3. Agreement with statements about beef, by social group

| | Agreement by Social Group | | | | | |
Statement	Rubber Tappers	Colo-nists	Ranchers	Cowboys	Policy Makers	NGOs
Beef gives more strength to work than other foods do.	45%	70%	65%	100%	35%	20%
A lunch with no meat leaves a person weak.	90%	70%	65%	75%	35%	15%
People who don't eat beef lack the will to work.	25%	55%	40%	55%	15%	0%
A lunch with no meat is not a real lunch.	55%	75%	70%	70%	60%	20%

$p < .05$ for each question.

group, who eat beef nearly every day, thought that beef gives a person more strength to work than other foods. Among the rural groups, the rubber tappers, who eat beef on less than one day a month, agreed the least with this statement (45 percent). Only 35 percent of policy makers and 20 percent of NGO workers agreed that beef gives you more strength.

Most rural groups, with the exception of the rubber tappers, said that they felt weak if they did not eat meat for lunch; this could be beef, chicken, pork, or game meat, but beef was associated with the most strength. At least 65 percent of all rural groups agreed that a meatless lunch left a person weak, but there was less agreement on the more strongly worded and more beef-specific statement "not eating beef leaves a person without the will to work."

When asked about the possibility of a lunch without meat, many did more than simply respond "yes" or "no"—they might also make a crinkled face or give drawn out moans of displeasure. It is not acceptable to not have meat for lunch, and, as one colonist put it: meatless meals are eaten "with our eyes closed." More than half the members of all groups, with the exception of NGO workers, agreed that a meal without meat of any kind is not a true meal. These results indicate distinct patterns of agreement: rural groups believe more in the positive social perceptions of beef than do urban NGO/policy maker groups.

By comparing these cultural data with personal attributes, we can see further differences. We would expect the NGO/PM groups to eat less meat because of their lower levels of agreement with positive perceptions of beef and their ideological opposition to cattle raising as a destructive practice. Instead, the NGO workers eat beef almost four days a week. This finding is surprising, but it shows that eating beef forms a part of the social fabric of Acrean and Brazilian society. Many environmentalists saw the contradiction in their perceptions and practices, but as one otherwise reserved government official exclaimed: "I can't help it, I am a carnivore!" For the rural groups, the many positive perceptions of beef were considered cultural facts, independent of their ideology.

Issues of access are also important. Rubber tappers cannot eat beef to the same extent as other groups because they are more isolated than other groups, have less money to buy it, and have no way to store it without electricity. The electrification project arrived in colonist communities that I worked in between 2007 and 2009. I saw in this short amount of time the increase in their consumption of beef now that they could store it. Another interesting trend was that some colonists' enthusiasm for beef cooled, and they had started eating a diet including both beef and other meats. Some explained that by watching television, also made possible by rural electrification, they had begun to hear about the health risks of eating too much beef.

YOU ARE WHO YOU EAT:
MEAT, METAPHOR, AND GRILL POWER

By analyzing patterns of consumption across groups, we have seen that eating beef reflects class hierarchies and is thought to fuel the advancement that will overcome them. You are, symbolically and materially, what you eat, but also *who* you eat (in a metaphorical sense). *Comer*, "to eat," also means "to have sex with" or "to consume sexually" in Brazilian Portuguese; this usually refers to the male, or penetrator, in sexual relations, who is said to have eaten the penetrated. To eat someone is to show dominance, and to extend the idiom of nourishment and prestige surrounding beef, it implies the ability to derive sustenance or appropriate some sense of power over the subject.

The ubiquitous *churrasco* provided many opportunities for me to observe how the idiom of eating or asserting power over others is expressed in social situations. There was a near-universal gendered division of labor in every *churrasco* that I went to. Men were usually in charge of preparing the meat and were designated as grillers. Women sometimes helped season or prepare the meat beforehand, but they always handed it off to the men for grilling.

If the *churrasco* was large, the sexes usually separated for at least part of the time. The women usually stayed in the kitchen preparing side dishes, while the men congregated around the grill, although there were intermediate areas where they mixed. Some of the items grilled at a *churrasco* by men were fried, baked, or prepared in other ways by women for normal meals. Social norms clearly structured this one event in such a way that a deviation from gender roles was expected during the *churrasco*. While cooking by a man under normal circumstances might be considered womanly or less manly, grilling was an unequivocal assertion of manliness.

As Limón (1989) demonstrated in his analysis of a small Mexican American barbecue in south Texas, in these spaces masculine wordplay focusing on double meanings associated with meat can be used to show domination, while simultaneously perpetuating and satirizing broader power inequalities. Given the double meanings of various meat cuts and "eating," for instance, accepting and eating meat, especially phallus-shaped items such as hot dogs or sausages, from a male server leaves one open to insults, principally to accusations of suppressed homosexual desires. One must be careful when responding to a griller or server's query: "Do you want some/my sausage/meat/ beef?" Accepting the offering in a deferential way or without reciprocating the barb signified an acceptance of their domination, and forced out the bated breath of the other men into a gale of laughter.

Although this would seem to imply that participants in this repartee were expressing homosexual desires, this was not how the dynamic was commonly perceived as filtered through gender roles in the region. Despite the fact that the griller's meat was eaten by the other person, who literally derived strength from their flesh, the griller/server would be the one who "ate" or penetrated the other person. It was not the actual use of the word "to eat" here that is important, but the act of penetrating, which was central to Brazilian notions of masculinity, regardless of who is being penetrated. Many did not consider a man who penetrated another man to be gay, but the receiver, considered the submissive partner in the dynamic, was often seen as being homosexual or associated with the qualities of a woman. By eating the meat that the griller/server metaphorically transformed into their instrument of penetration, one is "eaten" symbolically through a shared idiom of sexual domination, masculinity, and social standing.

One can safely accept a meat offering as long one responds with a statement that is similarly focused on the meat, but also has the underlying semantic power to return the insult. The basic rules are well understood, but a rebuttal could meet these criteria and still be considered a failure if it does not receive approval of other men around the grill. If one's return insult failed, the griller's status was further increased. Some examples of common ways of returning the griller/server offer of meat were to say that it was "too small," "rotten," or "not-filling."

Less frequently, the *churrasco* wordplay was aimed not at other men but at their wives and girlfriends (e.g., "Your girlfriend is looking skinny. Is she getting enough *carne*?"). Such statements are less a criticism of the absent woman than of the man addressed. The implications are that he is unable either to secure a healthy partner or to sustain one who would otherwise flourish from being with a man capable of buying meat for her and satisfying her sexually. On the rare occasions that I heard someone say that a woman "ate" a man, the woman was much bigger than her male partner or perceived to be more sexually experienced than him.

Interestingly, Acrean expressions for sexual infidelity involve metaphors referring to the animal world, and most commonly cattle. A person who cheats is said to have "jumped the fence" (*pular a cerca*), as when cattle leave their defined place in order to mate (where the grass may be greener). When a spouse has "jumped the fence," the cuckolded partner is said to "acquire horns." Being called a *chifrudo* or *corno* (horned one) is considered either a devastating insult or a term of chiding endearment among male friends. These horns are invisible but are often mentioned as if they are real. People say "Careful with the *chifres*!" to a friend who sticks his head out of a window, bumps his head, or tries on a hat. When a person has a blemish or bump on their forehead, friends say that their *chifres* are emerging, and that they had better watch their partner closely.

Although in other parts of the world strong, stubborn, or valiant men are compared to bulls, this association is rare in Brazil because, again, of the meaning of horns. Brazilians generally avoided relating themselves to cattle, and although T-shirts that depict a cowboy riding a bull are acceptable, wearing clothing with the image of cattle, especially those with horns, is avoided.

The dynamic of domination that characterizes human to human/cattle/animal/nature relations around cattle raising is employed symbolically and metaphorically to express similarly unequal social relationships of domination (Ortner 1974). While the *churrasco* is about the transition from "raw to cooked," it is also about jumbling nature–culture dichotomies and reveling in the in-between. The *churrasco* emphasizes physical pleasure attained in a very specific way: by searing the flesh of a powerful bovine while standing outside in the presence of friends. The exterior of the *picanha* is browned by the fire, but cutting into it reveals pink just below the surface and a blood-red center. This ritual is at once carnal and cerebral—it is about gorging on the tender meat of a savage beast that has been domesticated, and maybe "eating" one's friends through the use of language that is crude yet highly refined, and only successful when poetic.

CONCLUSION

The *churrasco*, the hamburger, and the *bife* in the lunch pail—each of these is a potential final destination of rural cattle, but the hamburger connection does not end at these places. Rather, urban consumption provides us a place where we may start disentangling the many features associated with the expansion of cattle ranching in Acre. Beef literally gives flesh to the key themes of materiality and meaning, as well as to structure and agency, which have provided the framework for this and previous analyses. Are there connections between the symbolic conquest of nature occurring in the countryside, the beef-centered connotations of sexual domination, and the belief that beef gives strength and shows one's social rank?

Think about that bulldozer on McNaldão's hamburger shack. What is the bulldozer plowing? It is unclear, but given my familiarity with images of the Amazon I cannot help but think of the forest. Regardless of the background, the bulldozer is a powerful tool of landscape transformation with which humans shape the natural world to their will and visions, no matter what is in the way. Work is fueled by food. Most Acreans believe that beef, above all foods, gives a person the most strength to work. Whether at a construction site in the city or a clearing in the forest, work is the process by which culture transforms and triumphs over nature. Acrean culture is reflected in the testaments to the power of men in this place that is so strongly tied to an intractable nature that never rests and will consume them if they stop working. Although people could eat other foods and receive similar physiological and nutritional benefits, it is the meaning of beef just as much as its material properties that is important.

The rubber tappers' perceived lack of productivity is often ascribed to undesirable traits related to physical weakness (*fraqueza*) or a *falta de coragem* (lack of will to work). These same attributes are often identified by Acreans as symptoms of a meatless diet. Especially in the countryside, creating cattle pastures and raising cattle brings one positive outcomes connected to individual advancement and generalized notions of development. Beef fuels "development" by giving people the strength to work, and through their working, links them to positive social values while simultaneously bringing them profits. Status, strength, and development are all melded into a commodity that has the power to give similar attributes to those who consume it.

CHAPTER 8

RUBBER-TAPPER AND COLONIST TRANSITIONS:
ENVIRONMENT, PRACTICE, AND IDENTITY

POLITICAL AND ECONOMIC FACTORS have combined with social and cultural changes to encourage cattle raising in Acre. Does being a rubber tapper—a "forest guardian"—have some bearing on one's decision to raise cattle? And as for the colonists, so integrally entwined with agriculture, how does their increasing reliance on cattle manifest itself in their perceptions of self? These are questions that young and old members of these groups are confronting as they shift to cattle raising.

Here I analyze the implications that changing economic practices have for colonists' and rubber tappers' notions of identity. I contextualize these changes as part of a long-term process in which people migrate and then adapt to a new environment. Changes in practice and identity were not by-products of adaptation to the Amazon rainforest ecology. Rather, as I will show, these groups' practices and identities were influenced by a unique configuration of ecological, political, economic, and ideological factors. Collectively, these constraints, both material and intangible, constitute a field of possibilities, or an "environment," that has structured their actions in specific ways at different times.

While my primary aim here is to elucidate this environment in relation to shifting practices and identities, I do not want to lose sight of the individuals who make up these groups. As I was writing this chapter, I was concerned that the unique and complex lives of the actual people I had come to know were being reduced to impersonal parts in a mechanical whole, and subsumed by generalities that matched no one person. Myriad factors went into their practices and decisions—chance meetings and accidents and sicknesses, personality quirks, the topography of their land, their age and health, and even the sex of their children. These people were living somewhere between structure and agency, motivated to varying extents by a singular configuration of economic, political, and sociocultural considerations as these were aligned at the specific moment I glimpsed their lives.

I have included a description of one member of each group. These profiles, which were originally written for a popular audience with little knowledge of the Amazon, provide an opportunity to reflect on the tensions involved in representing something as fluid and contested as identity in Amazonia.

POSITIONING AMAZONIAN PRACTICES

Practice theory (Bourdieu 1977) provides a means of conceptualizing the dialectical relationship between economic practice and social identity. Building on the political, ecological, and economic anthropological perspectives discussed in previous chapters, practice theory provides an overarching framework with which to locate Acrean practices in relation to political/economic structures as well as broader perceptions of practices, and a means to observe the agency of social groups, who respond to constraints through a sense of self fashioned over time (Knauft 1996; Ortner 2006).

"Social identity" is the way that members of a group perceive and express themselves culturally as part of a social collectivity. Social group identities are based on a number of features, including ethnicity, race, and connection with place (Barth 1965, 1969; Clifford 1988; Hale 1997; Tuan 1974). Non-indigenous and mixed-race Amazonian social groups show how these different features of identity change and are contextually expressed in relation to engagement with the dominant society and economy (Chibnik 1991; Cleary 1993; Harris 2000, 2004; Nugent 1993). As is the case for other Amazonian groups, the Acrean identity labels are related to ethnicity and race, place of origins, and class, but the key criterion for both internal and external perceptions is how they use their land to make a living (see Harris 2004).

Members of a group are situated within a collective "location" and possess a distinctive social memory, consciousness, and position within the social structure (Hale 1997). Within a shared biophysical setting, distinct identities also clash with, and are reinforced and otherwise influenced by, the other groups with whom they interact, each with different ways of perceiving, using, and contesting resources (Bennett 1969; Ingold 1980; Robben 1989; Schmink and Wood 1992).

The spaces that social groups exploit through distinct economic practices may be implicitly linked to their practice-based identities when they are institutionalized in land-tenure systems (Schwartzman 1987; Toni et al. 2007). Any encounter between groups, however, may produce changes in both perceptions and practices (Atran et al. 1999; Rudel et al. 2002). These changes could be at odds with traditional land-tenure systems and may or may not accurately reflect aspects of a group's putative identity. For example, political shifts that render the traditional practices of one group economically unviable could produce tensions between cultural identity and tenure rules (Ehringhaus 2005). Although in some cases a group's identity may denote an unchanging quality, Amazonians have been able to show that their own self-definition is fluid and contingent in an increasingly interconnected and changing world (e.g., Brubaker and Cooper 2000; Conklin and Graham 1995; Gupta and Ferguson 1992).

Identity is a slippery and problematic concept, but in Acre it remains a very salient emic and etic category with which to classify rural Acrean groups. The colonists and rubber-tappers described themselves with these labels. Members were thought to embody a suite of characteristics associated with that group identity, including residence in a specific place or land-tenure system and dedication to agriculture or extractivism. Specifically, the rubber-tapper and colonist identities were linked to the economic practices of agricultural and forest extractivism and to specific places in the form of institutional tenure systems—the settlement project and the extractive reserve. The rubber tappers were also strongly associated with the forest, as a place, as a focus of their practices, and as something with which they were assumed to have a cultural affinity.

RUBBER TAPPERS

CHANGES IN RUBBER-TAPPER PRACTICE AND IDENTITY

From the mid-nineteenth century up until the mid-twentieth, to be a rubber tapper meant that one tapped rubber. Rubber-tapper practice was highly constrained for much of this period, with *seringalistas*, or rubber barons, controlling rubber-tapper labor (Weinstein 1983). With the decline in the rubber economy, and the end of the oppression of

Table 8.1. Dominant economic practices of social groups, 1980–2009 and future (anticipated)

Group	Before 1980	1990	1995	2000	2009	2015	Future
Rubber tappers	E (r)	E (b)	E (b)	E (b)	E (b), C	E, C	E, C
Colonists	A	A	A	C	C	C	C, UW

A = agriculture; (b) = Brazil nut; C = cattle raising; E = extractivism; (r) = rubber; UW = urban wage labor.

the *seringal* system, many rubber tappers migrated to cities. Those who stayed behind began to incorporate agriculture, a practice previously forbidden by the rubber barons, into their extractive livelihood strategies (Bakx 1988).

Table 8.1 presents data from a survey in which members of each group were asked both to identify their primary economic practices at specific points in time from 1980 until 2009, and to anticipate future practices. In the interest of a consistent comparison between groups, I have defined "primary economic practice" as the one that contributed the most money to the household. In general, this was how most respondents in the survey defined the term.[1]

The rubber tappers in São Cristovão reported that they had relied primarily on extractivism, specifically rubber, prior to 1980. From 1990 to 2000, they maintained an extractivist orientation, but, because of the decline of rubber prices and the removal of the rubber subsidy, families were compelled to increase their reliance on Brazil nuts. During this period in other parts of the state, fishing and agriculture became important for rubber-tapper families (Salisbury and Schmink 2007).

By 2009, many families in São Cristovão were supplementing Bra-

1. "Primary economic practice" could otherwise mean many things. Among smallholders, this could mean the amount of labor or land dedicated to practice, or could refer to a subsistence activity, such as agriculture or hunting. These practices are essential to social reproduction of the household, but are not able to be captured as formal economic exchange. The majority of households surveyed were at least partially reliant on the cash exchange economy, but not all relied on subsistence activities.

zil nut harvesting with cattle raising, mirroring trends among rubber tappers inside and out of the RESEX in Acre (Gomes 2009; Salisbury and Schmink 2007; Toni et al. 2007; Wallace 2004). A state program had resuscitated rubber tapping for selected families in the area. Participants reported that rubber increased their household income somewhat, but that its contribution was minimal compared to those of other activities. Remittances from family members in the city now provided an important source of household income, and, for those still able to clear land, agriculture contributed to subsistence needs.

In the view of older rubber tappers, their way of life is related to a long history of forest-based existence. This feature of their group identity was galvanized during intergroup conflict and institutionalized with the establishment of the extractive reserves. The tappers who formed their identities around this confluence of factors are aging, and they are yielding control of their households to a younger generation that is less connected to previous forms of both practice and identity (Vadjunec, Schmink, and Gomes 2011; Gomes et al. 2012).

Many in São Cristovão viewed themselves as rubber tappers, regardless of whether or not they tapped rubber. This applied to aged tappers, who may not have been economically motivated or physically able to tap rubber, as well as their offspring, who often chose not to tap rubber because the endeavor was not worth much in comparison to other economic pursuits. Old and young alike said that their continued participation in extractive activities, particularly the harvesting of Brazil nuts, enabled them to define themselves as rubber tappers. Practice remained central to their ideals of self, but they felt, more or less, that being a rubber tapper was the same as being an "extractivist," a term describing forest-based resource management. Outsiders do not see extractivist activities as a divergence from rubber-tapper identity, as long as they are using the forest without destroying it. Despite changes in practice and the emergence of a generation that does not participate in the activity, older tappers told me that their children would be rubber tappers as long as they lived in the RESEX, regardless of how they used the land.

In a setting of demographic and economic change, rubber-tapper identity was naturally in a state of renegotiation, but everyone agreed that a man named old Pedro Perto was an example of a true rubber tapper.

RUBBER TAPPERS TOIL IN THE FOREST

The last time I saw Pedro Perto, he was tapping rubber in the forest.[2]

It was July [of 2009], and I was walking with Espimar, my guide in the rubber-tapper community of São Cristovão. As he walked, he played his new guitar and sang the few country songs that he had heard on the radio and somehow learned.

It was surreal walking through the forest as he sang, with little patches of light reaching through the canopy, our feet crunching on the leaves that had grown brittle in the dryness of the Amazon summer.

When the rains stop, rubber season begins.

As we came to the crest of a small hill, we spotted old Pedro Perto. He was smiling, as he always was, a smile that went to his eyes, which twinkled as he squinted. His brown skin was tight on his bones, his white hair as full as that of his sons, grandsons, and great-grandsons.

In his hand he held a *faca*, a knife for cutting rubber. He held the little handle in one hand and guided the blade with the other, working it diagonally across the tree bark. He left a line sure and straight, and the *leite*, or milk, began to bubble through. Gradually, a line of white liquid filled in the groove and began to run down a central vertical cut that channeled it to a cup or a nut shell (fig. 8.1).

He wore a long-sleeved plaid shirt against the early morning cold of the forest. As was his custom, a hand-rolled cigarette was stuck to his bottom lip, unlit. It moved with his lip when he talked. He had tied his shirt around his waist and pulled up the sleeves as the morning heated up, and the way it bloused out made him seem like a giant with skinny little legs.

He lit the cigarette and walked on to tap some more trees, which were scattered randomly throughout the forest, all connected by trails he had made. He spent less than a minute at each tree and was off again, walking at a jogging pace. There were about one hundred trees on each trail, and he had three trails. He would work each trail twice a week, resting on Sunday.

Pedro's ancestors came to Acre in the 1800s from the drought-stricken northeast of Brazil, lured by the promise of a better life. They were disappointed when they found out that the land and their labor was controlled by rubber barons, but they were trapped thousands of miles from home in the middle of the Amazon basin and had no way to get back.

In exchange for the rubber balls, the baron would give Pedro supplies, food, and medicine. He wasn't allowed to sell the rubber himself—that could get a rubber tapper killed.

2. From the series "Postcards from the Amazon"; published in the *San Angelo Standard-Times* on June 28, 2010. The original text has been maintained as it was originally published, with minor changes. The titles were chosen by the newspaper editors.

FIGURE 8.1. Rubber flows from a tree into a Brazil nut shell

"There were good barons and there were bad ones," he said. "The one that used to own the land here was really bad."

The price of natural rubber declined throughout the twentieth century because rubber seeds were stolen from the Amazon and used to create plantations in Southeast Asia. During World War II, when the Southeast Asian supplies were cut off, Amazonian rubber became important again and a new wave of migrants called "rubber soldiers" came to Acre to tap rubber for the Allied war effort.

The price of rubber gradually declined to the point that many rubber barons abandoned their lands, leaving the rubber tappers free. But when the government opened up the Amazon to settlement in the 1970s, the absentee barons sold their lands to ranchers, who came to cut down the forest, plant pasture, and raise cattle.

Violence erupted as the ranchers tried to kick the rubber tappers off the land that they had lived on for up to a century.

"When things got bad in one place, I moved to another. I even worked for a rancher for a while," Pedro said.

He moved seven times in all. Finally, when things calmed down, he came to settle in the reserve that the government set aside for the rubber tappers.

"It is good here now. We are free," he said. "We can sell to whoever we want and buy whatever we need." Earlier this year, I ran into Pedro Perto's son, Chico

Velho (Old Chico), in the city and asked about his dad. He told me that Pedro Perto had died.

Pedro lived the history of the rubber trade in Acre—from a time of debt servitude to, in the present, a time of freedom, but with new hardships.

Many rubber tappers would now prefer to raise cattle, which give them more money with less work. In the São Cristovão, however, there is a renewed interest in tapping rubber because the community has teamed up with a local factory that makes natural condoms.

Pedro's grandson now walks those same trails twice a day during the dry season, tapping rubber like his grandfather did.

THE MANY FACES OF THE RUBBER TAPPERS

Pedro was considered by everyone in São Cristovão to be a *seringueiro de pe rachado* (cracked-foot rubber tapper), a genuine backwoodsman whose authenticity was derived from years of interaction with the forest. I wanted to write the story about Pedro because he was a "true" rubber tapper, according to others in his community, and he also fit my own image of a tapper, especially as compared to others I met in the community. His story was one of many that I thought about writing, but it was only after I learned that he had passed away that I decided to put pen to paper; after he was gone I realized that he truly had been one of the last of a breed.

As I wrote the story, I was keenly aware that my articles would appear online and be read by both advocates of forest preservation and those promoting cattle raising and soy development in the Amazon, some of whom had written to me about the columns. The way that I represented the tappers would have implications. It would have been a challenge to create a profile representing this group around anyone else that I came to know in the *seringal*; for one reason or another, each of these defied the definition of the rubber tapper.

Ze Ovelha, another resident of São Cristovão, fit the description of a rubber tapper at the time I stayed with his family in 2009, but in 2010 he was working away from home as a cowboy. He had gone with Zafá, an orphan who bounced around the *seringal* from house to house, tapping the owner's rubber trees to earn his keep. The truth was that almost everyone that I came to know either tapped rubber or engaged in some form of extractivism, but many of them (fourteen out of the twenty interviewed) also relied on cattle.

There was the self-named Filé (Filet), a former truck driver who bought some rubber trails a few years ago and paid young men from the community to work them. His house was the only one in the town center, around which the school, rubber storage facility, and soccer field were also located. The rest of the community live up little walking paths through the forest. If you were to stop at the road's end and not go into the forest (as many governmental visitors to the community do), Filé, gold necklaces jingling on his bare chest, might be the only "rubber tapper" you would meet.

I was torn between presenting the tappers in accordance with dominant external perceptions—as unchanging forest guardians and the antithesis of the predatory cattle raisers—and showing them as a complex group comprising diverse and changing individuals. I chose to tell Pedro's story because it enabled me to describe rubber-tapper history and daily life. My primary objective in writing these columns was to share the complexity of Amazonian lives to a popular audience that viewed Amazonia as an exotic place. Pedro's story helped me convey the facts that (1) there were non-indigenous people living in the forest; (2) these people had found an economic way to use and sustain the forest; and (3) the things they did in the forest were important and relevant to the history of the United States.

In the end I chose to emphasize the continuity of the rubber-tapper lifestyle, by showing that the grandson taps rubber as his grandfather did. In this context, writing for a popular audience, did I do a disservice by presenting Pedro, a true rubber tapper, as a representative of a group that now goes by the same title but has very little in common with him in terms of history and practices? Was I propagating the same essentialisms that uphold the "forest guardian" image, which is in many ways integral to their land rights but which also limits their potential responses to an evolving political economy? I still have trouble reconciling these questions, but I think that it is important to raise them here: they evoke the very real dilemmas that anthropologists face when attempting to represent marginalized groups in the complex nexus of contemporary environmental and identity politics (see Hale 2006).

EXTERNAL PERCEPTIONS

Aged and young tappers may still tap rubber or harvest Brazil nuts, but there are few households that feel they would be able to survive without cattle. The shift to cattle—understood by at least some rubber tappers as somewhat consistent with what it is to be a rubber tapper—is less flexibly understood by outsiders.

The goal of the rubber-tapper movement and the establishment of the RESEX was to secure the land so that forest dwellers could make a living through the managed extraction of forest products, thus contributing to preservation of the forest (Ehringhaus 2005). Although rubber was already a marginal economic activity at the time, the rubber tappers rallied around their connections with the forest to defend their land against the ranchers. Rubber-tapper identity coalesced in a unique moment that corresponded with both increased international attention to environmental concerns and an opening in the Brazilian political scene (Allegretti 2002; Keck 1995). As a result of their international profile and the establishment of the extractive reserve system in Acre and throughout Amazonia, the rubber tapper "forest guardian" image was firmly established in external perceptions (Ehringhaus 2005; Tsing 2005).

The essentialization of identities may be an important tool in the struggle to gain access to land, but a change in identity or practice may undermine the legitimacy of a group's claim (Clifford 1988; Hale 1997). The expansion of cattle grazing into the RESEX, which prompted the threat of expulsion for some families, garnered national media attention, and was seen in the local press as a betrayal of rubber-tapper identity (Lobo 2008). The rubber tappers' adoption of cattle goes against not only their perceived identity, but also who they were supposed *not* to be—environmentally destructive cattle raisers. Although raising cattle in the RESEX is not a crime as long as the 10 percent deforestation limit is observed, the outcry among outsiders over cattle shows the potency of popular perceptions in which practice, identity, and land are linked (Gomes et al. 2012).

COLONISTS: AGRICULTURE, CULTURE, AND SETTLEMENT

The term *colono* (colonist) is strongly associated with the practice of small-scale agriculture, but the relationship between practice and identity is not as direct as it is for the rubber tappers. Similar to the label "settler" or "pioneer" in the United States, *colono* evokes images of migrating to a new place and carving out a space in the wilderness. A more generalized term, *agricultor* (agriculturalist), has sometimes been employed by colonists, but this label has different meanings in other parts of Brazil. Potentially, an agricultor could own much or little land and be rich or poor. Large-scale agriculture is almost nonexistent in Acre, so small-scale swidden agriculture is associated with both the *agricultor* and the *colono* throughout the state.

The Quixadá Directed Settlement Project was established on a former rubber estate of the same name in the upper Acre region. Its population is composed of both migrants and former rubber tappers, who were already living on or near the rubber estate and chose to enter into the settlement project when the land was appropriated by INCRA. Former rubber tappers have come to define themselves as colonists because of their residence in the settlement projects, contact with migrants, and dedication to agriculture. The migrants in Quixadá are mostly from central-southern and southern Brazil. At the time of my work they comprised displaced small-scale agriculturalists, those renting land from or working for large-scale landowners, and even urban residents. They all had come to the settlement project in search of their own "piece of land."

Many migrant colonists said that they came from a "culture of agriculture" and that agriculture was "in their blood." This foundational agricultural identity was strengthened by the developmentalist ideology of Amazonian colonization, a process in which self-reliant colonists are seen "taming the frontier." This mindset was further reinforced by the local institutional interventions of INCRA, which rewarded those who demonstrated productivity. Both colonists and INCRA staff spoke of the first president of INCRA-Acre, Moreno Maia, who supervised the settlement of the first wave of colonists to Acre. In tours of the settlements, he would threaten to take away colonists' land if they did not prove that they were being "productive," a concept synonymous in the settlement projects with converting forest to agricultural space.

Migrants with agricultural experience in the temperate south were initially overwhelmed by the Amazonian climate and ecology. They told of being dropped off somewhere along a little trail through the forest with their belongings, and of the struggles involved in adapting their practices to the new landscape. Former rubber tappers, who had some experience with swidden agriculture, were integral in transmitting local knowledge to many migrant families and helping them adapt.

As a result of institutional pressures and interactions with migrants, former rubber tappers in the settlement projects became primarily dedicated to agriculture. The small plots distributed by the project made it impossible to practice forest extractivism. Additionally, while previously the rubber tappers' properties had been determined by the distribution of forest resources, the plots on the settlement project were now uniform squares situated along a road, with little consideration given to the composition of the land. Furthermore, the migrants and INCRA administrators alike reinforced the developmentalist mindset and notions that "work" was equated with transformation of the wilderness to cultivated spaces.

As seen in table 8.1, colonists remained dedicated primarily to agriculture through 1995. Beginning in the late 1990s, however, many began to shift to cattle raising. As of 2009 cattle raising was the dominant economic practice and few colonists reported practicing agriculture on any scale, as a result of both the decline in agricultural support and the increased enforcement of deforestation and burning regulations. These developments have led to a sharp decline in agriculture, and exaggerated colonist reliance on cattle.

While cattle provide money to buy staple foods, many reported to me that agriculture provided greater self-sufficiency. Loss of self-sufficiency has led to feelings ranging from anger and frustration to worthlessness. A story recounted by multiple sources in Quixadá illustrated one of the most extreme consequences of colonist estrangement from agriculture. A man cut down a hectare of forest and burned it to plant his yearly *roça* (agricultural plot). This activity was detected by IBAMA officials, who swooped in and took him to jail. When he returned home, he killed himself. Narrators of this story said that this individual did not want to go on if he couldn't produce for himself. True or not, the often recounted story highlights the perceived decline of fundamental aspects of colonist practice and identity that has resulted from the inability to fulfill subsistence needs through agriculture. These migrants came thousands of miles to acquire their own land and become autonomous producers. The ideology of development and the institutional interventions of INCRA only reinforced this drive. The subsequent dramatic shift in policy has been difficult for many to swallow, and a great number have moved to the city.

The incorporation of cattle into colonist livelihoods has not been seen as a divergence from colonist identity. Many migrant families who came to Acre already had experience with cattle and relied on them to pull ox-carts and to provide milk and cheese. Despite their strong connection with agriculture, many considered cattle to be an integral part of a diversified rural livelihood. Those with cattle still refer to themselves as *colono* and even *agricultor*. Unlike the rubber tappers, some colonists now reliant on cattle seem comfortable calling themselves *pecuaristas* (cattle raisers) or *pequenos produtores* (small-scale producers). They only jokingly called themselves *fazendeiros* (large-scale ranchers), because this label has class and historical connotations beyond herd size.

While still reliant on cattle, others are expanding into novel practices: fish tanks, chicken farms, agro-forestry systems, and urban and rural wage labor. Many colonists accept these changes, saying that part of being a *colono* is being flexible and tough, and accepting that any practice could fit within the catchall *colono* label. As long as they can find ways to stay on the land, they are *colonos*. The true end of the *colono* comes, many say, when they sell their land and move to the city.

As with the rubber tappers, I could have described the life of any number of distinctive colonists, but I offer here a vignette on Leopoldo. Leopoldo's was one of the four different homes I stayed in when I was conducting research in different parts of Quixadá. I wrote this column about Leopoldo because of the simple fact that I came to know him well, and I found him to be interesting, as a former rubber tapper surrounded by migrants. Telling his story enabled me to emphasize one of the key objectives of writing the newspaper columns in the first place. It allowed me to highlight some of the cultural distinctions between native Acrean former rubber tappers and migrant colonists, and to show people with very different histories and ways of viewing the world living side by side.

BRAZIL NUT A VALUED RESOURCE

Early in the morning, Leopoldo lights the little earthen stove just outside the back door of his house.[3] He is making *mucuzá*, a corn gruel, with Brazil nut milk.

The sun has yet to make it over the distant wall of forest that surrounds his property, insulating a sea of pasture with his little house in the middle.

Out in the pasture, cows rub themselves clockwise around a towering *castanheira* (Brazil nut tree), rising straight and limbless a hundred feet up, and then exploding into a bushy crown. Calves run stiff-legged in the grass, heavy with moisture even though it hasn't rained here in a couple weeks.

When I arrived at Leopoldo's house, it was all closed up, but his bedroom

---

3. From the series "Postcards from the Amazon"; published in the *San Angelo Standard-Times* on May 1, 2010.

window was open, with a towel hanging out to dry. After having stayed with him last year, I knew this meant he wasn't far off.

If he was in town for the day, he would have closed all the openings to the house, securing them with a knot around a nail or a loosely nailed piece of wood turned like a valve against the window. Everything here is simple and efficient; sticks that are barely long enough sit in between fence openings and gates are secured with pieces of rope that are so short that only he can retie them.

After a few beeps of the motorcycle horn, he came weaving through the occasional Brazil nut tree or termite mound on the little dirt paths that traverse the pasture. He had been in his agricultural plot, where he spends most mornings and afternoons, cutting away weeds from the corn plants and pruning the banana trees.

At first, I wondered if it was him, because he was all alone and his trusty dog—gangly and white with a black patch over one eye—was not following behind. Turns out someone stole him. His two little kittens had also died since I had last seen him.

The dog and kittens used to snuggle up together on the highest step just outside the back door, waiting for him to wake up.

Leopoldo lives in a one-room house in a settlement project. Beginning in the early 1980s, areas of the Amazon were opened up for families that wanted their own land. The people that settled here are known as *colonos*, or colonists.

Each family got about one hundred acres of forested land, where they gradually built homes. All of Leopoldo's neighbors rely mostly on cattle; if they grow crops (corn, beans, rice, cassava), it is usually for their own consumption. Fish farms are increasingly popular and profitable among them.

Colonos are a mixture of native Acreans, usually former rubber tappers, and migrants from states to the south.

Many migrants were landless in their home states, which had temperate climates. Adapting to the Amazon rainforest without much support or knowledge of the local ecology was an incredible challenge.

Leopoldo, like many native Acreans in the settlement projects, has a good knowledge of the forest and uses and sells many forest products. He prefers the milk of the Brazil nut for *mucuzá*, while migrants from outside generally use cow milk and call the mixture *canjica*.

This illustrates the different traditions of native Acreans, who are more forest-oriented, and migrants, who brought agriculture and ranching with them. Despite these cultural differences, Leopoldo's land is very similar to that of his neighbors—about half pasture and half forest.

To make *mucuzá*, Leopoldo first grinds up a few handfuls of Brazil nuts. He then puts them into a strainer, squeezing as he runs water over them to create the Brazil nut "milk." Finally, he pours the milk into the pot of corn that he boiled last night, along with a spoonful of salt and heaps of sugar.

He harvested the nuts a few months ago, waiting until all the softball-sized

FIGURE 8.2. Leopoldo peels Brazil nuts with his machete in front of his barn

pods, which weigh about 2 pounds, had fallen from the tree. Like little cannon-balls, they can easily crack your skull, so everyone steers clear of the trees in the months when they are dropping.

He gathered them from the forest floor around the perimeter of the trees, chucking them into old rice sacks. Next, he made a big pile of the pods, sat down, arranged his legs, and struck each pod around the crown with his machete. After hacking through the half-inch-thick woody covering of the pod, he took out about fifteen nuts, nestled together like sections of an orange.

Back at home he sat down again and, with his machete, scraped the woody skins off the individual nuts.

Leopoldo gathers the nuts from the forest and sells them by the bucket. This year he got about 30 cents a pound for unpeeled Brazil nuts. Fresh Brazil nuts have the taste and texture of coconut meat.

Leopoldo has a gas stove, but he prefers to make *mucuzá* on his little earth oven, right outside his door. After the corn is swollen with Brazil nut milk, he takes it off and lets it cool for a time. He spoons some into a bowl for me and tops it with cinnamon.

In his little wooden house, Leopoldo sips his *mucuzá*. He then heads off, on a little dirt trail through the pasture, to his banana field, where he will thin out dead stalks and trim away weeds. Thus begins a day in the life of one colonist.

On this dirt road alone, six other families are beginning their days in entirely different ways.

I felt less handcuffed writing about Leopoldo than I did when describing Pedro the rubber tapper. Colonists are not romanticized or contested symbols of the international environmental movement. In fact, the colonists often felt forgotten by the government, and they were sometimes lost in the shuffle of Acrean rural research, as the SUVs whizzed by their homes on the way to the RESEX.

Leopoldo had a sense of connection with the forest that was not shared by his neighbors who had migrated to Acre. I enjoyed listening to him speak of the forest and his experiences. As we worked or sat around in the evening, I asked him any question that popped into my head. When I asked him how chickens got clean by rubbing themselves in the dirt and how the giant anteater got the ants from the huge anthills, he would go into joyful, detailed descriptions. He told me about an Amazon that I had imagined but never seen, especially in the settlement projects: a giant anteater and jaguar fighting to the death; the distinct pain inflicted by different snakes, ants, and spiders; and the biggest *sucuri* (anaconda) that he had ever seen. He loved talking about the forest and its creatures, concluding his explanations and stories by saying, "A natureza é muita perfeita" (Nature is very perfect).

THE CHANGING ENVIRONMENT: STRUCTURE AND PRACTICE

I have shown that former tappers and migrants viewed and used the forest in different ways, but I also emphasized that their lands looked the same and that they both relied primarily on cattle. The coexis-

Table 8.2. Average cattle herd size for migrants
and former rubber tappers in Quixadá

Group	Mean Herd Size
Migrants	81.12
Former rubber tappers	73.65
Total	78.58

$F = 0.106$

tence of both groups in Quixadá allows for an interesting comparison on the role of cultural factors in mediating broader political and economic forces. Do former rubber tappers, such as Leopoldo, tend to see the forest in a more positive light, compared to migrants? Are they less likely to raise cattle? Or, do structural factors overwhelmingly favor cattle to the point that there is no real difference between the number of cattle that each group owns? Table 8.2 shows the average number of cattle owned by respondents in a survey of fifty colonist households (comprising thirty-three migrants and seventeen former rubber tappers) in Quixadá.[4]

There is no statistically significant difference in average herd size between migrants and former rubber tappers. I think that rubber-tapper cultural perceptions of the forest continue to guide them to some extent, but these dispositions are subsumed by structural factors that overwhelmingly favor cattle raising over forest livelihoods. The former rubber tappers I came to know were markedly different from migrant colonists. They used their forest more than migrants, and had a detailed knowledge and appreciation for it. Despite this difference in forest perception and engagement, the former tappers called themselves colonists and their plots of land had a similar forest–pasture composition.

Cultural considerations do often guide the manner in which a social group engages with the opportunities and constraints emanating from changing environmental, political, economic, or normative structures. Distinctive cultures, and especially practice-based identities, are forged through practices across time, and these are, logically,

4. The data came from a survey of colonist households that I participated in as part of the NSF-HSD project "Infrastructure Change, Human Agency, and Resilience in Social-Ecological Systems."

constrained by the structures that facilitate such practices. If cattle raising becomes incentivized over extractivism for long enough, people will eventually shift to it or find another context in which they can continue doing what they once did. If a colonist migrates from the temperate south and attempts to do things the way they were done back home, he will be extremely frustrated, and eventually adapt to the new matrix possibilities that constitute the "environment."

When Quixadá changed from a rubber estate to a settlement project, the rubber tappers who stayed were shocked not by the natural environment, but by the manner in which it was now configured institutionally and ideologically: the forest was an obstacle, and it had to be transformed for them to keep their land. They were put on a specific path with the migrants, and they showed each other how to make it in a new system. The tappers taught the migrants about swidden agriculture and useful and dangerous aspects of forest life. The migrants showed the tappers how the system worked and how to navigate obstacles by "using your head"—getting profits from land, resources from politicians, and other strategies that ensured survival in a reconstituted matrix of possibilities. It was in this transformed environment of the settlement project and with the mutual assistance of culturally distinct groups that being a colonist cohered into an identity beyond common residence.

The ecological context has not changed markedly over the past century, but the environment as a series of constraints has evolved. Structural features were central to forging rubber-tapper practice and identity in the first place. In the *seringal* production system, rubber tappers, migrants from the arid northeast of Brazil, worked in a system of debt peonage under the owner of the *seringal*, the *seringalista*. Without access to the means of production, and with their production monitored by the rubber baron, they were forced to use the resources of the forest in a specific and highly structured way to ensure the continued production of rubber. Without the global connections of the capitalist rubber trade, this "environment" would not have existed in the middle of Amazonia, nor would the tappers have been there in the first place. These migrants from the parched northeast came to know the forest well and to identify with it, and with time these connections became a part of their identity. Their environment, then, was not simply the Amazonian ecosystem, but the way that it was configured in relation to the global economy and local systems of production.

After the flight of the rubber barons, the rubber tappers became the de facto owners of the land they occupied and worked. Although they may have had limited knowledge of agriculture and cattle raising, many of them slowly incorporated these systems into their livelihood strategies; however, they remained dedicated primarily to forest extractivism. It is likely that with the continued decline of rubber prices, many would have adapted to the structural constraints of the post-*seringal*, and increased these activities with time, but the encroachment of migrants onto rubber-tapper lands that began in the 1970s diverted their path again.

Forced to defend their lands and their homes, the rubber tappers first rallied around their class-based identities as small-scale rural producers. In a context facilitated by international environmental concerns and assisted by collaboration with international environmentalists, they hybridized their class-based discourse with emerging environmental and social justice agendas (Keck 1995; Cowell 1990). As a result of the rubber-tapper social movement, their lands were protected with the establishment of the RESEX, but they were also linked inextricably with forest extractivism and a forest-guardian identity.

Although cattle raising is on the rise in the RESEX, it is still markedly less present than in the settlement projects. Importantly, it is on the fringes of the RESEX, abutting the settlement projects, that the majority of cattle-driven deforestation has occurred (Gomes 2009). The marked difference between the RESEX and the settlement project highlights the importance of the land-tenure system in structuring practice in institutionally defined ways, while the fringe deforestation in the RESEX shows the influence of social groups across institutional boundaries. When viewed in tandem with the uniformity of migrant and former tapper practices in the settlement project, these data illustrate that the tenure area structures economic practices in important ways and has a greater influence than group-specific cultural considerations.

CONCLUSION

The shift to cattle has had different consequences for smallholder groups based on the distinct ways that the relationship between identity and practice is perceived internally and externally. For rural groups, the relationship may be flexible, and more broadly defined in terms of social and historical considerations. External perceptions, however, may be more rigid in their expectations that practices are consistent with purported identities, especially around forms of economic practice that were institutionalized in land-tenure systems and have political consequences. The strict external definitions of an identity–practice link have an effect on rubber-tapper practices, just as laws and regulations do. Rubber-tapper cattle raising is significant on symbolic and political levels, and the shift to cattle threatens to undermine use-based conservation initiatives.

It is often asserted that identity mediates the ways that groups respond to an evolving political economy. The rubber-tapper mobilization against ranchers clearly demonstrated such a dynamic, a case of agency in the face of structure. To what extent does a sense of shared identity now influence how the rubber tappers respond to structures that overwhelmingly favor cattle raising? Identity, practice, and structure are always in a dialectical relationship. Structures come together in unique ways to create an environment in which ecology is secondary to the way it is constituted politically and socially through laws, norms, and even essentialized external notions of identity. In the settlement project, this "environment" produced constraints in such a way as to lead to a uniformity of practice, despite the fact that cultural differences remained between migrants and former tappers.

CHAPTER 9

THE APPROPRIATION OF CATTLE CULTURE:
PERCEPTIONS, BEHAVIORS, AND
METHODOLOGICAL CONSIDERATIONS

AFTER A YEAR OF FIELDWORK I understood how the various pieces of cattle culture fit together into an overarching system of thought and action. What I wanted to know next was the extent to which aspects of cattle culture had been appropriated throughout Acrean society. For example, many ranchers and cowboys expressed the opinions that pastures were associated with hard work, and that leaving the forest intact was a sign of laziness. Was this belief widespread among the ranchers, or only among some of the more outspoken members of this diverse social group? I assumed that environmentalists would reject such statements, but perhaps I was confusing their overall disdain for cattle culture with perceptions of human–environment relations that everyone shared. Did the fact that I never saw anyone clomping down the hallway of the WWF in cowboy boots mean that they ate less beef, or that they were not fans of *sertaneja* music?

My participant observation, interviews, and survey had provided a wealth of information, but I wanted to collect data that would allow me to systematically compare groups in terms of their agreement with cattle-culture perceptions and their participation in its practices. I use cultural-consensus modeling to examine the extent to which groups agree with fundamental precepts of cattle culture. I then compare data from the perceptual and the behavioral realms to reveal the unique and contradictory ways in which different groups have appropriated cattle culture.

Such material, of course, means little in the absence of an ethnographic knowledge of the people and their setting with which to explain it. I analyze my results here in relation both to structural constraints and to distinctive group-level characteristics such as class, ideology, and access. A mixed quantitative and qualitative approach to methods and analysis (Bernard 2012) is especially important for research such as this, seeking as it does to communicate anthropological results to audiences working toward a better understanding of environmental issues (see Charnley and Durham 2010). In this chapter I discuss my results in relation to methodological considerations.

THE DOMAIN OF CATTLE CULTURE

After a year of fieldwork I began compiling a list of values and behaviors indicative or related to the cultural domain "cattle culture," which is not a unified concept. I chose this as an umbrella term because it avoids some of the regional and historical specificity of other such expressions, including "cowboy culture" (Dary 1981; Slatta 1990) and the "cattle complex" of East Africa (Herskovits 1926) and the Americas (Strickon 1965). Rifkin (1993) used the term "cattle culture" in his popular nonfiction book on human–cattle history and the contemporary beef industry. My conceptualization of cattle culture shares with these works an emphasis on a generalized cultural valorization of cattle and/or the characteristics associated with cattle-raising peoples.

My definition of cattle culture is derived from the statements and behaviors of people living in the Amazon, which differ substantively from those of other regional traditions, particularly in relation to local ecology. Here the preference for cattle raising is often framed in opposition to the forest as a space of nature. This positive = cattle/ negative = forest opposition is reflected in each of the following five themes:

1. *perceptions of practice*: the belief that raising cattle is the best way to use the land, socially (gives status) and economically (brings profit) (compared to other forms of land use, especially forest-based activity);
2. *perceptions of social groups*: the ascription of positive social attributes to people or groups who raise cattle, especially as compared to those who practice agriculture or extractivism;
3. *cattle-culture participation*: valorization of a cattle-based lifestyle through popular fashion and activities related to cattle (there is not a popular culture forest analog in Acre);
4. *beef consumption and perceptions*: frequent consumption of beef and belief in the positive social and symbolic meanings associated

with it, especially in relation to other foods and vegetarian-
ism; and

5. *human–nature interaction*: raising cattle is a preferable form of
   relating and interacting with nature, and is expressed through
   practices and a lifestyle that show human control of nature in the
   form of cattle-centered pasture or, more generally, any anthropogenic space that is not the forest.

I created a list of statements indicative of cattle culture in each of
these five areas. I next consulted with key informants in Acre, Amazonian specialists, and experts in cultural consensus in an effort to
refine my questions until I had confidence that my conceptualization
of cattle culture had construct validity (Handwerker 2002). My final
questionnaire consisted of seventy-one questions, with at least nine
questions in each area.[1]

CULTURAL-CONSENSUS MODELING

Cultural-consensus theory (CCT) is a collection of analytical techniques and models that can be used to measure cultural beliefs and
the degree to which individuals recognize or report those beliefs. A
comparison of the responses of individuals and the aggregate results
from the group can be used to estimate how well each individual corresponds to the group (Weller 2007:339). There are three assumptions
in CCT: (1) each informant answers questions independently of other
informants; (2) questions should all be on the same topic and have
the same level of difficulty; and (3) the method can only be utilized
if there is a single set of culturally defined answers to the questions
(in other words, there must be a high level of agreement in responses)
(Romney et al. 1986; Weller 2007:340).

The application of CCT is known as cultural-consensus modeling
(CCM) (Romney et al. 1986). Studies have empirically demonstrated
the ability of CCM to advance our knowledge of inter- and intra-
cultural differences and to complement traditional ethnographic approaches (e.g., Chavez et al. 1995; Dressler et al. 1996; Gravlee 2005).[2]

1. Intrigued by a possible association between the domination of nature and
authoritarianism, I also added two questions that would measure authoritarian
tendencies.
2. Examples of research employing CCM illustrate how the method functions and how resulting data are interpreted. In a study by Chavez and colleagues
(1995), the researchers asked respondents to rank the importance of risk factors

Critics of consensus modeling assert that it sacrifices intercultural variation in the search of an ideal informant (Aunger 1999).

I use CCM here as a tool to complement but not replace my ethnographic and qualitative research, because it allows me to determine the distribution of cattle-culture perceptions across diverse sectors of Acrean society. If my objective was to be able to say that there is consensus on cattle culture, I would not have included NGO workers and policy makers, many of whom found cattle culture to be reprehensible—I assumed.

In the formal model of CCM used for this analysis, it is necessary to include only responses that measure agreement with the cultural domain, and responses must be coded as dichotomous variables (Weller 2007). For example, the question "Does cattle raising give a person status?" measures agreement with a cultural domain, whereas "Do you wear boots?" measures a personal attribute. In the final count, the cultural consensus analysis thus includes thirty-nine questions and statements that measured agreement with the cultural domain of cattle culture; respondents had to answer either "yes" or "no." The survey also included eleven word associations. These measured cultural attributes, but did not follow the yes/no format, and so do not enter into the consensus analysis. Responses for these thirty-nine items were entered into UCINET 6 (Borgatti, Everett, and Freeman 2002) to determine overall and group-level consensus scores.

The number of informants per group needed to establish consensus depends on the strength of the cultural domain (Weller 2007). For example, if I were searching for consensus on the names of the months of the year or the days of the week, very few informants would be required to gain the correct responses. More informants are needed to learn the names of ethnic and racial groups. In an exploratory study, the strength of the domain is not known until the data have been analyzed, but having twenty respondents in each hypothesized group or subgroup was sufficient, according to consensus theory, to detect

---

for cervical and breast cancer. Using CCM, the researchers were able to measure shared cultural knowledge. Their results demonstrated that different groups (e.g., Chicana and Caucasian women) achieved specific levels of agreement on the elements of a cultural domain, or agreed on a cultural model, and the extent to which different groups shared similar features of other groups' cultural models. In a study of racial classification systems in Puerto Rico, Gravlee was able to "verify the existence and location of cultural boundaries and to justify the assumption of shared culture" (2005:962).

Table 9.1. Summary of mean scores for
competence in cattle culture, by social group

Social Group	Competence Mean
Cowboys	0.653
Policy makers	0.608
Colonists	0.595
Rubber tappers	0.593
NGOs	0.588
Ranchers	0.552

$F = 1.63$, $p = 0.16$.

the presence of a single cultural domain if it exists (Weller 2007). As mentioned throughout the earlier chapters, my sample consisted of twenty respondents for each of six groups, chosen by purposive sampling techniques (Bernard 2000:176).

Prior to conducting this analysis, I expected high cultural competence scores regarding the domain of cattle culture from (in anticipated order): cowboys, ranchers, and colonists. I expected rubber tappers to score lower in this broad category, but to nonetheless demonstrate some agreement with it. I thought that the policy group, with its diverse individuals, would be split, and that the NGO group would clearly reject cattle culture.

To my surprise, there was overall consensus on the domain of cattle culture (table 9.1). The ratio of the first eigenvalue to the second is used to determine if there is one set of answers present in the data, i.e., if there is cultural consensus. A standard assumption is that a ratio of greater than 3 to 1 indicates consensus (Weller 2007:346); analysis of competence scores in UCINET in fact indicated a ratio of greater than 3 to 1 for each group and for the entire sample. The difference between the competence mean of the highest- and lowest-scoring groups was only 0.101. It was also expected that there would be significant differences between the groups, but a one-way ANOVA (analysis of variance) confirmed that there was in fact no statistically significant difference among them. Appendix C shows the results for the entire survey, with a breakdown by group and question. The results are divided into three categories: strong, moderate, and low agreement.

METHODOLOGICAL CONSIDERATIONS

EXPERIENCE, IDEOLOGY, AND TRUTH

Figure 9.1 shows the distribution of competence scores within groups. It illustrates that although the overall group scores are similar, the internal cohesion of the groups varies. The policy makers in particular have a much wider range of scores than rural groups. Although there was consensus, it is instructive to look more closely at differences between groups. Here I discuss a handful of methodological and applied themes, largely in the category of human–environment interactions. At least 85 percent of the members of the rural social groups agreed that cattle raising was the most profitable way to use the land, but only around half of policy maker/NGO groups agreed. This survey was designed to capture agreement with the domain, but on this question, it appears that some groups are functioning in a different domain, bringing to light questions of epistemology, methodology, and cultural knowledge.

The lived experience of rural groups persuades them that as opportunities and constraints are currently structured, cattle raising is the most profitable way to use the land. Conversely, the policy maker/NGO groups were always hesitant to agree with such black-and-white

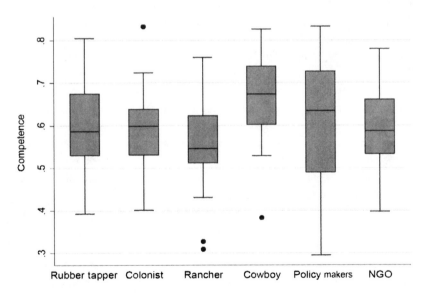

FIGURE 9.1. Competence range scores, by social group

statements, and almost universally began their responses with "It depends . . ." When they were forced to give a "yes" or "no" answer,
there was a 50/50 split in their responses to this question.

The reluctance of the policy maker/NGO groups to agree with
positive evaluations of cattle raising is related to three factors. First,
many policy maker/NGO respondents calculated "profitability" not
in terms of immediate economic returns, but by a more complex matrix that included economic and environmental sustainability. Cattle
raising may be profitable now, they said, but the pastures will become
degraded eventually, and profits will diminish. To them, agroforestry
and forest management scenarios would be more "profitable" in the
long run.

Policy maker/NGO responses also show the importance of both access to knowledge and ideological leanings. These groups are better
informed on alternatives to cattle raising that may be more profitable,
but which remain largely outside the knowledge, experience, or realm
of possibility of rural social groups. Third, it was painful for some policy makers in the "forest government," and for all of the NGOs workers, who are dedicated to environmental conservation and sustainable
livelihoods, to agree with positive statements about cattle raising.

Some of the statements from the human–nature interaction category reveal further differences between the rural and policy maker/
NGO groups (table 9.2). Item 1 asked respondents to agree or disagree
with the statement "It is dangerous to have forest close to the house."
About 61 percent of the members of the four rural groups agreed with
this statement, compared to 18 percent of the policy maker/NGO
groups. Item 2 states, "Pasture around the house is better than forest"; it received agreement from 70 percent of the rural groups but a
very low percentage of the policy maker and NGO group members.

The fact that the two groups who live in closest proximity to the
forest (rubber tappers and colonists) agree with these statements suggests that this statement is "true" according to those with more
knowledge of this topic. The data here and other results discussed
previously show that the policy maker and NGO groups are the most
coherent in their perceptions of questions related to the environment. While their values may match the rubber-tapper ideal, they do
not match the reality of forest life. That their responses contradict
those of rural groups, whose responses are based on the material realities of those environments, suggests that the policy maker/NGO
groups are at times guided by an ideology that is disconnected from
experiences of rural groups.

Table 9.2. Agreement with statements about forest–home proximity, by social group

Statement	Social Group						
	RTs[a]	Colonists	Ranchers	Cowboys	PMs[a]	NGOs	Overall
1. It is dangerous to have forest close to the house.	85%	65%	40%	55%	20%	16%	47%
2. Pasture around the house is better than forest.	85%	60%	70%	65%	20%	0%	50%

[a]RTs = rubber tappers; PMs = policy makers.

CULTURALLY TRUE OR POLITICALLY CORRECT?

I placed statements throughout the questionnaire that addressed similar subjects but were worded differently. For example, one asked whether a "rubber tapper lacks the will to work (*falta coragem de trabalhar*)" (table 9.3). Another asked the same question, but with the word "rubber tapper" replaced by "person who lives in the forest."

All social groups exhibited low levels of agreement when the question mentioned the rubber tapper. However, for the "person" the agreement jumps to between 60 and 75 percent among cowboys, rubber tappers, and colonists. The NGO, policy maker, and rancher groups responded in nearly the same way to these two similar questions.

NGO and policy maker groups do not agree with the underlying meaning of this question (that forest-dwellers are lazy). This was not the case for the ranchers; they detected the underlying semantic content of the questions and chose the politically correct response. Many ranchers did indeed say this sort of thing in conversations among themselves, as did colonists and cowboys.[3]

3. There is another possible explanation: groups' perceptions of the "forest," the "forest dweller," and the "rubber tapper" differ. Most people know that the rubber tapper lives in the "forest," i.e., as a defined geographical and ecological territory or space, but not actually *in* the forest, i.e., beneath the canopy. They know that the rubber tapper is surrounded by the forest, but that he carves out an anthropogenic space within the forest. Conversely, this "person who lives in the

Table 9.3. Agreement with statements about work ideology, by social group

	Social Group						
Statement	RTs[a]	Colonists	Ranchers	Cowboys	PMs[a]	NGOs	Overall
1. A rubber tapper lacks the will to work.	10%	25%	20%	10%	5%	0%	12%
2. A person who lives in the forest lacks the will to work.	74%	60%	20%	75%	5%	5%	40%

[a]RTs = rubber tappers; PMs = policy makers.

Different methods elicit different data, as I learned early on when I asked people if I could record our conversations. I stopped recording because people responded to my questions in a terse and guarded way while the recorder was on. They searched for responses that they thought would be most acceptable or "correct" to me, an outsider and perceived environmentalist, especially on controversial topics, such as deforestation, rubber tappers, and the government.

Cultural-consensus modeling can capture the majority of agreement among respondents, and give a researcher a general feel for the cultural domain. Controversial questions, however, may not elicit the "true" or "culturally correct" responses, but rather yield the "politically correct" responses. This is further evidence that formal methods (surveys) and quantitative data analysis (i.e., CCM) should be combined with traditional ethnographic methods and analysis to gain a balanced understanding of cultural phenomena.

CATTLE CULTURE PARTICIPATION AND PERCEPTIONS

Given my interest in connecting practices in the material world and cultural constructions, I now compare measures of cattle-culture

---

forest" had no social history or point of reference in the respondents' minds. They might have imagined a hermit of sorts, who could be considered lazy if he did not demonstrate observable separation between his home and the forest.

perceptions and participation among the groups surveyed. A comparison of agreement scores, which measure cultural data, with personal attribute data opens up new lines of inquiry. First, how does a group's degree of participation relate to their perceptions of cattle culture? Second, how do cattle-raising practices relate to the extent to which groups subscribe to and participate in cattle culture?

It seemed absurd to imagine someone working at the WWF or the Ministry of the Environment settling into bed to watch the late-night cattle auctions on TV, but I felt that it was important to understand to what extent cattle-culture activities and practices were actually distributed throughout Acrean society. Asking these questions of my environmentalist respondents enabled me to interrogate some of my assumptions. It also forced me to see the explanations for the high numbers of rubber tappers wearing cowboy boots, and to explain different features in relation to the complex social, political, economic, and geographical environment in which each group operated. Boots could be meaningful, but they could also be functional; for some, they could signify agency or reflect structural constraints.

My final list of cattle-culture activities included twenty-one activities or personal attributes, grouped according to five themes: (1) beef consumption (n = 4 questions); (2) wearing contri-, cattle-, or rodeo-themed clothing (n = 4); (3) participation in a cattle-based lifestyle (n = 3); (4) watching/listening to cattle culture–themed programming or music on TV/radio (n = 4); (5) participation in popular cultural events (n = 6). I focus here on seventeen questions from participation categories 2–5, excluding the beef category, which I discussed in detail in chapter 7. These questions were administered to members of the same groups as a part of the survey discussed above.

PARTICIPATION IN CATTLE CULTURE: QUESTIONS OF ACCESS, NOT IDEOLOGY

Table 9.4 summarizes reported group participation in activities in which cattle culture is valorized. The colonists, ranchers, and cowboys I interviewed all listened to sertaneja music, on either the radio or their own CDs or digital music. Battery-powered radios were much more common than televisions among the rubber tappers, 90 percent of whom reported listening to sertaneja music. Questions involving TV/radio, particularly the sertaneja and horse auction programs, and contri dress revealed strong links to cattle culture among the rural

Table 9.4. Reported participation in activities linked with cattle culture, by social group

Activity	RTs[a]	Colonists	Ranchers	Cowboys	PMs[a]	NGOs
			Social Group			
Listening to *sertaneja* music	90%	95%	95%	95%	70%	25%
Dancing to *sertaneja* music	15%	50%	45%	75%	35%	10%
Going to Expo-Acre	15%	20%	80%	85%	70%	35%
Going to rodeos	50%	85%	65%	100%	50%	20%

[a]RTs = rubber tappers; PMs = policy makers.

groups, while these queries were often met with laughter by NGO workers. They considered partaking in these activities to be in complete opposition to their identities as environmentalists and, also, as educated, "cultured" people. Those who chose these forms of expression were associated with a lack of taste and/or culture. One NGO worker referred to *sertaneja* music as *bestaneja* (*besta* means stupid) because listening to it "makes you *besta*."

Very few tappers or NGOs watched the late-night horse auctions that some rural families enjoyed. For the tappers, this likely reflects a material limitation more than a question of intentionally abstaining from certain activities, as is the case with NGO workers. The table reveals that around half of the colonists, ranchers, and cowboys danced to *sertaneja* music. Around a third of policy makers, and only 15 percent of rubber tappers and 10 percent of NGO workers, admitted to dancing to this music. Across groups, listening to *sertaneja* was more common than dancing to it, confirming that there is a range of ways to consume or participate in the same medium, from relatively passive to active.

Attendance at Expo-Acre shows differences again in terms of access, but this time extends to the colonists, who live at least around

300 kilometers from Rio Branco, where these events occur, and other groups, who live closer. For the first time, colonists are not among the highest percentages. Cowboys, who may live just as far away, often travel to these events with the ranchers who employ them. The 70 percent of policy makers who report attending Expo-Acre may do so either for recreation or because they are required to go as government employees. Most NGO workers dislike going to Expo-Acre, but may also be required to go by their job.

With the exception of NGO workers, at least half of each group attends rodeos. Distance was not an issue for colonists and rubber tappers because a number of rodeos have been created along the sides of the highways of rural Acre over the past few years. These rodeos form part of a statewide circuit, and people from local communities sometimes compete in them. Conversely, ranchers and policy makers attend national-level rodeos in the capital of Rio Branco, and usually only do so during Expo-Acre.

Overall, these findings reflect the ways in which the same cattle-culture activities take place in very different social contexts, and how participation in them can be related to access, class, ideology, and even employment.

Those rural groups who work most closely with cattle, the cowboys, participated in the greatest number of cattle-culture activities, followed by the other cattle-dependent groups: colonists, ranchers, and rubber tappers. Distinctions emerged in relation to social class, as wealthy ranchers sometimes reject certain features of cattle culture that they associate with the working class. Interestingly, rural smallholders and cowboys often linked themselves with cattle culture as part of their rural identity and as a form of class aspiration.

To what extent is participation related to perceptions? This measure is the sum of the activities for which members of each group indicated participation, divided by the total number of participation items. Figure 9.2 compares group perceptions (mean competence scores) with levels of participation.

The graph illustrates the relationship between what people do and how they think with regard to cattle culture, especially for cowboys. They are the cultural "experts" on the domain in terms of practices and values. This is encouraging because the cowboys, the face of cattle culture, should be the most knowledgeable and active in this domain. There is also great consistency across categories for the colonists, who rank either second or third in each category, and the

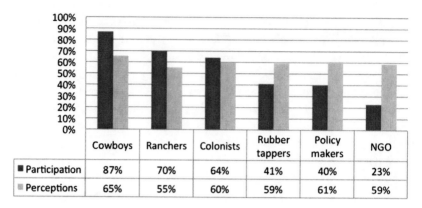

	Cowboys	Ranchers	Colonists	Rubber tappers	Policy makers	NGO
■ Participation	87%	70%	64%	41%	40%	23%
▨ Perceptions	65%	55%	60%	59%	61%	59%

FIGURE 9.2. Cattle-culture perception and participation, by social group

rubber tappers, who ranked fourth across the board. The graph shows that different groups perceive the cultural domain of cattle in basically the same way, but that they vary a great deal in terms of their participation.

Before I administered this survey, I had conducted a year of fieldwork and formed a general sense of the extent to which each group had appropriated (participation and perceptions) cattle culture. My ranking for the groups would have been similar for the participation measures, descending from cowboys to NGO workers in terms of both perception and participation. I could never have imagined that measurements of perception would indicate that groups agreed so much on the cultural domain, but the relationships revealed in the participation measures conform to my ethnographic expectations.

CONCLUSION

Survey data have established that there is overall consensus on the cultural domain of cattle culture, and no significant difference between groups in terms of their agreement with its ideals and values. Other forms of analysis revealed more about the similarities and difference between groups with regard to cattle culture; different factors, such as class, ideology, access, and employment, affect the ways that people participate in cattle culture.

The comparisons presented here have provided some clarity, but new questions have also emerged. Did I measure participation in cattle culture or in Brazilian or Acrean culture? To what extent do people consider what they are doing to be representative of cattle culture? Does a rubber tapper "choose" cowboy boots to the same extent that an NGO worker does? Are they even seeing the same object, or does functionality or other material quality in some way make it less meaningful to those who don't have a choice? My survey results showed me who wore boots, but my ethnographic research helped me interpret those results and move toward a fuller understanding of a complex reality in which a boot can be functional and meaningful; it can reflect class, ideology, or the fact that it is the only form of footwear available.

It would not have been possible to create this survey and conduct this analysis without an investment in ethnographic research that could establish the content and boundaries of this cultural domain, and then create appropriate measures of behavior and perception. Yet ethnographic methods alone do not provide a systematic comparison, and using them in concert with quantitative approaches provides another means of analysis.

Using mixed methods has enabled us to see to what extent different groups agree with one another, and thus understand to what extent cultural constructions surrounding cattle are shared across groups. In a context where the shift to cattle raising has not been fully reflected in group social identities, comparing group perceptions can help us to see the permeability of supposed boundaries between groups, and understand in what ways groups are different.

CHAPTER 10

THE FULL PICTURE

CATTLE ARE VISIBLE OVER the course of human history, "from the first archeological records, dating back to the Lascaux caves, to the assassination of Chico Mendez [sic] in the Amazon rainforests" (Rifkin 1992:3). The cow is the subject of political and economic structures, the vehicle to a better life, a source of sustenance, a status symbol, and the "eater of the forest." In this book I have "looked to the cow" in an attempt to better understand Amazonian cattle raising in the beginning of the twenty-first century. Whereas Evans-Pritchard found a depth of commitment to cattle pervading all aspects of Nuer social life, I found a range of recently formed behaviors and practices that were shared but also contested.

This animal appears in painted murals on the walls of bars and shops, and its skin holds up the cowboy's pants and covers his feet. Its milk has replaced the *leite* of the rubber tree, and the forested lands once measured in *pes* (feet) of rubber trees are now pastures valued for the heads per hectare they are able to sustain. Acreans say that the "hoof of the bull" opened Amazonia. I merely followed its tracks across group boundaries and attempted to locate it between economy and culture, between development and longing, and between the city and the forest. I have been able to draw out linkages and connections previously undetected in communities and even within the state of Acre, as I traced structures across scale and paths of diffusion. I have compared perceptions and practices of groups that I assumed to be very different, and found surprising similarities among them. Now, after building chapter by chapter, we can finally see how the pieces fit together, forming a detailed picture of Amazonian cattle raising.

Cattle are unrivaled in their unique ability to convert inedible vegetation into human food and products. They can be sold to provide income in times of need, and serve to store and reproduce wealth in good times—and they provide support throughout by their milk or muscle power. Such attributes are especially attractive to isolated groups, namely, the rubber tappers. Their agricultural and forest products cannot match this combination of value and flexibility, and when such items are to be sold, they usually have to be transported on the backs of oxen or horses.

The material value of cattle contributes to the strong cultural constructions that surround them across the world. Regardless of the region or the actual product—be it beef or bridewealth—the ecological and economic relationships between cattle and humans in subsistence settings inevitably give rise to intricate ties and celebrations of this bond, as seen in East Africa, India, and now Acre. The Acrean case shows that these forms of cultural expression can emerge in a relatively short time even among populations previously displaced or threatened by cattle raising.

The economic and cultural value of cattle is amplified by the current political and economic context in Acre. Other rural livelihoods are noncompetitive with cattle, especially in light of the transition from a period of land conflict to a situation in which social group boundaries first were clearly established and then became permeable, with all groups now participating and collaborating to some extent in the cattle industry. The ranchers brought the seeds of the cattle industry to the area, and they remain the richest and most powerful people in the countryside. Contemporary narratives of upward mobility focus on the reproductive capacity of cattle and how, unlike the case with agriculture and extractivism, a person can go from one cow to a big herd to buying more land to eventually becoming the rancher. Although the cowboy is the symbol of popular culture, the rancher embodies the *vida boa* (good life) in the countryside. The dream of owning land and cattle even pulls in judges, doctors, and other urban professionals, as well as urbanites displaced from the forest or drawn to the city.

Among the members of the rural groups I surveyed, a forest-based existence is strongly associated with poverty and other negative social qualities, which in fact are diametrically opposed to those surrounding cattle raising, such as progress, development, and wealth. These positive ideals have grown out of rural experiences and built on long-standing beliefs surrounding the nature–culture divide. Core Western ideals that place value on progress through the transformation of nature have been reinforced by developmentalist policies and religion. Negative characterizations of "stone age" forest-dwelling populations show the persistence of these ideals of transforming the forest wilderness into cultivated space. This transformation provides the owners food and perhaps wealth and, more important, also links them with positive ideals of "work" and bringing nature into the service of humanity. Maintaining the clear separation between one's home and the natural world is considered most desirable—from the dirt yards surrounding rural houses to the tiled yards and manicured lawns of the city.

The economic and social appeal of cattle is further bolstered by the growth of popular cultural expressions throughout the countryside and in the cities in such forms as rodeos, music, and *contri* dress. All of these forms, often built into traditional festivals and events, celebrate a cattle-based lifestyle over others, especially forest extractivism. Cattle culture has been further reinforced by the growth of an imported cultural model that blends rural ideas and practices into a recognizable expression of rural identity—the cowboy. As one rubber tapper put it, "The cowboy has his buckle and his boots. He has a costume. What would be the rubber tapper's costume? Tattered clothing!" This comment underscores the formidable challenge that the rubber tappers, the forest government, and other advocates of use-based conservation face—how to create economic value and cultural appreciation for a forest-based life. While the government and NGOs have sponsored projects, monuments, and museums to celebrate Acre's forest heritage, these attempts to valorize forest livelihoods and culture have not transitioned into popular cultural expressions.

Despite the increasing awareness of the importance of maintaining the forest, rural groups continue to be viewed with approval for their ability to clearly distinguish themselves from the forest through the establishment of "clean" pastures and cultivated spaces that show the separation of nature and culture.

In the cattle-culture conceptualization of human–nature relationships, humans are not only separate from nature, but they also seek to assert their dominance over nature by creating pastures, herding cattle, and eating their flesh for strength. Each of these features of the ranching mode of production is celebrated symbolically by cowboy clothing, *churrascos*, and rodeos events, particularly bull riding. This cattle-centered life is also recreated symbolically in the city, adding to its cultural appeal and providing a material foundation for rural cattle raising through beef consumption.

These positive social attributes arise from an idealized view of rural life that derives much of its meaning by framing itself in relation to that which it is not: the hustle and bustle, economic exploitation, and social fragmentation of the city. Many urbanites seek to cross the divide between nature and culture, but these boundaries also have temporal and spatial features. They long for a golden age of sorts, located someplace between "stone age" life in the forest and the decadence of the city.

Acreans regard the present in a number of different ways, but for those searching for this type of rural–urban reconciliation, cattle culture is the sole avenue for expressing a rural identity that is regionally, nationally, and internationally recognized. In contrast to the feckless and folkloric *caipira*, the cowboy is an assertive rural actor who is widely recognized throughout Brazil and North America. This idealization of the *peão* (peon) obscures the fact that these cow-less cowboys are not free to wander. This sense of connection and pride is appealing to those at the margins of Brazilian popular culture, in the rural areas, and even more so to Acreans, who are living at the "end of the world." By embracing cattle culture, urban populations connect with an idealized countryside and traditional beliefs that serve as a shield against urban decadence. While *florestania* is attempting to nurture a love and respect for forest life and culture, it does not have the historical, economic, and cultural foundations in popular culture that make cattle culture appealing.

Those still in the countryside also long for a different time and place—one in which they did face hardships, but were essentially free to use their land as they wished. The current emphasis on forest preservation presents an affront to their deeply held ideals of work and self-sufficiency. Deforestation regulations, and the lack of viable and proven support for other livelihoods, have strengthened resentment toward the government. Also blamed are *ecologistas* and urban "poets," who are disconnected from rural realities and have been made soft by the city. These extreme urbanites seek to maintain some "butterflies and monkeys" while rural people are forced to leave the country because they cannot use the land to provide for themselves.

Such resentment, once again, finds expression in cattle culture: in its disdain for urbanism, "don't fence me in" rhetoric, emphasis on autonomy and self-reliance, and idealization of a rural life that only exists for an individual once removed from it, or in *contri* and *sertaneja* songs. Cattle culture builds on the actual experiences and perceptions of Acreans as well as imported popular forms, and it is now becoming difficult to distinguish cattle culture from Acrean culture.

The way that economic, symbolic, perceptual, and structural components come together is revealed through beef. To raise beef, one must clear the forest and create pastures, which are worth more than the forest on the land market. These pastures are also judged positively as evidence of work, and of engaging nature in a way that is favorable in comparison with leaving the forest intact, which for many denotes laziness. With pasture, one is able to raise cattle, make more money, and participate in the "development" and "progress" that eventually lead to the "good life."

The material transformations taking place in the countryside are integrally linked to urban processes, specifically beef consumption. Beef consumption in Acre is the highest in Brazil, and 40 percent of the beef produced in its rural fields stays within the state. It is consumed by urban groups, such as NGO workers and policy makers, who eat it nearly four days a week. The decision to eat beef, regardless of one's ideology, provides another material foundation for cattle raising in the countryside, and also contributes to the growth of cattle culture by valorizing a cattle-based livelihood and the positive perceptions that surround it.

Beef is thought by many Acreans, especially those who engage in manual labor, to provide more strength to work, a process most clearly demonstrated through observable impacts on the material world. Eating beef is also an indicator of social class. Thus, there is a similar process of "development" occurring in the cities: beef fuels work, resulting in development (socioeconomic advancement), a process that is signified by the foods that one eats. These beliefs are held by both rural and urban working-class populations, reflecting a common thread of landscape transformation, development, and the ascription of positive social ideals through a process beginning with beef, be it through rural production or its urban consumption.

The conversations that occur while men roast meat over a fire map onto a system of thought in which humans capture strength through the appropriation of animal flesh. Yet, like other features of cattle culture, pleasure and affirmation are derived from doing so in a way that is traditional or even atavistic—standing in the open air, searing flesh on the fire, and perhaps talking about sex and humiliating each other. The payoff is the tender, *mal passada* (bloody, rare) *picanha* that is the ideal of *churrasco*. History sets the scene, as does the process of development, in towns of migrants and forest refugees whose standard of living is improving. It is the ability to connect with something more traditional that is no longer your life, and to do so in a way that inverts or temporarily suspends the oppressive conventions of the concrete jungle.

The search for sustainability requires finding methods for rubber tappers, colonists, and other rural peoples to make a living from their land in ways that balance environmental and economic concerns, but are also socially esteemed and culturally rewarding. As many in the forest government told me, achieving the ideals of the rubber-tapper movement means supporting forest livelihoods, and also trying to change the culture in which the forest and forest dwellers are viewed in a negative light. Changing our core perceptions is a formidable challenge, but it is likely to be more enduring and effective than cumbersome or coercive policy solutions. Cattle culture is but a recent expression of the thousands of years of ecological interactions that enabled humans to spread across the globe. The drama being played out in Acre is another chapter in the march of the West to "civilize the Indians," convert the forest to cultivated spaces, and progress, develop, and evolve. There is no equilibrium and certainly nothing resembling sustainability in the economic and ideological system that now proposes dichotomous preservation or market-based solutions. Moving toward sustainability requires that all reexamine the political, economic, and social evolutionary underpinnings of unequal accumulation, exaggerated consumption, and the hierarchical separation of the social and the natural.

I conducted field research in southern Acre, Brazil. Some ranches were located in Baixo Acre, lower Acre, which includes the capital city of Rio Branco, where I often met with key informants. These regions are named according to their location around the Acre River, which flows east from the city of Assis Brasil, on the Peruvian border, before passing through upper and then lower Acre. Upper Acre includes the municipalities of Assis Brasil and Brasiléia, where I conducted the majority of my research with colonists and rubber tappers.

Upper Acre covers 1,589,690 hectares, almost 10 percent of the state, and registers among the highest rates of anthropogenic disturbance in the state (Governo do Acre 2006). Lower Acre extends from the municipality of Capixaba to the Rio Branco to the north until reaching the borders of neighboring Rondônia and Amazonas. Lower Acre covers 13.55 percent of the state and 2,225,337 hectares (Governo do Acre 2006:100). The BR-317 highway, paved in 2002, runs the length of upper Acre, roughly following the course of the Acre River.

I chose to work primarily in the upper Acre region because of its history of land conflict surrounding cattle, the presence of all three social groups, and the rising popularity of cattle raising in the area. A number of suitable communities were identified based on the presence of various social groups, and the list was further narrowed by my ability to obtain governmental and community permission. I attempted to work with communities that were located in the same general area to limit differences in infrastructure, ecology, and access to markets and political resources. I accomplished this with respect to colonist and rubber-tapper communities, which were both located in the upper Acre region, between Brasiléia and Assis Brasil. Ranchers, however, because of their large, dispersed landholdings, did not constitute a sufficient sample in this area, although I did include those who were open to speaking with me. The majority of the ranchers I worked with lived in Rio Branco and owned ranches in either upper or lower Acre.

Acre is home to an estimated 14,451 indigenous Amazonians. There are none in the lower Acre region, except for a reported 271 individuals in the municipality of Assis Brasil (Governo do Acre 2006). I initially planned to include an indigenous community in my study, but this proved not to be feasible.

Each group is associated with a distinct land-tenure system. In order to demonstrate how groups are situated in relation to each other, I offer a schematic representation of social group spatial relationships (fig. A.1). The figure illustrates different social groups' landholdings in relation to each other within the research area. Groups have different-size landholdings, which vary from approximately eighty hectares (colonists) to three hundred hectares (rubber tappers), and around five thousand hectares for average ranchers. Rubber-tapper landholdings, the boundaries of which are determined by the distribution of rubber trees, are not uniform in their dimensions, and may overlap with those of their neighbors.

Figure A.1 also reveals the different levels of access to transportation among the groups. The BR-317 highway is passable throughout the year. Ranches are usu-

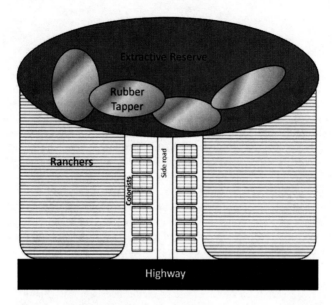

FIGURE A.1. Schematic diagram of social group spatial relationships

ally located near the highway. Colonists might also be located on the highway or farther up the unpaved side roads, which may not be passable by car during the rainy season. A side road might enter the extractive reserve, but most rubber-tapper households are accessible only by foot.

The rubber tappers in this sample live in the Chico Mendes Extractive Reserve (CMER), a sustainable-use conservation unit established in 1990, with a total territory of 930,203 hectares, or 5.66 percent of the state. Collectively, conservation units, including the extractive reserves (RESEX), and indigenous lands constitute over 45 percent of Acrean territory (Governo do Acre 2006:103).

I conducted research in two former *seringais*, or rubber estates, São Cristovão and Pindamonhangaba. After turning onto the *ramal* (unpaved side road) located at the 52-kilometer mark between Brasiléia and Assis Brasil, one passes through the landholdings of settlers from southern Brazil for about twenty-five kilometers before entering the CMER. The road penetrates into parts of São Cristovão, but not Pindamonhangaba, which is farther north. Rubber-tapper households are spread throughout the forest, close to their *colocações* (rubber holdings), which have socially defined boundaries within the community. Footpaths throughout the forest connect the rubber tappers to economically valuable rubber and Brazil nut trees and to the homes of their neighbors. Each family has about three hundred hectares of land, an amount that generally corresponds to three rubber trails.

I collected data over four separate seasons, from 2007 through 2010, during a total of eighteen months of fieldwork. In this appendix I will describe the primary methods I employed to collect data, the data collected, how data were analyzed, and how I have used the data to support my observations and conclusions.

The research area and social groups under study are described in appendix A. In addition to the rural spaces, inhabited by the three main social groups I worked with, I conducted research in the capital city of Rio Branco, where I interviewed key informants, policy makers, academics, and workers at socio-environmental NGOs. I also spent a great deal of time in Brasiléia, tracking commodities and relationships through interviews with family members who had moved to the city, and learning about regional history from governmental institutions.

PARTICIPANT OBSERVATION

My first two field seasons were primarily concerned with gaining an understanding of the economic and cultural roles of cattle in the lives of Acreans. I lived with rubber-tapper and colonist families for weeks at a time throughout the course of my fieldwork, which gave me an understanding of their lives and the context in which they make decisions. I participated in the daily productive lives of the residents, including tapping rubber, harvesting Brazil nuts, planting crops and clearing fields, and vaccinating and selling cattle. After these activities, back at their houses, we discussed the meaning, history, and functions of these practices. Living among the different groups, I saw the challenges that each faces, and the political and economic factors that most affect them. I also learned that although different people and households can be categorized as members of distinct social categories, there is a great deal of variation from household to household.

My experiences living with the families also revealed to me other important factors to be considered if I were to understand all economic and cultural aspects of cattle. I attended social events and rituals in which the cultural meanings of cattle took center stage, including *churrascos*, Expo-Acre (the state agricultural fair), and similar municipal-level events, as well as country music concerts and dances, and the annual *cavalgada* through Rio Branco to the fairgrounds to inaugurate Expo-Acre.

I also sought out places where cattle are valued economically and symbolically: agricultural supply stores, butcher shops, cattle auctions, country clothing stores, and country-themed bars and restaurants. Additionally, I analyzed the contents and messages of institutions/spaces that sought to articulate contrasting forest-based ideals, including the Museu da Borracha, the Museu dos Povos da Floresta, and the Biblioteca da Floresta. All represent attempts by the forest government to valorize forest-based citizenship (*florestania*). I also attended government events in which deforestation, burn bans, cattle raising, and rural issues were debated.

SURVEY ON HISTORY AND PERCEPTIONS OF CATTLE

In 2009 I conducted in-depth, semi-structured interviews with members of each social group (rubber tappers [n = 7], colonists [13], and large-scale ranchers [11]). The interviews covered their economic practices across time, the factors that caused them to change their practices, perceptions both of cattle and of their own and other social groups, and their relationships with other groups. These data gave me greater insights regarding the histories of each group, and the ways that they have been and continue to be affected by political and economic developments.

This survey also employed cognitive methods, specifically "pile sorts." I gave respondents cards representing "cattle/cattle raising," "agriculture," and "forest extractivism," and asked them which practices were most associated in their minds with words such as "poverty," "governmental support," and "progress." I also asked them to list characteristics of their own group and other groups, so that I might better understand their perceptions of themselves and others. I used these data to formulate my cattle survey, which I administered in 2010.

KEY-INFORMANT INTERVIEWS

I conducted key-informant interviews with functionaries and extension agents at governmental agencies, such as INCRA (Brazilian Institute for Colonization and Agrarian Reform), EMBRAPA (Brazilian Agricultural Research Corporation), SEAPROF (Secretariat for Agriculture and Family Production), SEMA (Secretariat of the Environment–Acre), IDAF (Institute for the Defense of Agro–Cattle Raising and the Environment), SEAP (Secretariat for Agro–Cattle Raising), IBAMA (Institute of Biodiversity and the Environment), and IMAC (Institute of the Environment–Acre). I also spoke with members of local NGOs: S.O.S. Amazonia, World Wildlife Fund (WWF), the Center for Amazonia Workers (CTA), the Group for Agro-Forestry Research of Acre (PESACRE), and the Pro-Indian Commission (CPI). Members of these institutions were included in my 2010 cattle-culture survey as "policy maker" and "NGO," respectively. I also spoke to private businesses that sell to rural producers, leaders of the rubber-tapper union, and the Federation of Agriculture, an interest group associated with the ranchers. These interviews revealed some of the broader processes at play, and the roles of institutions and their policies in the lives of rural social groups.

CATTLE-CULTURE QUESTIONNAIRE

Drawing on all of these experiences and data, I worked to identify the characteristics of the cultural domain of cattle culture. I searched the data for key themes related to or indicative of cattle culture, which I then divided into five categories. After consulting with key informants on the construct validity of my categories, I put together a questionnaire of seventy-one questions (see appendix C).

My sample consisted of twenty members from each of the following six groups: rubber tappers, colonists, ranchers, cowboys, people working at socio-environmental NGOs in Rio Branco (NGO), and policy makers (PM) working in governmental institutions focusing on rural issues in Rio Branco. The questions about participation were part of a survey that I administered in 2010, which also included a list of statements designed to measure agreement with perceptions associated with cattle culture (see chapter 9). The beef consumption category included one question on personal beef preferences and another on beef consumption, so these items do not fit neatly into this discussion of activities. Results from three additional urban surveys in different regions of Brazil (Rio Branco, Acre; Cerqueira Cesar, São Paulo; and Guaxupé, Minas Gerais) are not included in the analysis, but inform the discussion of cultural diffusion and rural/urban differences.

I analyzed thirty-nine questions dealing with cultural attributes using cultural-consensus analysis in the software program UCINET. A more detailed discussion of cultural-consensus analysis has been presented in chapter 9, where I also discuss the majority of the results, although data from this survey are employed throughout the book.

SURVEY OF COLONIST HOUSEHOLDS

I also draw on a survey of 266 colonist households conducted by myself and other members of an international research team studying the socioeconomic impacts of the BR-317 highway in 2008 and 2009. This was part of an NSF-HSD project entitled "Infrastructure Change, Human Agency, and Resilience in Social-Ecological Systems" (award number: 0527511; Stephen Perz, Principal Investigator). These interviews covered seven different communities that represent four different kinds of INCRA settlement models. This experience helped me to understand the general situation of colonists in southwestern Acre, and the differences between subregions and different types of settlement models. In chapter 8 I use data from one of the INCRA settlements, the Quixadá Directed Settlement Project, which was also my primary research site for research with colonists.

DRAWING OUT LINKS OF CATTLE CULTURE

In 2010 I attempted to draw out the origins of Acrean cattle culture by conducting research in traditional cattle-raising centers of Brazil. I traveled more than three thousand kilometers from São Paulo to Acre by land. I spent a week in small towns of Minas Gerais and São Paulo, areas where Acrean cattle culture originated, but which now are dedicated to agriculture (coffee and sugar cane, respectively). I was hosted by the families of Acrean ranchers who stayed behind in São Paulo and Minas Gerais, which gave me an understanding of the factors that had led some ranchers to Acre, the perspectives that they brought with them, and their family histories.

I also spent a week in the *pantanal*, the seasonal wetlands of central-western Brazil, and, with the assistance of the Brazilian Agricultural Research Corporation *pantanal* research station, I visited ranches and interviewed *pantaneiros* (cowboys of the *pantanal* region) and ranchers. I was also able to visit Argentina and Uruguay for a brief period in May 2010. Collectively, these experiences allowed me to trace some of the important origins and undercurrents of cattle culture, observe important regional cultural, historical, and economic differences in cattle economies and cultures, and draw out connections that otherwise I would have not have recognized in Acre.

"POSTCARDS FROM THE AMAZON"

From February through September 2010 I submitted a series of sixteen biweekly articles about Acre to the *San Angelo Standard-Times* newspaper. These accounts were designed to describe daily life in Acre to a foreign audience (my hometown). Topics were often related to my research, including profiles on the history and daily life of rubber tappers, colonists, and ranchers. I mention my writing these columns as a "method" because they provided valuable information, which is presented throughout the book.

Writing for the newspaper forced me to put my observations into a coherent form that could be understood by a non-academic audience, and to explore the foundations of issues that otherwise I might have taken for granted. The articles were published in print and online. I was surprised that some Acreans were alerted to my articles by Internet tags; their readings of my observations opened many new doors for discussion. The articles turned out to be useful in improving my rapport with the ranchers, who were initially distrustful of me as a foreign researcher. Once they saw that I was evaluating their situation critically, and searching for a characterization of them beyond the "villain" trope, my access to the ranchers increased considerably, although there were always issues of trust between us.

The knowledge that I was writing for diverse audiences forced me to come to grips with issues of representation, as I was often torn between essentialism and cultural relativism, the two opposing sides of a controversy, academic text and accessible story, and what I felt to be the "truth" and popular representation. Overall, not only was writing the columns a valuable method of data collection and cultural exchange, but the experience also forced me take a position as a researcher and find my authorial "voice."

I have incorporated some of the "Postcards" into the text, and these are differentiated in the chapters by format. My footnotes list their dates of original publication. These pieces provide additional context and depth for some members of the different social groups, and offer an interesting comparison between modes of academic and popular representation.

I here offer an illustration to aid in the interpretation of the results and clarify key concepts. In table C.1, I have included three statements showing distinct levels of agreement among members of each group and, in the far right column, the overall agreement across all respondents on the statement. Ideally there would be twenty members in each group responding to each statement, for a total sample of 120 respondents, but data are missing for some respondents on certain statements.

For item 1, we see extremely high agreement across groups. Only one individual, in the NGO group, in the entire survey did not agree that "if a person stops working, forest takes over the land." Averaging the responses of each group results in 99 percent overall agreement, or "high" overall agreement. In light of the near-universal agreement across this diverse sample, it is safe to assume that this statement is a cultural fact of life among Acreans.

It is important to remember that cultural-consensus analysis (CCA) measures agreement with the overall sample. By the precepts of CCA, the competence scores of those who agree with this statement will be boosted, raising the overall score of their group; the score of the one individual who disagreed with the majority will be lowered, as will the overall score of that person's group (in this case, NGO).

Item 2 is the statement eliciting the least agreement in my survey. Only 3 percent of the overall sample agrees with the statement posed, "Agriculturalists are rich around here." For this subject, I took a commonly uttered statement ("agriculturalists are poor") and reversed it, in order to set out a mix of positively and negatively worded questions as a means to reduce the effect of respondent bias. The results indicate that even when the meaning of the statement is reversed, a high percentage of respondents nonetheless agree with the underlying perspective.

The problem with this methodological step is that it does not give proof that the opposite statement is believed to be true ("agriculturalists are poor"), only that there is agreement that the false statement is, in fact, false. Despite this limitation, it is safe to assume that 97 percent of respondents agree that agriculturalists are not rich. For subjects on which there is high disagreement, or for which there is high agreement on negatively worded questions, I will reverse these figures and refer to them in terms of agreement in order to facilitate comparison. Thus, for item 2, there is 97 percent agreement (see the "adjusted" [adj.] column in tables C.2–C.4).

Item 3, inviting a true/false response to "Pasture around the house is better than forest," provides two pieces of information. First, there is no clear consensus on this statement, with 50 percent overall agreement and 50 percent disagreement. By requiring us to look closer at group-level responses, this item reveals that the overall results are not necessarily reflective of agreement within groups. Rural groups (rubber tappers, colonists, ranchers, and cowboys) all agreed with this statement at least 60 percent of the time. Conversely, no NGO members and

Table C.1. Levels of agreement with selected statements among social groups

	Social Group						
Statement	RTs[a]	Colonists	Ranchers	Cowboys	PMs[a]	NGOs	Overall
1. If a person stops working, forest takes over the land.	100%	100%	100%	100%	100%	95%	99%
2. Agriculturalists are rich around here.	5%	0%	0%	10%	0%	5%	3% [97%][b]
3. Pasture around the house is better than forest.	85%	60%	70%	65%	20%	0%	50%

[a]RTs = rubber tappers; PMs = policy makers.
[b]Inferred agreement with the contradictory statement (adjusted).

only 20 percent of policy makers agreed with the statement, bringing the overall average down and thus illustrating the ways in which groups differ in their perceptions.

Now that we have a good idea of the distribution of competence scores for each group, it is informative to compare group-level responses to individual questions. I discuss these data in terms of "agreement" (the percentage of a group agreeing or disagreeing with a statement) rather than "consensus" or "competence," terms derived specifically from CCM, although they basically measure the same relationships and trends. Examining group levels of agreement is useful because we can gain a better understanding of the similarities and differences between groups, beyond the fact that there was consensus. The findings presented in tables C.2, C.3, and C.4 represent the following distinct patterns: (1) strong agreement (more than 75 percent agreement) in each group (table C.2); (2) moderate agreement (more than 75 percent agreement for most groups, but less than 75 percent agreement for at least one group) (table C.2); and (3) lack of agreement (when at least one group is on the other side of the 50 percent agreement threshold) (table C.3).

Table C.2. Statements eliciting strong agreement across all social groups

| Statement | Percentage Agreeing, by Group | | | | | | |
	RTs[a]	Colonists	Ranchers	Cowboys	PMs[a]	NGOs	Total	Adj.
If a person stops working, forest takes over the land.	100%	100%	100%	100%	100%	95%	99%	99%
Agriculturalists are rich around here.	5%	0%	0%	10%	0%	5%	3%	97%
Ranchers can travel outside of Acre.	100%	95%	90%	100%	89%	100%	96%	96%
Most ranchers are black/mixed race.	0%	0%	5%	5%	15%	5%	5%	95%
It is not the dream of most Acreans to own land.	5%	5%	0%	5%	10%	5%	5%	95%
It is the dream of most Acreans to be a rubber tapper.	25%	5%	0%	5%	10%	0%	8%	93%
Raising cattle gives a person the good life.	95%	90%	100%	100%	80%	89%	92%	92%
Raising cattle gives a person social status.	90%	95%	85%	100%	90%	90%	92%	92%
It is the dream of most Acreans to own cattle.	95%	84%	95%	100%	85%	85%	91%	91%
Rubber tappers lack the will to work.	10%	25%	20%	10%	5%	0%	12%	88%

[a]RTs = rubber tappers; PMs = policy makers.

Table C.3. Statements eliciting moderate agreement across all social groups

Statement		RTs[a]	Colonists	Ranchers	Cowboys	PMs[a]	NGOs	Total	Adj.
	Percentage Agreeing, by Group								
Rubber tappers are the group that best preserves forest.		100%	95%	60%	100%	95%	95%	91%	91%
Government should never limit the voice of the people.		63%	94%	100%	95%	100%	90%	90%	90%
Agriculture has more tradition here than cattle raising.		30%	15%	0%	5%	5%	5%	10%	90%
It is healthy to live in the forest.		100%	90%	55%	90%	95%	95%	88%	88%
A person with a clean pasture is a hard worker.		95%	90%	100%	100%	85%	55%	88%	88%
Converting forest to pasture shows control over nature.		15%	10%	33%	26%	0%	10%	16%	84%
Prejudice against non-Acreans has decreased.		70%	85%	95%	85%	80%	68%	81%	81%
Rubber tappers have the good life.		11%	5%	5%	15%	42%	56%	22%	78%
Ranchers come from outside Acre.		100%	90%	58%	75%	70%	70%	77%	77%
Ranchers caused conflict in the past.		90%	70%	53%	55%	95%	100%	77%	77%
Extractivism is the way to better life for forest dwellers.		25%	20%	15%	25%	40%	40%	28%	73%
Agriculturalists are miserable (*coitados*).		40%	50%	45%	5%	10%	20%	28%	72%

[a]RTs = rubber tappers; PMs = policy makers.

Table C.4. Statements eliciting little agreement across all groups

| | Percentage Agreeing, by Group | | | | | | | |
Statement	RTs[a]	Colonists	Ranchers	Cowboys	PMs[a]	NGOs	Total	Adj.
A vegetarian can have good health.	85%	47%	50%	80%	82%	90%	72%	72%
Cattle raising is the most profitable way to use land.	85%	95%	90%	95%	50%	45%	77%	77%
Rubber tappers are more respected than ranchers.	35%	15%	58%	25%	10%	26%	28%	72%
Ranchers have calloused hands.	30%	70%	25%	10%	25%	20%	30%	70%
People who don't eat meat lack the will to work.	25%	55%	40%	55%	15%	0%	32%	68%
Rural people would rather live in the city.	20%	10%	80%	20%	55%	40%	38%	68%
A person who lives in the forest lacks the will to work.	74%	60%	20%	75%	5%	5%	40%	60%
The forest gives tappers everything they need.	70%	32%	15%	60%	20%	45%	40%	60%
Lunch with no meat leaves a person weak.	90%	70%	65%	75%	35%	15%	58%	58%
Lunch with no meat is not a real lunch.	55%	75%	70%	70%	60%	20%	58%	58%
Cowboys are more courageous than other rural workers.	55%	55%	30%	85%	25%	0%	42%	58%
The government makes it difficult for rural folk to make a living.	65%	70%	55%	30%	20%	17%	43%	57%
Tappers don't have a culture of cattle raising.	45%	45%	55%	65%	60%	70%	57%	57%
Beef gives more strength to work than other food does.	45%	70%	65%	100%	35%	20%	56%	56%
Women should not contradict a man in public.	40%	80%	47%	85%	40%	30%	54%	54%
It is dangerous to have forest close to the house.	85%	65%	40%	55%	20%	16%	47%	53%
Pasture around the house is better than forest.	85%	60%	70%	65%	20%	0%	50%	50%

[a]RTs = rubber tappers; PMs = policy makers.

Adams, Ryan. 2008. "Large-Scale Mechanized Soybean Farming in Amazonia." *Culture and Agriculture* 30 (1): 32–37.

———. 2010. "Elite Landowners in Satarém: Ranchers, Gaúchos, and the Arrival of Soybeans in the Amazon." PhD diss., Indiana University.

Allegretti, Mary. 2002. "A construcão social de políticas ambientais: Chico Mendes e o movimento dos seringueiros" (The social construction of environmental policy: Chico Mendes and the rubber-tapper movement). PhD diss., Universidade de Brasília.

Almeida, Ana Luisa de Ozorio. 1992. *The Colonization of the Amazon.* Austin: University of Texas Press.

Alves de Souza, C. A. 2008. *História do Acre* (History of Acre). Rio Branco: Carlos Alberto Alves de Souza.

Arima, Eugenio, Paulo Barreto, and Marky Brito. 2006. *Cattle Ranching in the Amazon: Trends and Implications for Environmental Conservation.* Belém, Brazil: IMAZON.

Arima, Eugenio Y., Peter Richards, Robert Walker, and Marcellus M. Caldas. 2011. "Statistical Confirmation of Indirect Land Use Change in the Brazilian Amazon." *Environmental Research Letters* 6 (2): 024010.

Atran, Scott, Douglas Medin, Norbet Ross, Elizabeth Lynch, John Coley, Ediberto Ucan Ek, and Valentina Vapnarsky. 1999. "Folkecology and Commons Management in the Maya Lowlands." *Proceedings of the National Academy of Science* 96 (13): 7598–7603.

Aunger, Robert. 1999. "Against Idealism/Contra Consensus." *Current Anthropology* 40:S93–S101.

Bakx, Keith. 1988. "From Proletarian to Peasant: Rural Transformation in the State of Acre, 1870–1986." *Journal of Development Studies* 24 (2): 141–160.

Balée, William. 2006. "The Research Program of Historical Ecology." *Annual Review of Anthropology* 35:75–98.

Barona, Elizabeth, Navin Ramankutty, Glenn Hyman, and Oliver T. Coomes. 2010. "The Role of Pasture and Soybean in Deforestation of the Brazilian Amazon." *Environmental Research Letters* 5 (2): 024002.

Barth, Fredrik. 1956. "Ecological Relationships of Ethnic Groups in Swat, North Pakistan." *American Anthropologist* 58 (6): 1079–1089.

———. 1969. "Ecological Relationships of Ethnic Groups in Swat, North Pakistan." In *Environment and Cultural Behavior: Ecological Studies in Cultural Anthropology,* ed. A. P. Vayda, 362–376. Garden City, NY: Natural History Press.

Bennett, John W. 1969. *Northern Plainsmen: Adaptive Strategy and Agrarian Life.* Chicago: Aldine.

Bernard, H. Russell. 2000. *Social Research Methods: Qualitative and Quantitative Approaches.* Thousand Oaks, CA: Sage.

———. 2012. "The Science in Social Science." *Proceedings of the National Academy of Sciences* 109 (51): 20796–20799.

Biersack, Aletta. 1999. "Introduction: From the 'New Ecology' to the New Ecologies." *American Anthropologist* 101 (1): 5–18.

Bishko, C. J. 1952. "The Peninsular Background of Latin American Cattle Ranching." *Hispanic American Historical Review* 32 (4): 491–515.

Blaikie, Piers, and Harold Brookfield. 1987. *Land Degradation and Society.* London: Methuen.

Borgatti, Stephen P., Martin G. Everett, and Linton C. Freeman. 2002. *UCINET 6 for Windows: Software for Social Network Analysis.* Harvard, MA: Analytic Technologies.

Bourdieu, Pierre. 1977. *Outline of a Theory of Practice.* Cambridge: Cambridge University Press.

Brazilian Federal Public Ministry. 2012. *Carne legal* (Legal beef). http://www.carnelegal.mpf.gov.br/. Accessed Aug. 29, 2012.

Browder, J. O., and B. J. Godfrey. 1997. *Rainforest Cities: Urbanization, Development, and Globalization of the Brazilian Amazon.* New York: Columbia University Press.

Brubaker, R., and F. Cooper. 2000. "Beyond 'Identity.'" *Theory and Society* 29: 1–47.

Butzer, Karl. 1988. "Cattle and Sheep from Old to New Spain: Historical Antecedents." *Annals of the Association of American Geographers* 78 (1): 29–56.

Campbell, D. G. 2007. *A Land of Ghosts: The Braided Lives of People and the Forest in the Far Western Amazon.* New Brunswick, NJ: Rutgers University Press.

Campbell, D. G., and H. D. Hammond, eds. 1989. *Floristic Inventory of Tropical Countries.* New York: New York Botanical Garden.

Cancian, Frank. 1989. "Economic Behavior in Peasant Communities." In *Economic Anthropology,* ed. Stuart Plattner, 127–170. Stanford, CA: Stanford University Press.

Charnley, S., and W. H. Durham. 2010. "Anthropology and Environmental Policy: What Counts?" *American Anthropologist* 112 (3): 397–415.

Chavez, Leo, F. Allan Hubbell, Juliet McMullin, Rebecca Martinez, and Shiraz Mishra. 1995. "Structure and Meanings in Models of Breast and Cervical Cancer Risk Factors." *Medical Anthropology Quarterly* 9 (1): 40–74.

Chayanov, A. V. 1986. *The Theory of the Peasant Economy.* Madison: University of Wisconsin Press.

Chibnik, Michael. 1991. "Quasi-Ethnic Groups in Amazonia." *Ethnology* 30 (2): 167–182.

Cleary, David. 1993. "After the Frontier: Problems with Political Economy in the Modern Brazilian Amazon." *Journal of Latin American Studies* 25 (2): 331–349.

Clifford, James. 1988. *The Predicament of Culture: Twentieth-Century Ethnography, Literature, and Art.* Cambridge, MA: Harvard University Press.

Cohen, Abner. 1981. *The Politics of Elite Culture: Explorations in the Dramaturgy of Power in a Modern African Society.* Berkeley: University of California Press.

Colson, Elizabeth. 1955. "Native Cultural and Social Patterns in Contemporary Africa." In *Africa Today,* ed. C. G. Haines, 69–89. Baltimore, MD: Johns Hopkins University Press.

Comaroff, Jean, and John L. Comaroff. 1990. "Goodly Beast, Beastly Goods: Cattle and Commodities in the South African Context." *American Ethnologist* 17 (2): 195–216.

Conklin, Beth A., and Laura R. Graham. 1995. "The Shifting Middle Ground: Amazonian Indians and Eco-politics." *American Anthropologist* 97 (4): 695–710.

Cosgrove, Denis. 1984. *Social Formation and Symbolic Landscape.* London: Croom Helm.

Cowell, Adrian. 1990. *The Decade of Destruction.* London: Hodder and Stoughton.

"The Cradle of Life." 2011. *Wild Amazon.* TV. Produced by Mitch Turnbull. National Geographic Channel.

Cronon, William. 1983. *Changes in the Land: Indians, Colonists, and the Ecology of New England.* New York: Hill and Wang.

Crumley, Carol. 1994. *Historical Ecology: Cultural Knowledge and Changing Landscapes.* Santa Fe, NM: School of Advanced Research.

Cunha, Euclides da. 1944. *Rebellion in the Backlands [Os sertões].* Trans. Samuel Putnam. Chicago: University of Chicago Press.

Daly, Douglas C., and Ghillean T. Prance. 1989. "Brazilian Amazon." In *Floristic Inventory of Tropical Countries*, ed. D. G. Campbell and H. D. Hammond, 401–426. New York: New York Botanical Garden.

Dary, David. 1981. *Cowboy Culture.* New York: Knopf.

Davis, Shelton. 1977. *Victims of the Miracle: Development and the Indians of Brazil.* Cambridge: Cambridge University Press.

Dean, Warren. 1987. *Brazil and the Struggle for Rubber.* Cambridge: Cambridge University Press.

Denevan, William M. 1992. "The Pristine Myth: The Landscape of the Americas in 1492." *Annals of the Association of American Geographers* 82 (3): 369–385.

Dent, Alexander Sebastian. 2009. *River of Tears: Country Music, Memory, and Modernity in Brazil.* Durham, NC: Duke University Press.

Descola, Philippe. 1994. *In the Society of Nature: A Native Ecology in Amazonia.* Cambridge: Cambridge University Press.

———. 2013. *Beyond Nature and Culture.* Trans. Janet Lloyd. Chicago: University of Chicago Press.

Deshler, W. W. 1965. "Native Cattle Keeping in Eastern Africa." In *Man, Culture, and Animals*, ed. Anthony Leeds and A. P. Vayda, 153–168. Washington, DC: American Association for the Advancement of Science.

DeWalt, B. R. 1983. "The Cattle Are Eating the Forest." *Bulletin of the Atomic Scientist* 39:18–23.

Dove, Michael, and Carol Carpenter. 2007. "Introduction: Major Historical Currents in Environmental Anthropology." In *Environmental Anthropology: A Historical Reader*, ed. Michael Dove and Carol Carpenter, 1–86. Oxford: Wiley-Blackwell.

Dressler, William, Jose Ernesto dos Santos, and Mauro Campos Baleiro. 1996. "Studying Diversity and Sharing in Culture: An Example of Lifestyle in Brazil." *Journal of Anthropological Research* 52 (3): 331–353.

Durning, Alan B., and Holly B. Brough. 1991. *Taking Stock: Animal Farming and the Environment.* Worldwatch Paper 103. Washington, DC: Worldwatch Institute.

Dyson-Hudson, Rada, and Neville Dyson-Hudson. 1980. "Nomadic Pastoralism." *Annual Review of Anthropology* 9:15–61.

Edelman, Marc. 1995. "Rethinking the Hamburger Thesis: Deforestation and the Crisis of Central America's Beef Exports." In *The Social Causes of Environmental Destruction in Latin America*, ed. Michael Painter and William H. Durham, 25–62. Ann Arbor: University of Michigan Press.

EDF (Environmental Defense Fund). N.d. "Ready for REDD: Acre's State Programs for Sustainable Development and Deforestation Control." Environmental Defense Fund. http://www.edf.org/sites/default/files/Acre_Ready_for_REDD_EDF.pdf. Accessed Sept. 20, 2013.

Ehringhaus, Christiane. 2005. "Post-Victory Dilemmas: Land Use, Development, and Social Movement in Amazonian Extractive Reserves." PhD diss., Yale University.

Ensminger, Jean. 1992. *Making a Market: The Institutional Transformation of an African Society*. Cambridge: Cambridge University Press.

Evans-Pritchard, E. E. 1940. *The Nuer*. Oxford: Oxford University Press.

Fabian, Johannes. 2002. *Time and the Other: How Anthropology Makes Its Object*. New York: Columbia University Press.

Faminow, M. D. 1998. *Cattle, Deforestation, and Development in the Amazon: An Economic, Agronomic, and Environmental Perspective*. New York: CAB International.

FAO (Food and Agriculture Organization of the United Nations). 2006. "Cattle Ranching and Deforestation." Livestock Policy Brief 3. ftp://ftp.fao.org/docrep/fao/010/a0262e/a0262e00.pdf. Accessed April 19, 2012.

Fearnside, Philip. 2005. "Deforestation in Brazilian Amazonia: History, Rates, and Consequences." *Conservation Biology* 19 (3): 680–688.

Ferguson, James. 1985. "The Bovine Mystique: Power, Property, and Livestock in Rural Lesotho." *Man*, n.s., 20 (4): 647–674.

———. 2006. *Global Shadows: Africa in the Neoliberal World Order*. Durham, NC: Duke University Press.

Foweraker, Joe. 1981. *The Struggle for Land: A Political Economy of the Pioneer Frontier in Brazil from 1930 to the Present Day*. Cambridge: Press Syndicate of the University of Cambridge.

Galvin, Kathleen A. 2009. "Transitions: Pastoralists Living with Change." *Annual Review of Anthropology* 38:185–198.

Gezon, Lisa, and Susan Paulson. 2005. "Place, Power, Difference: Multiscale Research at the Dawn of the Twenty-first Century." In *Political Ecology across Spaces, Scales, and Social Groups*, ed. Susan Paulson and Lisa Gezon, 1–16. New Brunswick, NJ: Rutgers University Press.

Glacken, Clarence J. 1973. *Traces on the Rhodian Shore: Nature and Culture in Western Thought from Ancient Times to the End of the Eighteenth Century*. Berkeley: University of California Press.

Goldschmidt, Walter. 1969. *Kambuya's Cattle: The Legacy of an African Herdsman*. Berkeley: University of California Press.

Gomes, C. V. 2009. "Twenty Years after Chico Mendes: Extractive Reserves' Expansion, Cattle Adoption, and Evolving Self-Definition among Rubber Tappers in the Brazilian Amazon." PhD diss., University of Florida.

Gomes, C. V., J. M. Vadjunec, and S. G. Perz. 2012. "Rubber Tapper Identities:

Political-Economic Dynamics, Livelihood Shifts, and Environmental Implications in a Changing Amazon." *Geoforum* 43 (2): 260–271.

Gonçalves, D. N., and Franco Iacomini. 1997. "O Brasil cowboy" (The Brazilian cowboy). *Veja*, Aug. 27. http://veja.abril.com.br/270897/p_092.html. Accessed Jan. 15, 2011.

Governo do Acre. 2006. *Zoneamento ecológico-económico, fase II* (Ecological-economic zoning, phase II). Rio Branco: SEMA.

Gravlee, Clarence. 2005. "Ethnic Classification in Southeastern Puerto Rico: The Cultural Model of 'Color.'" *Social Forces* 83 (3): 949–970.

Greenpeace Brasil. 2009. *O farra do boi na Amazonia* (The Festival of the Oxen in Amazonia). São Paulo: Greenpeace Brasil.

Gupta, Akhil, and James Ferguson. 1992. "Beyond 'Culture': Space, Identity, and the Politics of Difference." *Cultural Anthropology* 7 (1): 6–23.

Hale, Charles R. 1996. *Resistance and Contradiction: Miskitu Indians and the Nicaraguan State, 1894–1987.* Palo Alto, CA: Stanford University Press.

———. 1997. "Cultural Politics of Identity in Latin America." *Annual Review of Anthropology* 26:567–590.

Hames, Raymond. 2007. "The Ecologically Noble Savage Debate." *Annual Review of Anthropology* 36:177–190.

Handwerker, W. Penn. 2002. "The Construct Validity of Cultures: Cultural Diversity, Culture Theory, and a Method for Ethnography." *American Anthropologist* 104 (1): 106–122.

Harris, Mark. 2000. *Life on the Amazon: The Anthropology of a Brazilian Peasant Village.* Oxford: Oxford University Press.

———. 2004. "Introduction." *Some Other Amazonians: Perspectives on Modern Amazonia,* ed. Mark Harris and Stephen Nugent, 1–11. London: Institute for the Study of the Americas.

Harris, Marvin. 1956. *Town and Country in Brazil.* New York: Norton.

———. 1966. "The Cultural Ecology of India's Sacred Cow." *Current Anthropology* 33 (1): 261–276.

———. 1985. *Good to Eat: Riddles of Food and Culture.* New York: Simon and Schuster.

Hecht, Susanna. 1982. "The Environmental Effects of Cattle Development in the Amazon Basin." PhD diss., University of California, Berkeley.

———. 1993. "The Logic of Livestock and Deforestation in Amazonia." *Bioscience* 43 (10): 687–695.

———. 2012. "From Eco-Catastrophe to Zero Deforestation? Interdisciplinarities, Politics, Environmentalisms and Reduced Clearing in Amazonia." *Environmental Conservation* 39 (1): 4–19.

Hecht, Susanna, and Alexander Cockburn. 1989. *The Fate of the Forest: Developers, Destroyers, and Defenders of the Amazon.* London: Verso.

Heckenberger, Michael, Afukaka Kuikuro, Urissapá Tabata Kuikuro, J. Christian Russel, Morgan Schmidt, Carlos Fausto, and Bruna Franchetto. 2007. "Amazonia, 1492: Pristine Forest or Cultural Parkland?" *Science* 301:1710–1713.

Herskovits, Melville J. 1926. "The Cattle Complex in East Africa." *American Anthropologist* 28 (1): 230–272.

Hobsbawm, E. J. 2013. *Fractured Times: Culture and Society in the Twentieth Century.* London: Little, Brown.

Hutchinson, Sharon. 1996. *Nuer Dilemmas: Coping with Money, War, and the State.* Berkeley: University of California Press.

IBGE. 2008. Brazilian Institute of Statistics and Geography. http://www.ibge.gov.br/english. Accessed July 1, 2009.

Ingold, Tim. 1980. *Hunters, Pastoralists, and Ranchers: Reindeer Economies and Their Transformations.* Cambridge: Cambridge University Press.

Jarvis, Lovell. 1986. *Livestock in Latin America.* New York: Oxford University Press.

Jordan, Terry G. 1993. *North American Cattle-Ranching Frontiers: Origins, Diffusion, and Differentiation.* Albuquerque: University of New Mexico Press.

Kaimowitz, David, B. Mertens, Sven Wunder, and Paulo Pacheco. 2004. *Hamburger Connection Fuels Amazon Destruction.* Bogor, Indonesia: CIFOR.

Kainer, Karen, Marianne Schmink, A. C. Pinheiro Leite, and M. J. da Silva Fadell. 2003. "Experiments in Forest-Based Development in the Western Amazon." *Society and Natural Resources* 16:869–886.

Kawa, Nicholas C. 2012. "Magic Plants of Amazonia and Their Contribution to Agrobiodiversity." *Human Organization* 71 (3): 225–233.

Keck, Margaret E. 1995. "Social Equity and Environmental Politics in Brazil: Lessons from the Rubber Tappers of Acre." *Comparative Politics* 27 (4): 409–424.

Knauft, Bruce. 1996. *Genealogies for the Present.* New York: Routledge.

Kottak, Conrad. 1990. *Prime-Time Society: An Anthropological Analysis of Television and Culture.* Belmont, CA: Wadsworth.

Krech, Shepard. 2000. *The Ecological Indian: Myth and History.* New York; London: Norton.

Lawrence, Elizabeth A. 1990. "Rodeo Horses: The Wild and the Tame." In *Signifying Animals,* ed. Roy Willis, 222–235. London: Unwin Hyman.

Lea, Tom. 1957. *The King Ranch.* Vol. 1. Boston: Little, Brown.

Lévi-Strauss, Claude. 1969. *Totemism.* Boston: Beacon.

Limón, José E. 1989. "'Carne, carnales,' and the Carnivalesque: Bakhtinian 'batos,' Disorder, and Narrative Discourses." *American Ethnologist* 16 (3): 471–486.

Little, Paul. 1999. "Environments and Environmentalisms in Anthropological Research: Facing a New Millennium." *Annual Review of Anthropology* 28: 253–284.

Loker, William. 1993. "The Human Ecology of Cattle Raising in the Peruvian Amazon: The View from the Farm." *Human Organization* 52 (1): 14–24.

Loy, Jane M. 1981. "Horsemen of the Tropics: A Comparative View of the Llaneros in the History of Venezuela and Colombia." *Boletín Americanista* 31:159–171.

Luzar, Jeffrey. 2006. "Roads, Governance, and Land Use in the Brazilian State of Acre." PhD diss., University of Florida.

Mahar, Dennis. 1989. *Frontier Policy in Brazil: A Study of Amazonia.* Washington, DC: World Bank.

Marcus, George. 1983. *Elites: Ethnographic Issues.* Albuquerque: University of New Mexico Press.

Martinello, Pedro. 2004. *A batalha da borracha na Segunda Guerra Mundial* (The rubber battle in the Second World War). Rio Branco: EDUFAC.

Marx, Karl. 1977 [1867]. *Capital.* Vol. I. New York: Random House/Vintage.

Mazza, Cristina, Carlos Mazza, Jose Sereno, Sandra Santos, and Aiesca Pellegrin.

1994. *Etnobiologia e conservação do bovino pantaneiro* (Ethnobiology and conservation of Pantaneiro cattle in Brazil). Brasília: EMBRAPA.

McCabe, Terrance. 2004. *Cattle Bring Us to Our Enemies: Turkana Ecology, History, and Raiding in a Disequilibrium System.* Ann Arbor: University of Michigan Press.

McCann, Bryan. Forthcoming. "Popular Culture in Emergent Brazil." In *Emergent Brazil*, ed. Jeffrey Needell. Gainesville: University of Florida Press.

Meggars, Betty. 1971. *Amazonia: Man and Culture in a Counterfeit Paradise.* Arlington Heights, IL: AHM.

Meillassoux, Claude. 1980. "From Reproduction to Production: A Marxist Approach to Economic Anthropology." In *The Articulation of Modes of Production*, ed. H. Wolpe, 189–201. London: Routledge.

Mitchell, S. T. 2010. "Paranoid Styles of Nationalism after the Cold War: Notes from an Invasion of the Amazon." In *Anthropology and Global Insurgency*, ed. J. D. Kelly et al., 89–104. Chicago: University of Chicago Press.

Moog, Clodomir Vianna. 1994. "Bandeirantes and Pioneers." In *Where Cultures Meet: Frontiers in Latin American History*, ed. David J. Weber and Jane M. Rausch, 165–172. Wilmington, DE: Scholarly Resources Books.

Moore, S. F. 1993. "Changing Perspectives on a Changing Africa: The Work of Anthropology." In *Africa and the Disciplines*, ed. Robert Bates, V. Y. Mudimbe, and Jean O'Barr, 3–57. Chicago: University of Chicago Press.

Moran, Emilio. 1981. *Developing the Amazon.* Bloomington: Indiana University Press.

———. 1982. "Ecological, Anthropological, and Agronomic Research in the Amazon Basin." *Latin American Research Review* 17 (1): 3–41.

———. 1993. "Deforestation and Land Use in the Brazilian Amazon." *Human Ecology* 21 (1): 1–21.

Mortiz, Mark, Kristen Ritchey, and Saidou Kari. 2011. "The Social Context of Herding Contracts in the Far North Region of Cameroon." *Journal of Modern African Studies* 49 (2): 263–285.

Mosca, Gaetano. 1939. *The Ruling Class.* New York: McGraw-Hill.

Mullin, Molly H. 1999. "Mirrors and Windows: Sociocultural Studies of Human–Animal Relationships." *Annual Review of Anthropology* 28:201–224.

Myers, Norman. 1981. "How Central America's Forests Became North America's Hamburgers." *Ambio* 10 (1): 3–8.

Nader, Laura. 1972. "Up the Anthropologist—Perspectives Gained from Studying Up." In *Reinventing Anthropology*, ed. Dell H. Hymes, 284–311. New York: Pantheon.

Nations, James, and Daniel Komer. 1983. "Rainforests and the Hamburger Society." *Environment: Science and Policy for Sustainable Development* 25 (3): 1983.

Nepstad, Daniel, Britaldo S. Soares-Filho, Frank Merry, Andre Lima, Paulo Moutinho, John Carter, Maria Bowman, et al. 2009. "The End of Deforestation in the Brazilian Amazon." *Science* 326:1350–1351.

Netting, Robert. 1993. *Smallholders, Householders: Farm Families and the Ecology of Intensive, Sustainable Agriculture.* Stanford, CA: Stanford University Press.

Nichols, Madaline Wallis. 1968. *The Gaucho.* New York: Guardian Press.

Nugent, Stephen. 1993. *Amazonian Caboclo Society: An Essay on Invisibility and Peasant Economy*. Providence, RI: Berg.

Oliven, G. O. 2000. "'The Largest Popular Culture Movement in the Western World': Intellectuals and Gaúcho Traditionalism in Brazil." *American Ethnologist* 27 (1): 128–146.

Olwig, Kenneth. 2002. *Landscape, Nature, and the Body Politic: From Britain's Renaissance to America's New World*. Madison: University of Wisconsin Press.

Orlove, Benjamin S. 1980. "Ecological Anthropology." *Annual Review of Anthropology* 9:235–273.

Ortner, Sherry B. 1974. "Is Female to Male as Nature Is to Culture?" In *Readings in Ecology and Feminist Theology*, ed. Mary Heather McKinnon and Moni McIntyre, 36–55. Kansas City, MO: Sheed and Ward.

———. 2006. *Anthropology and Social Theory*. Durham, NC: Duke University Press.

Pace, Richard. 2009. "Television's Interpellation: Heeding, Missing, Ignoring, and Resisting the Call for Pan-National Identity in the Brazilian Amazon." *American Anthropologist* 111 (4): 407–419.

Pace, Richard, and Brian Hinote. 2013. *Amazon Town TV: An Audience Ethnography in Gurupá, Brazil*. Austin: University of Texas Press.

Pacheco, Pablo, and René Poccard-Chapuis. 2012. "The Complex Evolution of Cattle Ranching Development amid Market Integration and Policy Shifts in the Brazilian Amazon." *Annals of the Association of American Geographers* 102 (6): 1366–1390.

Pareto, Vilfredo. 1968. *The Rise and Fall of Elites: An Application of Theoretical Sociology*. Totowa, NJ: Bedminster.

Pärssinen, M., D. Schaan, and A. Ranzi. 2009. "Pre-Columbian Geometric Earthworks in the Upper Purús: A Complex Society in Western Amazonia." *Antiquity* 83 (322): 1084–1095.

Perramond, Eric. 2010. *Political Ecologies of Cattle Ranching in Northern Mexico*. Tucson: University of Arizona Press.

Perz, Stephen G., Liliana Cabrera, Lucas Araujo Carvalho, Jorge Castillo, and Grenville Barnes. 2010. "Global Economic Integration and Local Community Resilience: Road Paving and Rural Demographic Change in the Southwestern Amazon." *Rural Sociology* 75 (2): 300–325.

Perz, Stephen G., Liliana Cabrera, Lucas Araujo Carvalho, Jorge Castillo, Rosmery Chacacanta, Rosa E. Cossio, Yeni Franco Solano, et al. 2011. "Regional Integration and Local Change: Road Paving, Community Connectivity, and Social-Ecological Resilience in a Tri-national Frontier, Southwestern Amazonia." *Regional Environmental Change* 12 (1): 35–53.

Phillips, O., A. H. Gentry, C. Reynel, P. Wilkin, and B. Galvez-Durand. 1994. "Quantitative Ethnobotany and Amazonian Conservation." *Conservation Biology* 8 (1): 225–248.

Plattner, Stuart. 1989. "Marxism." In *Economic Anthropology*, ed. Stuart Plattner, 379–398. Stanford, CA: Stanford University Press.

Polanyi, Karl. 1958. "The Economy as an Instituted Process." In *Trade and Markets in the Early Empires*, ed. Karl Polanyi, Conrad Arensberg, and Harry Pearson, 243–270. Glencoe, IL: Free Press.

Porro, Noemi. 2002. "Rupture and Resilience: Gender Relations and Life Trajectories in the Babaçu Palm Forests of Brazil." PhD diss., University of Florida.

Posey, Darrell. 1985. "Indigenous Management of Tropical Forest Ecosystems: The Case of the Kayapó Indians of the Brazilian Amazon." *Agroforestry Systems* 3 (2): 139–158.

Raffles, Hugh. 2002. *In Amazonia: A Natural History*. Princeton, NJ: Princeton University Press.

Redford, Kent H. 1991. "The Ecologically Noble Savage." *Cultural Survival Quarterly* 15 (1): 46–48.

Resor, Randolph. 1977. "Rubber in Brazil: Dominance and Collapse, 1876–1945." *Business History Review* 51 (3): 341–366.

Revkin, Andrew. 1990. *The Burning Season: The Murder of Chico Mendes and the Fight for the Amazon Rainforest*. Boston: Houghton Mifflin.

Rifkin, Jeremy. 1993. *Beyond Beef: The Rise and Fall of the Cattle Culture*. New York: Plume.

Rimas, Andrew, and Evan Fraser. 2008. *Beef: The Untold Story of How Milk, Meat, and Muscle Shaped the World*. New York: HarperCollins.

Rival, Laura. 2002. *Trekking through History*. New York: Columbia University Press.

Rivière, Peter. 1972. *The Forgotten Frontier: Ranchers of North Brazil*. New York: Holt, Rinehart, and Winston.

Robben, Antonius C. G. M. 1989. *Sons of the Sea Goddess: Economic Practice and Discursive Practice in Brazil*. New York: Columbia University Press.

Robbins, Paul. 2007. *Lawn People*. Philadelphia: Temple University Press.

Romney, A. K., S. C. Weller, and W. H. Batchelder. 1986. "Culture as Consensus: A Theory of Culture and Informant Accuracy." *American Anthropologist* 88 (2): 313–338.

Roseberry, William. 1989. *Anthropologies and Histories: Essays in Culture, History, and Political Economy*. New Brunswick, NJ: Rutgers University Press.

Rudel, Thomas K., Diane Bates, and Rafael Machinguiashi. 2002. "Ecologically Noble Amerindians? Cattle Ranching and Cash Cropping among Shuar and Colonists in Ecuador." *Latin American Research Review* 37 (1): 144–159.

Sahlins, Marshall. 1972. *Stone Age Economics*. New York: Aldine de Gruyter.

Said, Edward. 2003. *Orientalism: Western Conceptions of the Orient*. London: Penguin.

Salisbury, David, and Marianne Schmink. 2007. "Cows versus Rubber: Changing Livelihoods among Amazonian Extractivists." *Geoforum* 38 (6): 1233–1249.

Santos, Roberto. 1980. *História econômica da Amazônia* (History and economy of Amazonia). São Paulo: Queiroz.

Sarmiento, Domingo. 1868. *Life in the Argentine Republic in the Days of the Tyrants; or, Civilization and Barbarism*. New York: Hurd and Houghton.

Sayre, Nathan. 1999. "The Cattle Boom in Southern Arizona: Towards a Critical Political Ecology." *Journal of the Southwest* 41 (2): 239–271.

Schmink, Marianne. 1982. "Land Conflicts in Amazonia." *American Ethnologist* 9 (2): 341–357.

———. 2011. "Forest Citizens: Changing Life Conditions and Social Identities in the Land of the Rubber Tappers." *Latin American Research Review* 46: 141–158.

Schmink, Marianne, and Mancio Lima Cordeiro. 2008. *Rio Branco: A cidade da florestania* (Rio Branco: The city of the forest). Belém, Brazil: Universidade Federal do Pará.

Schmink, Marianne, and Charles Wood. 1992. *Contested Frontiers in Amazonia.* New York: Columbia University Press.

Schneider, Harold K. 1957. "The Subsistence Role of Cattle among the Pakot and in East Africa." *American Anthropologist* 59 (2): 278–300.

Schwartzman, Stephan. 1989. "Extractive Reserves: The Rubber Tappers' Strategy for Sustainable Use of the Amazon Rainforest." In *Fragile Lands of Latin America: Strategies for Sustainable Development,* ed. J. O. Browder, 150–163. Boulder, CO: Westview.

Scott, James C. 1998. *Seeing Like a State.* New Haven, CT: Yale University Press.

Shane, Douglas. 1986. *Hoofprints on the Forest.* Philadelphia: Institute for the Study of Human Issues.

Sheridan, Thomas E. 2007. "Embattled Ranchers, Endangered Species, and Urban Sprawl: The Political Ecology of the New American West." *Annual Review of Anthropology* 36:121–138.

Shore, Chris, and Stephen Nugent. 2002. "Introduction: Towards an Anthropology of Elites." In *Elite Cultures: Anthropological Perspectives,* ed. C. Shore and S. Nugent, 1–21. London: Routledge.

Shoumatoff, Alexander. 1990. *The World Is Burning.* Boston: Little, Brown.

Slater, Candace. 2002. *Entangled Edens: Visions of the Amazon.* Berkeley: University of California Press.

Slatta, Richard. 1990. *Cowboys of the Americas.* New Haven, CT: Yale University Press.

———. 1997. *Comparing Cowboys and Frontiers: New Perspectives on the History of the Americas.* Norman: University of Oklahoma Press.

Smeraldi, Roberto, and Peter H. May. 2008. *O reino do gado* (The cattle kingdom). São Paulo: Amigos da Terra.

Smith, Nigel. 1982. *Rainforest Corridors: The Transamazon Colonization Scheme.* Berkeley: University of California Press.

———. 2002. *Amazon Sweet Sea: Land, Life, and Water at the River's Mouth.* Austin: University of Texas Press.

Spear, Thomas. 1993. "Introduction." In *Being Maasai: Ethnicity and Identity in East Africa,* ed. Thomas Spear and R. Waller, 1–18. Athens: Ohio University Press.

Sponsel, Leslie E. 1986. "Amazon Ecology and Adaptation." *Annual Review of Anthropology* 15:67–97.

Steward, Julian, ed. 1946. *Handbook of South American Indians.* 7 vols. Washington, DC: US Bureau of American Ethnology/Government Printing Office.

Stoeltje, Beverly J. 1989. "Rodeo: From Custom to Ritual." *Western Folklore* 48 (3): 244–255.

Strickon, Arnold. 1965. "The Euro-American Ranching Complex." In *Man, Culture, and Animals,* ed. Anthony Leeds and A. P. Vayda, 229–258. Washington, DC: American Association for the Advancement of Science.

Tinker, Edward Larocque. 1961. *Life and Literature in the Pampas.* Gainesville: University of Florida Press.

Toni, Fabiano, Jair Carvalho dos Santos, Ronei Sant'Ana de Menezes, Charles H. Wood, and Henrique Sant'Anna. 2007. *Expansão e trajetórias da pecuária na Amazônia: Acre, Brasil* (Expansion and trajectories of cattle raising in Amazonia: Acre, Brazil). Brasília: Editora Universidade de Brasília.

Tribuna. 2008. "RESEX: 300 famílias podem ser expulsas" (300 families could be expelled from RESEX). Oct. 14. http://www.amazonia.org.br/noticias/noticia .cfm?id=288124. Accessed Aug. 15, 2010.

Tsing, Anna Lowenhaupt. 2005. *Friction: An Ethnography of Global Connection.* Princeton, NJ: Princeton University Press.

Tuan, Y.-F. 1974. *Topophilia: A Study of Environmental Perception, Attitudes, and Values.* New York: Columbia University Press.

Turner, Frederick Jackson. 1920. *The Frontier in American History.* New York: Henry Holt.

Vadjunec, Jacqueline, Marianne Schmink, and C. V. Gomes. 2011. "Rubber Tapper Citizens: Emerging Places, Policies, and Shifting Rural–Urban Identities in Acre, Brazil." *Journal of Cultural Geography* 28 (1): 73–98.

Vadjunec, Jacqueline, Marianne Schmink, and A. L. Greiner. 2011. "New Amazonian Geographies: Emerging Identities and Landscape." *Journal of Cultural Geography* 28 (1): 1–20.

Valentim, J. F. 2008. "Evolução da produção agropecuária no Acre" (Evolution of agricultural production in Acre). Oct. 2, 2008. http://www.cpafac.embrapa.br /imprensa/artigos_tecnicos/artigos-de-midia-3/artigos-de-midia-2008 /evolucao-da-producao-agropecuaria-no-acre/?searchterm=Evolu%C3 %A7%C3%A3o%20da%20produ%C3%A7%C3%A3o%20agropecu%C3 %A1ria%20no%20Acre. Accessed Sept. 21, 2011.

Valentim, J. F., and C. M. Andrade. 2009. "Tendências e perspectivas da pecuária bovina na Amazônia brasileira" (Tendencies and perspectives on cattle raising in the Brazilian Amazon). *Amazônia: Ciência e Desenvolvimento, Belém* 4 (8): 9–32.

Vivieros de Castro, E. 1998. "Cosmological Deixis and Amerindian Perspectivism." *Journal of the Royal Anthropological Institute*, n.s., 4 (3): 469–488.

Wagley, Charles. 1971. *An Introduction to Brazil.* New York: Columbia University Press.

Walker, Robert, John Browder, Eugenio Arima, Cynthia Simmons, Ritaumaria Pereira, Marcellus Caldas, Ricardo Shirota, and Sergio de Zen. 2009. "Ranching and the New Global Range: Amazonia in the 21st Century." *Geoforum* 40:732–745.

Walker, Robert, Emilio Moran, and Luc Anselin. 2000. "Deforestation and Cattle Ranching in the Brazilian Amazon: External Capital and Household Processes." *World Development* 28 (4): 683–699.

Wallace, Richard. 2004. "The Effects of Wealth and Markets on Rubber Tapper Use and Knowledge of Forest Resources in Acre, Brazil." PhD diss., University of Florida.

Weber, David J., and Jane M. Rausch. 1994. "Introduction." *Where Cultures Meet: Frontiers in Latin American History*, ed. David Weber and Jane M. Rausch, xiii–xli. Wilmington, DE: Scholarly Resources Books.

Weinstein, Barbara. 1983. *The Amazon Rubber Boom, 1850–1920.* Stanford, CA: Stanford University Press.

Weller, S. C. 2007. "Cultural Consensus Theory: Applications and Frequently Asked Questions." *Field Methods* 19 (4): 339–368.

West, Paige, James Igoe, and Dan Brockington. 2006. "Parks and Peoples: The Social Impact of Protected Areas." *Annual Review of Anthropology* 35 (1): 251–277.

Wilk, Richard R., and Lisa C. Cliggett. 2006. *Economies and Cultures: Foundations of Economic Anthropology.* Boulder, CO: Westview.

Williams, Raymond. 1975. *The Country and the City.* New York: Oxford University Press.

Wolf, Eric. 1982. *Europe and the People without History.* Berkeley: University of California Press.

Wolpe, Harry. 1980. *The Articulation of Modes of Production.* London: Routledge.

CPSIA information can be obtained
at www.ICGtesting.com
Printed in the USA
FFOW02n0439150717
37778FF

9 781477 310601